Ilse Born-Lechleitner | Sally Brunner | Anna Harkamp
Eva Holleis | Andreas Kaplan

way2go! 7

Coursebook

So arbeiten Sie mit *way2go!*

Jede der 10 Units beginnt mit einer **Vorschau** auf die Inhalte und einer **anregenden Aufgabe**, die Sie zu einer ersten Auseinandersetzung mit dem Thema motivieren soll.

Die Units sind in **Unterthemen** gegliedert, in welchen die verschiedenen sprachlichen **Kompetenzen** systematisch aufgebaut werden und auf niveaurelevante *Language* (Grammatik und Vokabular) eingegangen wird.

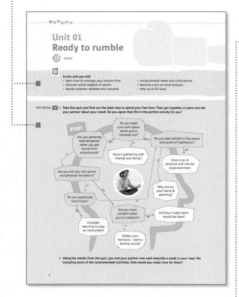

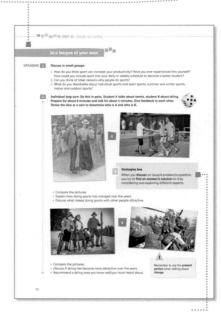

B   *By the way* bietet Ihnen interessante Informationen zu Aspekten des **englischsprachigen Kulturkreises**.

L   *Language*-Abschnitte greifen aus dem Kontext wichtige **grammatische Strukturen** heraus, die wiederholt oder gelernt werden sollten. Auch **Vokabel-Schwerpunkte** werden so gekennzeichnet.

S   *Strategies boxes* sollen Sie bei der Bearbeitung der verschiedenen Aufgabentypen und der Operatoren der Schreib- und Sprechaufträge unterstützen. **Längere *Strategies*-Abschnitte** beinhalten umfangreichere Informationen auch zu Lern- und Arbeitsstrategien. Die *Strategies*-Seiten im Anhang wiederholen zentrale Arbeits- und Prüfungsstrategien.

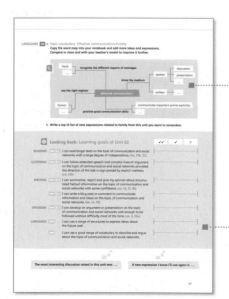

L   Am **Ende jeder Unit** sammeln und erweitern *Topic vocabulary*-Felder das für das angestrebte Sprachniveau relevante Themenvokabular.

◎   Den Abschluss der Kapitel bilden *Looking back*-Tabellen, die der Selbsteinschätzung Ihres Kompetenzstandes dienen. Die Beschreibungen, die Sie dort finden, entsprechen den Lernzielen bzw. Teilkompetenzen des **Lehrplans**. Um diese für Sie transparenter zu machen, wurden sie in *way2go!* möglichst kurz gehalten und mitunter auf mehrere Formulierungen aufgeteilt. In Klammern werden jene Aufgaben angeführt, die die jeweilige Teilkompetenz trainieren. Es sind immer nur die wichtigsten Teilkompetenzen des Kapitels angegeben, eine vollständige Liste finden Sie online.

Mit den beiden *Semester checks* und dem dazugehörigen Lösungsschlüssel am Ende des Buches können Sie sich selbstständig eine **Rückmeldung** zur Erreichung der **Lernziele** einholen.

Die Seiten *Literature along the way* möchten Ihnen Lust auf die Beschäftigung mit klassischer und moderner englischsprachiger Literatur machen.

Grammar revisited gibt einen Überblick über die Grammatik-Themen der Units und vertieft sie mit zusätzlichen Informationen.

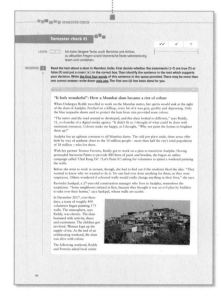

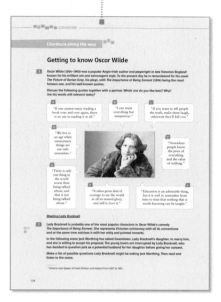

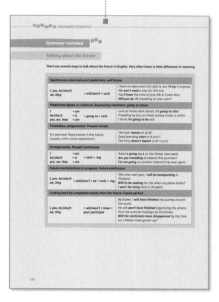

Der *Writing coach* macht Sie mit den Besonderheiten verschiedener **Textsorten** vertraut. Authentische Schreibaufträge und Modelltexte zeigen Ihnen exemplarisch, worauf es bei der Bearbeitung ankommt.

Das *Vocabulary* im Anhang enthält den Lernwortschatz in der Reihenfolge, wie er in den Units vorkommt. Wörter, deren Aussprache sich vielleicht nicht gleich erschließt, sind durch Angaben zur Lautschrift ergänzt.

Symbole

Registrieren Sie sich mit dem Nutzerschlüssel (hintere Umschlagseite innen rechts unten) auf *Mein öbv*.

i9597d Online-Code, der zu den Audio- und Video-Dateien im Internet führt. Geben Sie den Code einfach in das Suchfeld auf www.oebv.at ein.

 03 Verweis auf die CD Ihrer Lehrkraft

radio FM4 Hierbei handelt es sich um einen original FM4-Beitrag.

01 Verweis auf die DVD Ihrer Lehrkraft mit Videobei-trägen (u. a. von der BBC)

 p. 12 Verweis auf weiter-führende Übungen im Practice Pack

Kennzeichnung von Aufgaben, die die Formate der standardisierten Reifeprüfung üben

 Hinweis auf eine sprach-liche Besonderheit

Hinweis zu **SRP-ähnlichen** *Listening*-**Aufgaben**: Um eine flexible Handhabung im Unterricht (oder auch zu Hause) zu ermöglichen, besteht der Audio-Track immer aus einer einmaligen Aufnahme des Hörtextes mit nur einer kurzen, thematischen Einleitung. Der Track kann jedoch beliebig oft abgespielt werden, um auf individuelle Bedürfnisse einzugehen.

Contents

Listening

- Balancing school and leisure time
- Sports trivia
- ... and viewing: Ruqsana, a female Muslim kickboxer

Writing

- Choose one of the situations and just ... write!
- Describing a sport
- A voice-over for a video
- A comment on an article
- Analysing a chart

Speaking

- Quiz: The ideal free time activity
- School-life balance
- ILT[1]: Sports over the years
- Women's vs. men's sports
- A female Muslim kickboxer
- Professional athletes
- Describing charts

Way more

- **Strategies:** Analysing charts/graphs; Welcome to B2!; The function word 'discuss'
- **By the way:** Sports in Ireland

Listening

- My favourite person in the family
- Family structures that will change society
- Who are they talking to? (Recognising register)

Writing

- The 'average' Austrian family/ Fun facts about your own family
- A blog post about a particular family form
- A blog comment about register in text messages

Speaking

- The average family
- Families over time
- Your favourite person
- Families of the future
- ILT[1]: Ways of communicating
- PA[2]: Living together

Way more

- **Strategies:** The function words 'speculate' and 'state'
- **By the way:** All together now! (Collective nouns)

Listening BBC

- Popular ways to live after school
- ... and viewing: London's waterways; A building in Mozambique (BBC) (4W)

Writing

- A flatmate ad
- Responding to a flatmate ad
- A timeline
- Summarising an article/a video
- An article about living in the country/city
- A report about a new park

Speaking

- Flatmates
- Current/future living arrangements
- City life or life in the country?
- Homes at different stages in life
- Inadequate housing
- ILT[1]: Housing and growing up
- PA[2]: When should you move out?

Way more

- **Strategies:** Summarising a text; 400-word writing tasks

Listening radio FM4

- A blind world traveller (FM4) (MM)
- Public transport in a rural community
- ... and viewing: An unusual mode of transportation in London

Writing

- Travel dos and don'ts
- An ad promoting your favourite leisure activity
- An article on travelling safely
- An email to the manager of a local bus service company
- A report about public transport in your area

Speaking

- "Your ticket, please!" – A cartoon
- Travelling without being able to hear or see
- ILT[1]: Different ways of travelling
- Public transport: Pros and cons
- PA[2]: Persuading car drivers to use public transport
- Public transport in small towns
- Transporting goods
- Travelling with a pet

Way more

- **Strategies:** The function word 'consider'
- **By the way:** Driving on the left

Listening

- A debate on education
- ... and viewing: Should teenagers get a job?
- University ads (MM)
- Making plans for the future

Writing

- An email applying for a job in a pub
- Writing to a concerned parent
- A blog post on strict education
- Writing a uni ad (and performing it)
- Conversations

Speaking

- Education and learning
- A debate about what school should teach their students
- ILT[1]: School and general education
- PA[2]: Popular Saturday jobs
- Parents and education
- Future plans
- What are you looking for in a university?

Way more

- **Strategies:** Multiple choice tasks; The function word 'examine'; Discussing a quote
- **By the way:** Freshers' Week

---

[1] **ILT:** individual long turn   [2] **PA:** paired activity

Contents

Listening **radio FM4**	Writing	Speaking	Way more
▪ An editorial meeting of a youth magazine ▪ A family argument ▪ The Kennel Club Library (FM4) (MC) ▪ Excerpts from *Romeo and Juliet*	▪ Advocating a lifestyle ▪ An essay on why teenagers should be encouraged to keep a pet ▪ The story behind the argument ▪ An email about reading a modern piece of literature	▪ Lifestyles ▪ Cat and dog owners ▪ Pets – pros and cons ▪ The relevance of Shakespeare today ▪ ILT¹: Family conflicts ▪ PA²: How to work on *Romeo and Juliet* in class	▪ **Strategies:** Discovering the essay ▪ **By the way:** Famous dogs

Listening **radio FM4**	Writing	Speaking	Way more
▪ … and viewing: Skateboarders forced out of city centres ▪ Gun laws in the US ▪ Sacred Stone Camp (FM4) (4W)	▪ An email to a mayor ▪ The camera's story ▪ A blog comment: Is spray painting art or a crime? ▪ An essay on CCTV cameras at school ▪ Standing Rock: Tweets/An email to One Mind Youth	▪ WANTED people ▪ Discussing offences and crimes ▪ ILT¹: Crime ▪ PA²: Preventing burglaries ▪ Gun control ▪ Safety solutions for school ▪ Non-violence and famous activists	▪ **Strategies:** The function word 'emphasise'

Listening	Writing	Speaking	Way more
▪ An interview with a musician about culture ▪ A lecture about Neil Gaiman (4W)	▪ Is art important? ▪ Formal writing ▪ An essay about going to the theatre vs. streaming a play ▪ An email to a literary agent ▪ A dark fiction story	▪ A cartoon about (modern) art ▪ The theatre – then and now ▪ Presenting an idea for an exhibition ▪ Superstitions ▪ Presenting your favourite author ▪ ILT¹: Reading/Popular culture ▪ PA²: Good books for young people	▪ **Strategies:** The function word 'argue' ▪ **By the way:** Tap your toes in Ireland

Listening **radio FM4** BBC	Writing	Speaking	Way more
▪ Biased reporting ▪ Comic book journalist Sarah Glidden (FM4) (MC) ▪ A radio report on threats to journalists ▪ … and viewing: Predictive advertising (BBC) (MM)	▪ An email on comic journalism ▪ An essay on being a foreign correspondent ▪ Imagine living in a country with limited press freedom ▪ A blog post on online advertising ▪ A report on a project on advertising	▪ Reader and media bias ▪ News as comics instead of articles? ▪ Difficulties of critical journalism ▪ Press freedom worldwide ▪ Collecting personal data ▪ PA²: Advertising for young people ▪ Using feelings to sell sth. ▪ Interpreting a cartoon	▪ **Strategies:** Interpreting a cartoon

Listening BBC	Writing	Speaking	Way more
▪ A lecture on the Iceberg Model of Culture ▪ … and viewing: An Aboriginal community in Australia (BBC)	▪ A note apologising for hurting someone's feelings ▪ A blog post about intercultural experiences on holiday ▪ Aboriginal vs. Australian culture ▪ An email applying to work for a project with Aboriginals	▪ Discussing culture from different perspectives ▪ The Iceberg Model of Culture ▪ ILT¹: Getting to know other cultures ▪ PA²: The most challenging aspects of culture ▪ Indigenous peoples ▪ Indigenous art	▪ **Strategies:** The function word 'encourage'

¹**ILT:** individual long turn ²**PA:** paired activity

Unit 01
Ready to rumble

 i9597d

In this unit you will:
- learn how to manage your leisure time
- discover social aspects of sports
- decide whether athletes are overpaid
- revise phrasal verbs and collocations
- become a pro at chart analysis
- step up to B2 level

SPEAKING **1** **a** Take this quiz and find out the ideal way to spend your free time. Then get together in pairs and tell your partner about your result. Do you agree that this is the perfect activity for you?

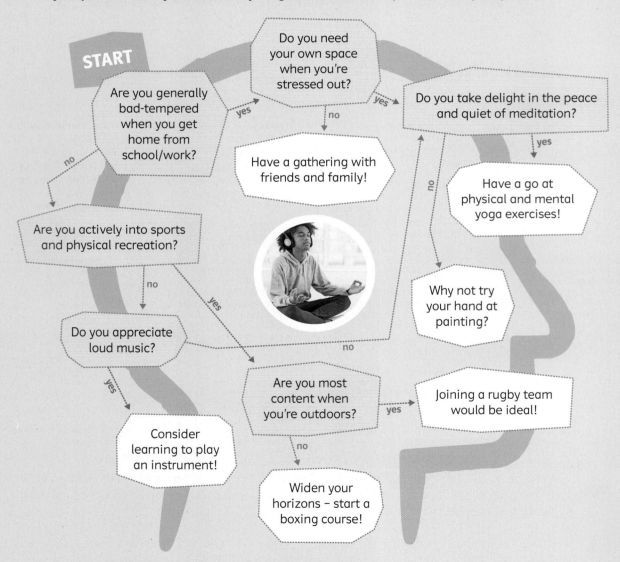

START

Are you generally bad-tempered when you get home from school/work?

Do you need your own space when you're stressed out?

Do you take delight in the peace and quiet of meditation?

yes — Have a gathering with friends and family!

yes — Have a go at physical and mental yoga exercises!

no

Are you actively into sports and physical recreation?

Do you appreciate loud music?

Consider learning to play an instrument!

Are you most content when you're outdoors?

Why not try your hand at painting?

Joining a rugby team would be ideal!

Widen your horizons – start a boxing course!

b Using the results from the quiz, you and your partner now each describe a week in your 'new' life including some of the recommended activities. How would you make time for them?

READING 2 **Read these forum posts and decide what kind of leisure activity the people are writing about.**

James Lee
Fountain Valley
June 11

Ever since I was a child, I have loved … . I enjoy the feeling of satisfaction I get (1) **creating** things that are (2) **appealing to look at**, and … lets me do just that. Once I pick up my materials and get started, I can (3) **let my imagination run free**, trying out new ideas and techniques. Sometimes I look up stuff on the internet to find some (4) **inspiration**. I also post pictures of my own pieces in the hope they might encourage other people to take up my hobby. … makes me happy because it feels like I can make my fantasies come true. Sometimes I'm amazed at what I create and feel really proud of myself, and occasionally I get frustrated when things don't go well. … is full of mystery, because every time I create a new piece, there's a new outcome. I can never predict quite how it will turn out!

Gracie
Oxford MS
May 15

Yes, I do have (5) **hobbies** that I don't use for college applications or to make money. One of my hobbies is … . I took it up when I was five and have always loved it, but until recently I didn't really (6) **appreciate** how it helps me (7) **strike a balance between** my school work and my free time. It took me some time to figure that out! It's the most relaxing and exciting activity to do, in my opinion. Some of my favourite styles of … are contemporary and ballet. … makes me really happy because I'm doing something I love with the people I love, so it's a win-win. Sometimes we perform in schools or hospitals to (8) **entertain** people. It's my way of giving something back to the community. I'm going to carry on doing it for as long as I can.

Priscilla
US
May 21

My hobby is … . I found out I was good at … at an early age as relatives would often comment on it when I got up to entertain them at family gatherings. It's something that (9) **makes me feel alive**, and it makes me feel good about myself. I like … because it (10) **relieves stress** and allows me to (11) **release all my emotions**. I feel like I'm letting everything go and switching off from all my everyday worries. … is something that I do when I'm sad and upset. My mother often points out that I have a beautiful voice, so I (12) **take advantage of** it and vocalise every chance I get. I'm starting to wonder whether I could make my interest into a career one day. How cool would it be to do your hobby as a paying job?

LANGUAGE 3

Expand your vocabulary: Leisure activities
Match the highlighted expressions in the posts to one that has a similar meaning below.

L

a amuse	e new ideas	i be original/artistic
b beautiful	f give equal importance to	j pastimes/interests
c enjoy as much as possible	g gives energy	k realise
d express myself	h making/forming	l relaxes

LANGUAGE 4

Expand your vocabulary: Phrasal verbs
There are at least three phrasal verbs (e.g. *look at*, *find out*, …) in each of the three posts above. Write them into your notebook and add an expression with the same meaning to each of them.
Example: *to pick up sth. – to take sth. in your hands*

WRITING 5

What's your favourite hobby? Describe it in a few sentences without naming it and let your classmates guess what it is. Use at least two phrasal verbs and two expressions from exercises 2 and 3.

LISTENING **6**
◉ 01
⊕
⎘
p. 5

You are going to listen to an interview with Dr Patrik Byrne, an expert on balancing school with the rest of your life. First you will have 45 seconds to study the task below, then you will hear the recording twice. While listening, choose the correct answer (A, B, C or D) for each question (1–5). Put a cross (☒) in the correct box. The first one (0) has been done for you.

After the second listening, you will have 45 seconds to check your answers.

Balancing school and leisure

0 Dr Byrne works

A at St Cuana's National School. ☐
B for the School Advisory Board. ☒
C for the radio station. ☐
D as an independent consultant. ☐

1 Malachi

A is really close to his mother. ☐
B finds it difficult to fall asleep. ☐
C can't manage his time successfully. ☐
D plays in a school band. ☐

2 Patrik suggests that Malachi should

A spend more time on team sports. ☐
B find more time to be by himself. ☐
C keep all his commitments. ☐
D think hard about what is important. ☐

3 Malachi should also

A organise his days better. ☐
B stop going to theatre group. ☐
C reduce his circle of friends. ☐
D increase his pace of life. ☐

4 Aileen wants advice on how to

A plan her days more successfully. ☐
B find more time to practise music. ☐
C apply for university. ☐
D improve her grades at school. ☐

5 Patrik gives Aileen tips on how to

A study in more efficient ways. ☐
B keep written records of her day. ☐
C focus more on school demands. ☐
D manage her negative emotions. ☐

LANGUAGE **7**
⎘
p. 5

Expand your vocabulary: School-life balance
Listen to the radio feature again and tick the expressions you hear.

L
a breathing space
b me time
c peace and quiet
d improve your productivity
e slow down

f unwind
g don't overtax yourself
h sleep eight hours
i cut down on
j schedule time for

k set clear priorities
l manage your time well
m give your brain some rest
n fit in a hobby
o don't procrastinate

SPEAKING **8**

Discuss in pairs:

1 Which of the strategies suggested in the radio feature do you find useful/don't you find useful? Why? Which of them do you practise yourself?
2 What other advice would you give Malachi and Aileen?

WRITING **9**

Choose one of the tasks below and write about 100 words.

a Aileen's best friend is really upset that Aileen didn't come to her birthday party. Write the text message(s) that she sends to Aileen.
b Aileen's wipe-off calendar suddenly started talking to her. Do you think it'll praise her for being so organised or tell her to relax? Write down what it says.
c Malachi's mother talks to him about never being home. Write his diary entry afterwards.

10 **a** You are going to read a blog post on how to avoid putting off things that need to be done.
Some words are missing. Complete the text by writing <u>one</u> word for each gap (1–11) in the spaces
provided. The first one (0) has been done for you.

Stop procrastinating!

Do you sometimes procrastinate? Be honest.
Everyone (0) _____ . Maybe you put things
off when you're overwhelmed with too much
to do, or when you're distracted, upset, tired,
or uncertain. Maybe you need some help
(1) _____ organisation or setting goals.
Or maybe you need more encouragement or
direction in order to move forward. We all
procrastinate at (2) _____ point. But when
does procrastination become problematic?

Procrastination is a (3) _____ of avoidance behaviour. It can short-circuit motivation and forward
momentum. It can also interfere with learning, happiness and overall well-being. When that
happens, it's important to find ways to (4) _____ procrastination's hold and potential impact.

Make up your mind to get things done
A (5) _____ in mindset from "I can't" or "I won't" to "I can, and I will!" can increase your
productivity. Take a deep (6) _____ and exude purpose and self-confidence, and there's no end to
what you can achieve.

Stay calm
This is important because it (7) _____ you to be in the right frame of mind. You are in control.
Navigating difficult times, putting forth effort and being resilient are better alternatives than
(8) _____ a procrastinator. You can become riled up, or you can calm yourself down. Go for the
latter.

Be open to communication and collaboration
Talk with people you respect and trust and who can (9) _____ you as you tackle challenges.
Listen. Ask questions. Be resourceful. Share ideas. Chat about procrastination. Use a steady tone
of voice. Don't be afraid to seek help from various sources (10) _____ you feel you need it.

Consider what really matters to you
Then work out how to make (11) _____ for those things. What propels you toward
accomplishment? Curiosity? Encouragement? Competition? Become familiar with your feelings,
attitudes and habits. The better you know yourself, the sooner you can get down to the business
of tapping your strengths, bolstering your weaknesses and doing what you have to do to learn
how to stop procrastinating.

0	does	6	
1		7	
2		8	
3		9	
4		10	
5		11	

b Write down three things you will do to avoid procrastination and share them with a partner.

In a league of your own

SPEAKING **11** **Discuss in small groups:**

1 How do you think sport can increase your productivity? Have you ever experienced this yourself? How could you include sport into your daily or weekly schedule to become a better student?
2 Can you think of other reasons why people do sports?
3 What do you like/dislike about individual sports and team sports, summer and winter sports, indoor and outdoor sports?

12 *Individual long turn:* Do this in pairs. Student A talks about tennis, student B about skiing. Prepare for about 8 minutes and talk for about 4 minutes. Give feedback to each other. Throw the dice or a coin to determine who is A and who is B.

A

S **Strategies box**

When you **discuss** an issue/a problem/a question, you try to **find an answer/a solution** to it by considering and exploring different aspects.

- Compare the pictures.
- Explain how doing sports has changed over the years.
- Discuss what makes doing sports with other people attractive.

B

- Compare the pictures.
- Discuss if skiing has become more attractive over the years.
- Recommend a skiing area you know well/you have heard about.

! Remember to use the **present perfect** when talking about **change**.

READING + WRITING **13** **a** Read through the three descriptions of different sports. What kind of sport do you think is meant here?

1

is a stand-up combat sport based on kicking and punching, historically developed from karate and boxing. It is often practised for self-defence or general fitness.

2

is a mixture of swimming, dance and gymnastics, with athletes performing a routine of elaborate[1] moves in the water accompanied by music. It requires advanced water skills.

3

is a sport in which two or four players hit a lightweight ball back and forth across a table using small bats. It is fast and you need good reflexes.

b Get together with a partner and write your own description of a sport. Let your classmates guess what sport you're referring to.

SPEAKING **14** Discuss these questions in small groups:

1 Which of the sports mentioned would you rather consider 'women's sports' and which 'men's sports'?
2 What kinds of sports are generally rather seen as 'male' or 'female'? Why is that so? Find some more examples.

LISTENING + VIEWING
⌔ 01

15 **a** Watch a video about Ruqsana Begum, a female kickboxer from London. How many women can you spot in the video? How many of them are exercising in front of the camera?

b Watch the video again and find out whether it's Ruqsana or someone else who talks about the things below. Correct any sentences that are wrong.

1 When Ruqsana started, there weren't many kickboxing women.
2 Her parents weren't supportive when she told them what she was doing. They wanted her to move out.
3 Ruqsana's specially designed sporting hijab has already encouraged lots of young women to train.
4 She never planned on being a role model, and it really scares her.
5 The Muslim community needs more female role models.

Ruqsana

SPEAKING **16** Discuss in small groups:

1 Why has it been controversial for a young woman to start kickboxing?
2 Why does it make a difference whether that woman is religious?
3 What challenges might Muslim women face that aren't usually an issue for others?

WRITING SPEAKING **17** Turn the first minute of the video into an advertisement for kickboxing by writing a new voice-over (the spoken words of a person you can't see) for it. Record it using a computer/your phone and play it alongside the video. Which voice-over is the best advertisement?

[1] **elaborate:** kompliziert, raffiniert

READING **18** Read this opinion piece by a feminist writer about women and sports. Some parts are missing. Choose the correct part (A–N) for each gap (1–11). There are two extra parts that you should not use. Write your answers in the boxes provided. The first one (0) has been done for you.

Why women don't do sports

Most women would say that they have precious little time to themselves. The time they don't spend working for an employer, they do something called 'housework', and, for most women between 25 and 50, 'childcare' is additional. There is also the task of (0) _____, tidy, deodorised, made up, not to mention toned and well-dressed, plus the exhausting business of hair and hairiness management. Work, all of it. Women either don't do leisure or they do activities that aren't too expensive, and they (1) _____ between work and leisure. Men spend their free time relaxing, but for women it's just another form of work.

There are powerful reasons why women steer clear of leisure activities, including sports. The majority of women worldwide – who are still illiterate and unpaid family workers – know only too well that if they are ever seen (2) _____, a job will be found for them. In more traditional societies, the holidays on which menfolk are permitted to straighten their backs and get dressed up smartly are the days when women have to work hardest, cleaning up the house and (3) _____. It is not so long ago that on Sundays, while the rest of the family played cricket on the village green, the woman of the house had to cook and serve a three-course Sunday lunch and subsequently clean up after it.

Today, everybody male is occupied with leisure and sports activities. Has the woman of the house grabbed a kitbag and followed their example? No. Women don't go fishing. Women do play golf, but not much. Women (4) _____. Women don't buy sports cars, boats, jetskis, trailbikes, guns, crossbows … Women do not listen to the call of sports and leisure. But it is also true that the sports and leisure industry does not address women that much. Their argument comes full circle: it is that no female market exists.

Sport has traditionally been regarded as male territory, and women doing sports have always had to fight against gender stereotypes

(5) _____ than men. Among the 258 athletes lining up at the start of the first Winter Olympics held in 1924 in Chamonix, only 11 were female, all of them figure skaters. And it was not their sports achievement, but the length of their skirts, reaching just below the knee, which caused a furore[2].

Things have changed a little, but researchers have discovered that sports that are beautiful, graceful, non-aggressive or pleasing to the eye are typically considered (6) _____ . On the other hand, face-to-face competition, aggression and body contact are seen as masculine. Researchers say people automatically associate male games with competitive spirit, discipline, stamina and loyalty to a team.

There are other barriers to women doing sports than that it is traditionally considered (7) _____ . For instance, there are marked differences between men's and women's feet as women generally have a narrower heel. Typically, women also have wider hips. Wearing shoes that aren't designed to take these differences into account may actually cause injuries, yet manufacturers claim that there is no demand for women's football boots, for example. Another example of discrimination of female sports would be that TV stations claim there is no demand for (8) _____ , leaving the female professional teams without the financial backing that male teams regularly receive by selling advertising spots.

Other restrictions women interested in sports face (9) _____ . In India, for example, a country where a light skin colour is still something prestigious, the myth that chlorine darkens one's skin keeps status-conscious women out of – admittedly rare – public swimming pools. Religious issues also come into play: (10) _____ in swimsuits might be difficult not only for body-conscious western females, but also for women of different religions. Create a garment like the burkini

---

[2] **to cause a furore:** für Aufregung/Furore sorgen

that allows Muslim girls the freedom to do sports and provides modesty at the same time, and it becomes a political issue. That's why it is important that high-profile sports equipment companies like Nike have decided to create a 'Pro Hijab' for the (11) _____ who want to do sports but still remain accepted in their community. As Aheda Zanetti, the creator of the Burkini, says of her invention: "Anyone can wear this, Christian, Jewish, Hindu. It's just a garment to suit a modest person, or someone who is afraid of skin cancer, or a new mother who doesn't want to wear a bikini, [...]."

A	as male territory	H	putting together giant meals
B	with their hands in their laps	I	going out in the public
C	have the perfect body	J	portraying them as weaker
D	keeping the female body clean	K	don't buy sports equipment
E	broadcasting female football games	L	have to do with cultural prejudices
F	appropriate for women	M	don't see the difference
G	do a lot of work	N	growing number of women

0	1	2	3	4	5	6	7	8	9	10	11
D	M	B	H	K	J	F	A	E	L	I	N

a Expand your vocabulary: Sports

p. 7

Read the text again and find the expressions that fit these explanations.

L

a making you feel extremely tired
_____

b the businesses providing recreation- and entertainment-related products and services
_____

c a person very good at physical activity who takes part in organised events
_____

d not using force or violence
_____

e an event in which people try to win sth.
_____

f the ability to control yourself and follow rules
_____

g the strength to do sth. tiring for a long time
_____

h damage to a person's body
_____

i a group of people who do a certain sport for money
_____

j getting a lot of attention
_____

b **Write sentences with the expressions using examples to explain them.**
Example: *Running, weightlifting or playing squash are <u>exhausting</u> activities.*

READING **20** Read the opinion piece in 18 again and try to summarise the main point of each paragraph in one sentence. Compare your sentences with a partner and agree on the best ones.

SPEAKING **21** Discuss these questions in pairs. Give reasons for your answers.

1 Do you agree with the main message(s) of the text?
2 What sport can you think of that is totally unsuitable for men? Why is that so?
3 Do you watch professional women's sports events on TV?
4 Should female athletes earn the same as their male colleagues?
5 Should all women wear 'westernised' clothes when doing sports?

WRITING **22** Choose one of the arguments in the opinion piece and write a PEEL paragraph disagreeing with it. Try to use at least two expressions from 19.

B **By the way: Sports in Ireland**

In Ireland, Gaelic games lie at the heart of who the Irish are and what it is to be Irish. The games are truly unique and exciting, and visitors to Ireland are fascinated by them. The two main Gaelic games are Gaelic football and hurling.

In a conventional game of football, what would the referee say if a player picked up the ball and ran with it? The whistle would be blown and the player penalised[3]. However, in Gaelic football, both hands and feet can be used by the players to control the ball. Moreover, the teams consist of 15 people on each side, and goal-scoring is also very different to the football you are probably used to. Getting the ball over the bar of the H-shaped goal gets one point, and getting it under the bar scores three points.

Another uniquely Irish game is hurling, which is one of the world's oldest field sports and has been played in some form in Ireland for more than 800 years. The women's version of the game is known as 'camogie'. The game is often compared to field hockey, but other than the fact that both games involve a stick and a ball, there is no similarity. Some people have called it a mixture of hockey and war! The curved wooden stick with a flat end is known as a 'hurl' or 'hurley', or, in Irish, a 'camán' (pronounced 'come-awn') and is made from a single piece of wood. The ball, or 'sliothar' (pronounced 'shlit-her') is about the size of a tennis ball and is covered in leather. As well as striking the ball with the hurley, players can kick or hit it with their hand. An impressive hurling skill is the ability to bounce or balance the ball on the hurl while running at full speed before finally flipping it high into the air and whacking it over or under the H-shaped crossbar. It's no wonder that players usually wear protective helmets these days!

The other two Gaelic games are rounders and Gaelic handball. Every weekend club matches of all these sports are played in towns and villages all over Ireland, with the biggest Gaelic football and hurling games regularly attracting crowds of over 40,000 viewers.

Do you know any sports that are only played in our part of the world? How could you describe them to people who have never seen them before?

---

[3] **to be penalised:** bestraft werden

Going for gold (or cash)

SPEAKING 23 Brainstorm in small groups:

1 What kinds of sport are popular in Austria? Why?
2 What kinds of sport are popular in other countries?
3 Can you name any professional athletes? What makes them popular?

READING 24 a Check your knowledge on professional ball sports. Read the questions below and guess.
LISTENING Then listen to the correct answers.
⊙ 02
⊕

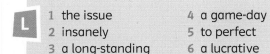

1 Which ball game came to the United States in the 1850s through New Orleans,
probably introduced by immigrants from Scotland, Ireland and Germany?
  a basketball   b soccer   c American football

2 Which is the only country to have taken part in every Soccer World Cup?
  a Germany   b Italy   c Brazil

3 In which ball sport is the Super Bowl the most important game?
  a baseball   b basketball   c American football

4 Where are about 80% of soccer balls produced?
  a Pakistan   b Turkey   c Mexico

5 In which sport do the best-paid female athletes compete?
  a tennis   b soccer   c skiing

6 In which sport does the average male athlete earn most?
  a American football   b basketball   c soccer

b Work in pairs.

1 Which of these facts did you find surprising? Give reasons for your answers.
2 Do some quick research: How much do popular professional athletes currently earn?
3 Women athletes still earn less than their male counterparts. Can you think of reasons?

LANGUAGE 25 a Expand your vocabulary: Collocations – part 1
🔖 You are going to read an article on whether professional athletes are overpaid.
p. 7 Together with a partner, match the pairs. There is more than one correct answer.

L
1 the issue	4 a game-day	7 short
2 insanely	5 to perfect	8 wear
3 a long-standing	6 a lucrative	9 to fund

a someone's paycheck	c snack	e at hand	g one's skills	i debate
b and tear	d priced	f career spans	h salary	

b Find the collocations above which mean the same as:

1 to finance someone's income
2 to work hard on one's competence
3 unreasonably expensive
4 a profitable income
5 damage resulting from normal use
6 the key question

LANGUAGE **26** Expand your vocabulary: Linking devices
Read the article and fill in the missing linking devices from the box.

> **L** actually ▪ as much as ▪ as well as ▪ because ▪ but ▪ but as long as ▪ no matter ▪ of course ▪ so why ▪ though ▪ whether ▪ until

Are professional athletes getting paid too much?

(1) _Whether_ or not professional athletes are overpaid has been a long-standing debate. And in a world where some professional athletes are paid almost 100 times the salary of the average US teacher, it comes as no surprise. (2) _No matter_ whether or not you think athletes are overpaid, the issue at hand is not how much they're being paid, but why they're being paid that way. (3) _So why_ are professional athletes making more money than most of us could ever dream of? (4) _Actually_,

there are many factors that go into it, such as the amount of time athletes put into perfecting their skills, the wear and tear on their bodies, and their short career spans.

As fans, we encourage and allow for athletes to get paid higher and higher salaries each year (5) _because_ we keep coming back for more. (6) _Though_ a good portion of this money comes from TV deals signed with major networks, a lot of it also comes from ticket sales and merchandise. As a fan of Chicago sports, I can tell you that I have purchased insanely priced tickets to Cubs and Blackhawks games, averaging around $30–$60, with no regrets. I'm guilty of watching college football every Saturday during the season, and I own gear from at least three different colleges. I, (7) _as well as_ other fans, are still a part of the reason athletes get paid so much. (8) _As much as_ I would like to sit here and say that athletes are overpaid, considering even some rookies[4] make more than the president of the United States, I am partly responsible for funding their paychecks.

Professional athletes have been paid lucrative salaries for years. (9) _Of course_, it seems crazy that a player would make more money than a doctor, lawyer, fireman, police officer, teacher, or even our president. (10) _But_ as fans and consumers, we keep putting the money in their pockets. We keep returning to our favorite spot on the couch, with our good friends and our usual game-day snacks every week just to watch our favorite teams play. (11) _Until_ we as fans decide to give up on our teams, we will continue to help these players make this type of money. (12) _But as long as_ they keep playing, I'll keep paying.

[4] **rookies:** Neulinge, Anfänger/innen

Discuss the following questions in small groups:

1 What is the main source of income for professional athletes?
2 Why do you think these athletes make so much money only because their fans are watching them on TV?
3 Which examples does the author give to explain how athletes might be overpaid?
4 How does the author feel about funding the athletes?

READING 28 **Read the statements below and decide which of them give the main facts of the article.**

1 The author tries to give answers as to why athletes earn so much money.
2 The article deals with the fact that professional athletes are overpaid.
3 Athletes invest a lot of time in improving their skills.
4 Most of the athletes' salaries come from TV contracts, sales and merchandise.
5 Athletes earn more than the president of the USA.
6 The author confesses that he enjoys funding his favourite teams, although he admits that they might be overpaid.

WRITING 29 **Having read the article 'Are athletes getting paid far too much?', you have decided to start a blog on this topic.**

In your blog post you should:

- outline the main facts of the article
- explain why professional athletes should **or** should not be funded
- convince your readers that female athletes should earn as much as male athletes

Write around 250 words. Use some linking devices from 26. Underline them in your blog post.

→ See *Writing coach, Blog post*, p. 180.

ANGUAGE 30 *Expand your vocabulary: Collocations – part 2*
You are going to do a pair discussion on whether professional athletes are overpaid. The following collocations should help you find good arguments. Match the adjectives, verbs and phrases to the keywords and write the collocations in your notebook. There is more than one correct answer. You can find an example below the table.

Verbs	Adjectives	Phrases	Keywords (nouns)
A achieve	1 considerable	a in professional sports	career
B damage	2 excellent	b a form of	effort
C deserve	3 exceptional	c a great deal of	entertainment
D increase	4 immense	d an increase in	health
E recover from	5 long-term	e a drop in	injury
F require	6 physical	f bad for one's	popularity
G risk	7 poor	g the peak of one's	salary
H suffer from	8 pure		talent
I waste	9 severe		

Example: *career: a career in professional sports; an exceptional/a long-term/a poor career; to risk/waste your career; (to be at) the peak of your career; bad for your career, …*

SPEAKING 31 **Have a discussion with a partner. Student A argues that professional athletes are overpaid, student B argues that they deserve the money they earn. Throw the dice to determine who is A and who is B. Prepare for 2 to 3 minutes before you start the discussion. Tick off the collocations you used.**

STRATEGIES + LANGUAGE

pp. 8/9

32 Describing and analysing charts

Look at steps 1–3 and decide which of the aspects (A, B or C) refer to each of these steps. The language below the table will help you to describe and analyse charts.

S	1 Describe the nature of the chart/graph _____	2 Focus on the essential information _____	3 Analyse the chart/graph _____
	A What is the most noticeable thing about the chart/graph? Which of the details are really relevant? Talk about details only if they are significant, and group similar things. What major differences or changes does the chart/graph show?	B What are possible reasons for the differences or changes? What do the results/trends tell you about the topic or the participants of the survey? Why and for whom are they relevant? Can you give a future outlook?	C What kind of chart (bar chart/pie chart/line graph) is it? What is the survey about? What information is given on the participants of the survey? What do the different sections of the graph refer to?

Starting:
The chart shows/depicts/gives an overview of/illustrates/highlights/deals with/compares …

Describing numbers (e.g. percent):
A large proportion; a significant majority; a small number; only a minority; approximately two thirds; almost half; just over a third; exactly a quarter; only one in ten; more/less than a fifth …

Describing change:
The numbers increase/go up/climb/reach a peak …
The numbers decrease/go down/fall/decline …
The numbers don't change/remain stable/remain steady/stay constant …

Pointing out the significance of the information given:
There has been a dramatic change …;
In comparison to …, the number of … has fallen considerably; There is a remarkable difference between … and …; The number of … is certainly impressive …

SPEAKING **33** a Work with a partner to describe the following charts/graphs. Use expressions from above.

Chart 1

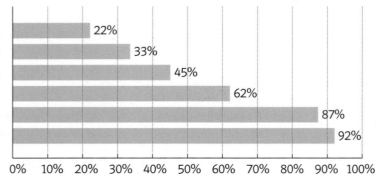

Why professional athletes deserve the money they make

They are international celebrities	22%
They have exceptional talent	33%
They put in considerable effort	45%
They risk their health	62%
They are role models for kids	87%
They provide excellent entertainment	92%

0% 10% 20% 30% 40% 50% 60% 70% 80% 90% 100%

Chart 2

Sports coverage on a US TV channel according to a recent survey

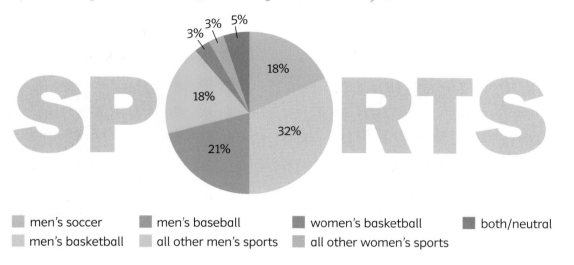

3% 3% 5%
18%
18%
32%
21%

■ men's soccer   ■ men's baseball   ■ women's basketball   ■ both/neutral
■ men's basketball   ■ all other men's sports   ■ all other women's sports

Chart 3

Austrian students' interest in sports according to a survey done at different schools

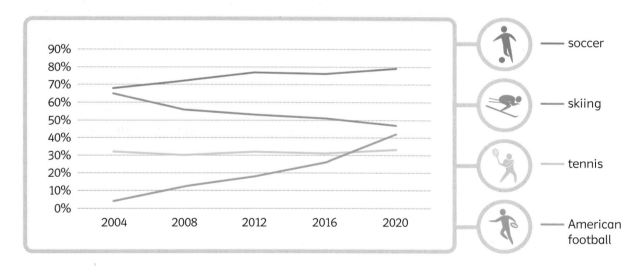

soccer

skiing

tennis

American
football

b Now analyse the charts. Try to find answers to some of the following questions together.

1 What is the essential information given in the data?
2 Why is the data interesting?
3 Who might be interested in the data? For what reason?
4 Who might have been asked/interviewed to provide the data?
5 What are possible reasons for the answers?
6 What are possible future trends?

WRITING 34   **Choose one of the three charts and explain it.**
Focus on the essential information and try
to interpret it to some extent. Write around 100 words.

LANGUAGE 35 a Topic vocabulary: Spending time meaningfully/Athletes
Complete the words with the missing letters.

p. 9

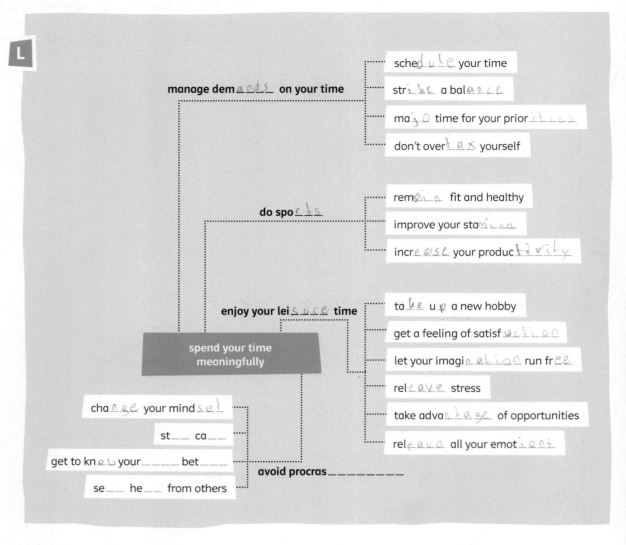

L

manage dem**ands** on your time

- sched**ule** your time
- stri**ke** a bal**ance**
- ma**ke** time for your prior**ities**
- don't over**tax** yourself

do spo**rts**

- rem**ain** fit and healthy
- improve your sta**mina**
- incr**ease** your produc**tivity**

enjoy your lei**sure** time

- ta**ke** u**p** a new hobby
- get a feeling of satisf**action**
- let your imagi**nation** run fr**ee**
- rel**ease** stress
- take adva**ntage** of opportunities
- rel**ease** all your emot**ions**

spend your time meaningfully

cha**nge** your mind**set**

st___ ca___

get to kn**ow** your _____ bet___

se___ he___ from others

avoid procras_____

b Make your own map on professional athletes: What do they need, risk and get for their job?

c *Word families.* Complete the table of word families.

Noun (idea/concept)	Verb	Adjective
	benefit	
appreciation		
		relieved
		perfect
courage, encouragement		
	pay	
		injured, uninjured
risk		

A new school year – a new set of learning goals. But there's something special about them now: listening and reading are now at level B2 – the pass level of your Matura exam. Writing and speaking at B2 will follow in the summer term. Therefore, you can expect this year to be more of a challenge than last year, but it also means you've now got two school years to practise and improve your skills at this level. Let's get started!

S

1   **Go over your work in this unit and then study the new learning goals below.**
- Which areas do you feel confident in?
- Which goals will need the most work?

2   **Reflect on your study habits of the last two years.**
- Did you make the most of your time in class?
- How much time and effort did you spend on your homework?
- How regularly did you study outside of class?

3   **Now it's time for New (school) Year's resolutions.**
- What good habits do you want to continue this year?
- How are you going to improve?

Write down at least three plans for how you are going to improve your English this year.

◎ **Looking back:** Learning goals of Unit 01

			✓✓	✓	!!
READING ▶▶▶ B2	I can read longer texts on the topic of sport and leisure with a large degree of independence. (ex. 18, 20)				
LISTENING ▶▶▶ B2	I can understand most broadcast audio material on the topic of sport and leisure delivered in standard dialect. (ex. 15b)				
WRITING ▶▶▶ B1+	I can write a blog post to explain a problem somewhat precisely. (ex. 29)				
SPEAKING ▶▶▶ B1+	I can maintain a conversation or discussion, compare and contrast alternatives and give brief comments on the views of others. (ex. 1a, 8, 14, 16, 21, 27, 31)				
▶▶▶ B1+	I can develop an argument or presentation on the topic of sport and leisure well enough to be followed without difficulty most of the time. (ex. 12, 33a/b)				
LANGUAGE ▶▶▶	I can use a good range of linking devices to structure my texts well.				
▶▶▶	I can use a good range of collocations to make my texts more idiomatic.				
▶▶▶	I can use a good range of vocabulary to describe and argue on the topic of sport and leisure.				

My main aim for this school year is . . .	Working with charts is . . .

Unit 02
It's all relative

 t5h9tf

In this unit you will:

- read and blog about modern families
- pick a family favourite
- learn about a blessing of unicorns

- make predictions about the future
- compare different types of register
- get your message across

SPEAKING **1** Here's what a British newspaper has to say about British families. Work with a partner. Read the statements and discuss which figures should go where.

14 ▪ 7 ▪ 1,435 ▪ 452 ▪ 72 ▪ 52

🥧 MODERN FAMILIES

The average British family has (1) 452 arguments a year – but fortunately enjoys 1,492 kisses.

(2) 52 % of British families own a pet, with dogs being the most popular.

489 hours

Brits watch 489 hours of TV, and wait (3) 14 hours for the kettle to boil.

Parents spend more than a week taking kids to clubs or parties, and (4) 7 hours waiting for the bathroom.

(5) 72 % of parents say technology prevents real conversations with their kids, and 51% of kids say the same about their parents.

But there is time for (6) 1,435 hugs and saying "I love you" on 1,036 occasions.

WRITING **2** Choose one of these tasks and share your results in class:

a Do some research and write similar statements about the average Austrian family.
b Create some fun facts about your own family that could go on a similar list.

SPEAKING 3 **Talk about these questions in pairs:**

1 How many people are part of your family? Who are they?
2 How do you celebrate Christmas, birthdays or other holidays in your family? How has this changed since you were young?
3 How do you communicate with members of your extended family (e.g. uncles or cousins)?

LISTENING 4 a **Listen to four teenagers talking about their favourite person in their families. Match the sentence parts to the person who says them.**

◎ 03

p. 12

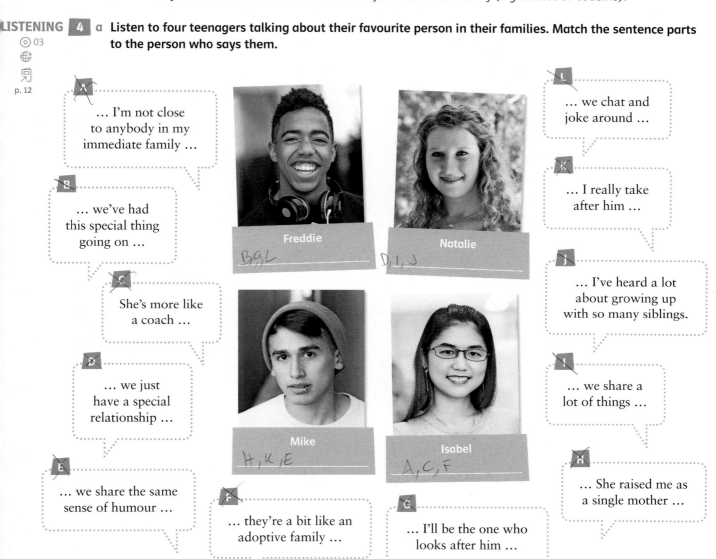

A … I'm not close to anybody in my immediate family …

B … we've had this special thing going on …

C She's more like a coach …

D … we just have a special relationship …

E … we share the same sense of humour …

F … they're a bit like an adoptive family …

L … we chat and joke around …

K … I really take after him …

J … I've heard a lot about growing up with so many siblings.

I … we share a lot of things …

H … She raised me as a single mother …

G … I'll be the one who looks after him …

Freddie — B, g, L

Natalie — D, I, J

Mike — H, K, E

Isabel — A, C, F

b Insert the names:

1 _Mike_ looks a lot like his father.
2 _Freddie_ lives in a blended family.
3 _Isabel_ doesn't get on with her parents.
4 _Natalie_ has 12 great-aunts and -uncles.

SPEAKING 5 **Prepare a short statement (1 to 2 minutes) on your favourite family member. Explain clearly and in detail why he/she is important to you. Talk in pairs and give each other feedback.**

!

The term '**Patchwork Family**' is only used in German (like '**Handy**'). In English you would use the expressions '**stepfamily**' or '**blended family**'.

LANGUAGE **6** a Expand your vocabulary: Relationships

p. 12

A newspaper asked teenagers what 'family' meant to them. Read the different posts and unscramble the words.

Order by **Newest** ⌄   1 2 3 4 ... »

JOE | 3m ago

My family doesn't necessarily include all of my (1) blood *ravetelis*. Really, my family are the people that love and take care of me. They don't have to be (2) *lisibgsn* or live in the same (3) *hoolushed* to be my family. I consider a lot of my friends part of my family. Call me crazy, but I also include my dog. We have a really (4) *oslce* bond and are (5) *ensarilepab*. My parents have recently (6) gone *outghhr* separation and (7) *dovrice*. People I once considered close family members are now people I no longer (8) have *cnatcot* with. My (9) nuclear *fmilay* as a whole is dysfunctional, but the family that I've made for myself is very loving and reliable, even if we're not (10) *eletrad*.

↳ Reply   ⇆ Share

IVONA | 24m ago

Family is my mum shouting that we live in a pigsty, but she always knows what to do when I'm in trouble, so I can always (11) *epnded* on her. It's my dad cracking jokes that nobody understands; it's my brother telling me that I can't go out in a skirt that length, but then saying he's proud of me after my exams; it's my other brother walking me home when I'm out late. It's not that we live (12) in perfect *ormhnay*, but we definitely (13) *tiskc* together when push comes to shove. Truthfully, I'd say that most of the time my family is pure madness, but it's a madness that I can't live without. I'm really (14) *thataecd* to them all.

↳ Reply   ⇆ Share

ROBERT | 1h ago

My parents have always worked very hard to (15) establish strong *seit* and honest communication with me. Nearly every night before I went to bed, one of them sat at my bedside and asked, "How are you? Anything you need to talk about?" This was a good (16) *prinigubgn* for me because it meant that my parents were also my friends and confidants and we could (17) *larete* to each other. Although this may not be common in many families, I fully believe good communication is crucial for healthy relationships among family members in order for them to (18) *nbod*.

↳ Reply   ⇆ Share

KEANI | 1h ago

I want to go to Oxbridge and I hope my parents understand that I must do everything I can to get there. Though I don't want to create any (19) *nientso* between us, my family's going to have to take a backseat. I'm also attempting to figure out what my family life will look like when I'm at university. Will I still be able to talk to my parents in the same way? Will I be able to manage on my own? Who will I (20) *xmi* with at university? I wonder what my new (21) social *irlcec* will look like.

↳ Reply   ⇆ Share

---

b **Copy the green expressions (e.g. *blood relatives*) into your notebook. Add an explanation or a translation.**

READING **7** **On the newspaper's website, the original posts had titles. Choose one of the titles below for each post by writing the first letter of each name next to it. There are two extra titles you won't need.**

1 Families can really be annoying   ☐   4 Still, we love them   J
2 It's hard, but we need to talk   ☐   5 Growing up, leaving home   K
3 Teenagers are under pressure   I   6 Adolescence is tough   R

WRITING **8** a **Choose one of the headlines and write a similar post about your family. Use as many of the green + LANGUAGE   expressions as possible.**

b **Blank out some of the expressions from the text you've written and give it to a partner to fill in.**

a **You are going to read an article on changing family structures. First, work with a partner and look at the headline only. What could 'new family structures' be? What is a 'traditional family'?**

b **Read the headline again. What is meant when someone says that a child 'does well'? How do you measure this? Discuss some ideas you have and compare them with another pair.**

READING **10** a **Read the article. What is the author's opinion? How does she support it?**

Children do just as well in 'new family structures' as in the traditional family

by Susan Golombok

For a long time, people believed that the traditional two-parent family with married heterosexual mum and dad and biologically related children was important for the well-being of children. So 'non-traditional' variants of this family structure, be they, for example, single-parent families or stepfamilies, took second place, at best. More recent variations, known as 'new family forms', involving same-sex parents and families created by reproductive technologies, have also been stigmatised. However, research on these more modern family forms supports them as equivalent to the traditional family structure.

The research on new family forms gathered over the last 35 years has shown that children in these families do just as well as children raised in traditional families. The evidence also reveals that boys are no less 'masculine' in terms of identity and behaviour, and girls are no less 'feminine', when they grow up with single parents or with same-sex parents.

To some, these findings will hardly be surprising. Children in these new family forms are typically very wanted children with dedicated parents. They are not born casually. Some studies even find more positive relationships in these partnerships than in traditional families.

I am not saying that children in new family forms always do well. The research simply shows that they are just as likely to do well or have problems as children in traditional families, depending on factors such as the quality of parenting, the children's own personal characteristics and, importantly, the social environment in which they are raised. That includes society's attitudes towards the family. Society's prejudice and stigmatisation can harm these children – even though there is actually nothing in their families that puts them at risk. Research on new family forms contradicts conventional wisdoms and prejudice, confirming what many parents in those families have long known – the kids are typically doing fine.

b **Go through the article again. What factors does the author mention that can impact a child's life in a positive or negative way? Can you think of any other factors that might influence a child's life?**

LANGUAGE **11** a Expand your vocabulary: Types of family
Which types of family below are mentioned in the article? Underline them.

a blended family	d nuclear family	g stepfamily
b childless family	e <u>family of same-sex parents</u>	h <u>traditional family</u>
c extended family	f <u>single-parent family</u>	

b **Write a short definition of all types of family listed in the box above.**

LISTENING **12** **a** **You are going to listen to Beryl Stephenson, a sociologist, talking about four different family structures that will change society in the future. Before you listen, match the expressions with their explanations.**

p. 10

1 backbone
2 professionals
3 infrastructure
4 breadwinner
5 living space
6 convenience
7 lifestyle
8 living costs

a something that makes things easier

b the person in a family who earns the money the family needs

c something that provides strength and support

d the type of life you have

e people with special skills and qualifications, often working in management positions in companies

f the money you spend on food, rent, clothes, etc.

g an area like a room, flat or house

h the systems and services, such as public transport or power supplies, that a country needs to work effectively

04

b **Now listen to Beryl Stephenson talking about how family structures might change in the future. Take notes to answer the questions below.**

1 Why will the young professionals not buy the flats they live in? *because they are flexible they change and they stay there like in hotels*
2 What kind of services will they expect in addition to their flats? *fitness studios, cleaning services, take away*
3 What are the advantages of two single-parent families living together? *more flexible, support each other, ethics*
4 What is the biggest challenge for urban family units consisting of multiple generations? *organise the and the living space*
5 Where does the last type of new family mentioned live? *country side*
6 How will the changing family structures influence society? *decision making, personal space will be limited*

SPEAKING **13** **Which of the four types of new families would you like to be part of? Give three reasons.**

14 *Paired activity:* **You are taking part in an international discussion forum on different forms of living together. Discuss with a partner which one might be most accepted by young people your age and agree on two or three.**

- traditional families
- blended families
- single-parent families
- families of same-sex parents
- childless couples

S **Strategies box**

Remember to **observe the context**: It's not about which form of living together *you* like or dislike, but which form might be most accepted *by young people your age.*

WRITING **15** **You have taken part in the international discussion forum on different forms of living together and decide to share your ideas in a blog.**

In your blog post you should:

- describe one of the family forms you discussed
- point out possible advantages of living in it
- speculate how people will feel about it in the future

Write around 250 words. Give your blog post a title.

S **Strategies box**

To speculate means **to form ideas and theories about something**, or to consider possible answers to a question, especially when you don't have enough information about it to be certain.

→ See *Writing coach, Blog post,* p. 180.

Make sure you know the meaning of the expressions below, then go through the previous section again and collect more to put in the four categories.

L

People	What they do	Things you need	How things can be
father-in-law spouse ancestor	raise children stand by each other keep sb. company	a home living space infrastructure	positive caring hospitable

b **Look at the expressions in your table for one minute and close your book. Write down as many as you can remember. Then compare your expressions in small groups and make up sentences using them.**

WRITING 17 **What does family mean to you? Write your own definition. Use words and phrases you've collected.**

B **By the way: All together now!**

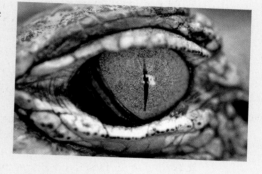

There are many collective nouns for humans, some of which are positive, such as *a club* or *a party*, and some of which are less positive like *a gang* or *a rabble*[1]. You probably know some collective words for animals too, such as *a pride of lions* or *a herd of cattle*, but there are a few you probably haven't heard of. For example, there may be *a mischief*[2] *of mice* living in your cellar, eating away at your food supplies. Not to worry, just get yourself *a clowder of cats* to chase them away. The cats may have babies which would then be *a kindle of kittens*. In the cellar, there may also be *a clutter of spiders*, but they'll be busy feeding on *a business of flies*.

If it's starting to feel a little crowded at home, you might go outside and see *a gaggle of geese* or *a scurry of squirrels*. *An army of frogs* might be in the river, along with *a shoal of fish*. Rather worryingly, there could be *an unkindness of ravens* or even worse, *a murder of crows*! Further away from home, there's *a shrewdness*[3] *of apes* and *a congregation of alligators*.

Some words for groups of animals seem obvious. For example, if you've ever tried to move a buffalo, you'll know why a group of them is *an obstinacy*[4]! Equally, *a shiver of sharks* and *a stand of flamingos* make perfect sense. As elephants never forget, maybe that's why a group is *a memory of elephants*, and *a crash of rhinoceroses* speaks for itself.

Let's end on a pleasant note. Who could resist *a charm of hummingbirds*[5]? And wouldn't you love to meet, in your perfect fantasy world, *a blessing*[6] *of unicorns*?

Work with a partner to make up your own fun collective nouns, for example *a rabble of pupils*, *a depression of teachers*, etc.

---

[1]**rabble:** Gesindel, Pöbel
[2]**mischief:** Unfug
[3]**shrewdness:** Schläue, Klugheit

[4]**obstinacy:** Bockigkeit, Sturheit
[5]**hummingbird:** Kolibri
[6]**blessing:** Segen

LANGUAGE **18** a **Expand your vocabulary: Predicting the future**

p.13

The following three sentences all predict the same event in the future. Try to explain the difference in meaning.

a Frank and Alice will get married.
b Frank and Alice are about to get married.
c Frank and Alice are bound to get married.

L	**+ infinitive**	**+ noun or gerund**
	be sure to be set to be certain to be due to be about to be bound to	be on the brink of be on the verge of be on the point of

b **Study the expressions in the box and the sentences below. Decide which expressions say that something 'is definitely going to happen' and which ones that something 'will happen soon or any minute'.**

a Over the next decades, the percentage of single households in Austria is due to <u>increase</u>. By 2060 they will make up around 41% of all households in the country.
b Europeans are having fewer children, so Europe's population is on the verge of <u>reaching</u> a new low point. As a consequence, the societies of the EU countries are about to <u>change</u> dramatically.

19 a **A pessimist is predicting the future of families. Fill in the expressions to make sentences.**

The divorce rate is (1) c_____ to rise over the next years. Millions of families are

(2) b_____ to split up, and depression among children is (3) s_____ to become

a frequent issue. We are on the (4) v_____ of disaster!

b **What would an optimist say? Rewrite the pessimistic prediction about the future of families.**

c **Are you a pessimist or an optimist? Make your own predictions about the future of families using the appropriate expressions.**

LANGUAGE **20** **Future perfect and continuous**

p.13

What is the difference in meaning? Match each example sentence with the appropriate explanation (a or b) and timeline (A or B).

1 By the time I'm 35, I will have built the house of my dreams.
2 When I'm 35, I will be building the house of my dreams.

a You are imagining yourself in the future and looking back at what you have achieved in the present/past.
b You are predicting what will be going on at a specific time in the future.

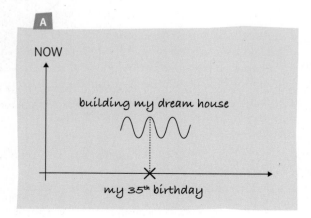

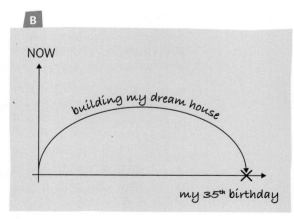

→ See *Grammar revisited, Talking about the future*, p. 172.

WRITING **21** **Write a paragraph about your dreams for your life in two years and one for your life ten years from now. What will you have done by then, and what will you will be doing at that time?**

LANGUAGE **22** Expand your vocabulary: Formal and informal register

📑 p. 14

Work with a partner. Which of the adjectives below describe language rather used in formal contexts, which in informal contexts? Which kinds of language could be used in both? Highlight the adjectives in different colours. What other words can you think of that describe language?

L

a appropriate   d conversational   g polite   j impolite   m rude
b chatty   e disrespectful   h inappropriate   k insulting   n vague
c colloquial   f euphemistic   i incoherent   l proper   o emotional

23 **a** Collect expressions that you would use when talking to an English friend, but never when talking to your English teacher. Give examples of inappropriate phrases that you could change to make them appropriate for the teacher (e.g. *I screwed up – I made a mistake*).

    b Summarise the differences between written and spoken language that you are aware of.

24 **a** Study the questions and statements below and decide whether they are rather formal (F) or informal (I). Are they written (W) or spoken (S) language? Circle the correct answers. Sometimes there is more than one correct answer.

<u>Situation 1</u>: You are interested in a particular job and ask a friend who works there about the salary.

1 Could you let me know how much I'd earn?   **F**/ I   **W**/ S
2 Oh, by the way, how much money would I make?   F /**I**   W /**S**
3 And what will I take home at the end of the month?   F /**I**   W /**S**
4 I would like to enquire about the salary.   **F**/ I   **W**/ S
5 How much?? 😜   F /**I**   **W**/ S
6 Could you please tell me what the salary is?   F /**I**   W /**S**

<u>Situation 2</u>: You want to complain about a burger you had at a restaurant.

1 This burger was just horrible.   F /**I**   W /**S**
2 Eww! How gross!   F /**I**   W /**S**
3 I didn't enjoy my meal at all.   **F**/ I   **W**/ S
4 Burger: 🤢   F /**I**   **W**/ S
5 Ugh! This burger was really crap.   F /**I**   W /**S**
6 The burger tasted extremely unpleasant.   **F**/ I   **W**/ S

    b Compare your answers with a partner and give reasons for your choices. What makes these statements formal/informal? Highlight the elements that distinguish formal language from informal language in different colours.

SPEAKING **25** Discuss with a partner which of the phrases below you would rather use to tell a teacher or a friend that you don't like the book you are currently reading in class.

a a bit tedious   d can't stand it   g it really sucks   j not inspiring
b a real drag   e dead boring   h not especially enjoyable   k rubbish
c a real pain   f hardly motivating   i suitable for younger children   l a waste of time

WRITING **26** Use expressions from above to write two short texts:

    a a feedback note to a teacher complaining about a school trip you didn't enjoy
    b a text message to a friend while on the trip

READING 27 a Imagine you have to prepare a presentation on register for school. During your research, you come across the article below. Go over it quickly: Why could this be a useful source?

How did that register?
Five levels of formality in language

We've all experienced the occasional verbal slip-up, whether we're nervous or the words just don't come out right. In casual speech between friends, a faux pas like that is usually laughed off and moved on from as quickly as it appeared. However, in business meetings and professional speeches, they're a little harder to overlook. A major source of faux pas encountered in interpretation work is the tricky element of language known as 'register'. It's the difference between walking up to a colleague and saying "What's up?" instead of "How are you doing?"

Spoken language takes on different levels of formality depending on the social situation and the relationships between those involved. Register is the form that language takes in different circumstances, and 'code switching' is the ability to go from one register to another guided by context. Register is an essential social skill that provides flexibility and demonstrates competence in speech and appropriate social norms.

However, even for experienced interpreters, register is difficult to master as it relies not only on the language itself but also on social customs, culture, and even personal preferences. As a relationship progresses between individuals, the register they use will usually evolve to be more informal.

There are two basic forms of register: informal and formal. Contexts where one might use the informal register are with friends, family, and meeting people at casual venues, like a bar. The formal register is reserved for professional settings like classrooms, the workplace and interviews. Place isn't the only determinant of register: Factors like how long the people have known each other, their previous relationship, if any, and their purpose in speaking to each other affect how formal or informal the speech will be. Speaking with parents and teachers would require less formal speech than at a company networking event, but more formal speech than a peer group. Linguists have actually determined that there are five different levels of formality in most languages:

Register	Definition	Examples
1 Frozen	Language that never changes	Wedding vows, the wording of a law
2 Formal	Standard English	Speeches, language spoken in court
3 Consultative	Less formal standard English	Pupil to teacher, employee to employer
4 Casual	Language between friends	Conversation in a café, chatting on the way to school
5 Intimate	Language between partners or other close family and friends	Pet names, inside jokes

b Read the article again closely to do the tasks below. Compare your answers with a partner.

1 Explain what 'code switching' involves.
2 Give reasons why it is important to be able to recognise and use different registers.
3 Name some factors on which register is based.
4 Name some factors which influence the register used between two partners.

c What (other) examples of written texts for the five levels of formality can you think of?

Listen to some people talking in five different situations.

1 What register are the people using?
2 Where do these conversations take place?
3 What is the apparent relationship between the two people?
4 Why are they talking to each other?

SPEAKING **29** a **Discuss the following questions in small groups:**

1 Can you think of an occasion when you misjudged the register needed and created a faux pas? Share your experience of such a situation with the other students.
2 In English there is no polite 'Sie' or informal 'du'. What other methods do you think English speakers use to show an informal or formal register when they're speaking?

b **Create some pictures in which people are using the wrong register. Compare them in class and vote for the most creative ones.**

> Hey, ma'am, smile a bit. People are taking pictures.

> Sorry, dude, we totally forgot about the assignment. Can you cut us some slack⁷?

WRITING **30** **Browsing the internet, you have read the following lines in a blog post on teenagers' way of communicating.**

Anonymouse

… This is what really worries me. The only way for teenagers to communicate seems to be by writing text messages in which they use a register of their own. Have they forgotten how to write properly?

reply

You have decided to comment on the blog post above. In your blog comment you should:

- explain why many teenagers prefer texting to talking
- specify what language teenagers use in text messages
- state that teenagers are able to use the right register if needed

Write around 250 words.

→ See *Writing coach, Blog comment*, p. 182.

S **Strategies box**

To state means **to express** or **declare your opinion clearly**, formally and in a definite way.

---

⁷ **to cut sb. some slack** (*infml.*): mit jmdm. nachsichtig/nicht so streng sein

I hear you (not?)

SPEAKING **31** The diagram on the right shows the four-sides model of interpersonal communication according to F. Schulz von Thun. Work with a partner to interpret the diagram and express its message in your own words.

What do I inform about?

Factual information

What do I reveal about myself?

Self-revelation

Sender → **Message** **Appeal** → Receiver

What do I want you to do?

Relationship

How do we interrelate?

READING **32** Read the article about this model of communication. Complete the sentences (1–7) using a maximum of four words. Write your answers in the spaces provided. The first one (0) has been done for you.

p. 15

Lend me your ears

If you're asked how many tongues or pairs of ears you have, you'll doubtless answer, "One," but not according to Friedemann Schulz von Thun, a German psychologist. His 'four-sides model of interpersonal communication' suggests that we have four different 'tongues' and 'ears' as ways of transmitting and receiving messages. Schulz von Thun's overall message is, if you're speaking, you should anticipate possible misinterpretations and explicitly say what you do and don't mean. Equally, if you're listening, before being hurt and getting all defensive straight away, you should ask how something was meant.

According to Schulz von Thun, the speaker sends a message which has four different aspects: the self-revelation (what I'm saying about myself), the facts (what happened, matter-of-fact information), the relationship (what I think of the other person) and the appeal (what I want the listener to do, or not do). The listener hears with four different ears, also related to the four aspects of the message: the self-revelation (what is the speaker showing of themselves?), the facts (what do I know or need to know?), the relationship (what does the speaker think of me?) and the appeal (what is the speaker asking me to do, or not do?).

When all is good and the conversation flows, there is a balance between the four aspects and the speaker/listener roles swing back and forth. Both sides are sensitive to what they are saying and what they are hearing. Problems occur when the speaker and listener emphasise different (mismatching) sides of the model, when there are too many implicit (hidden) messages, when the speaker and listener are not sensitive to each other and which side the other is emphasising. Explicit messages are openly expressed, whereas implicit ones are hidden.

The classic example Schulz von Thun uses is a car passenger telling the driver that "the traffic light is green" while waiting at a junction:

Factual information: The green light is on.
Self-revelation: I want to get going.
Relationship: You need my help.
Appeal: Go!

So, how can we avoid misunderstandings in a conversation? When we say something, we should try to be clear about what it is that we want to say and try to avoid too many implicit messages. This makes it easier for the receiver to identify which side of the square you are coming from. That includes body language and facial expressions that match your message so as not to confuse the listener. As the speaker you can prepare the listener for your message by clarifying, for example, saying, "My personal feeling about this is …" or "I want to express my standpoint …" when you want to emphasise self-revelation. If you want something from someone, try to say it explicitly: "I need your help with …" instead of "I have to do this project all by myself". If you see that the listener hasn't picked up the message you have sent – and often this shows itself with annoyance with the relationship ear –, go to the emotional level and try to identify the feeling of the other person and why they are feeling that way ("You're feeling … because …").

As the listener you have choices to make about which ear you are going to hear emphasised. It is often helpful to first try to identify which side of the square the speaker is coming from, i.e. to really listen. Is the speaker giving me information and/or telling me about themselves (self-revelation)? It is then essential to help them identify their feelings. Are they asking me to do something (appeal)? Are they saying something about our relationship? Then I can go to the emotional level and use attentive listening skills, "You're feeling …" messages, until the relationship aspect is

clarified and the conversation can move on to other aspects: self-revelation, information or appeal.

0	Schulz von Thun says that speakers need to _____ .	say what they mean
1	According to Von Thun, listeners should avoid _____ .	being defensive straight away
2	After an 'appeal', listeners should know whether or not _____ .	sth should be done
3	Communication problems arise when neither person _____ .	is sensitive
4	Listeners can be confused by _____ .	body language mis matching
5	If you notice the listener hasn't understood your message, you should _____ .	go to the emotional level
6	The secret of really listening lies in _____ .	identifiying intentions
7	If someone is revealing personal information about themselves, you have to _____ .	listen carefully

LANGUAGE **33** Expand your vocabulary: Communication
Use the article to create a collection of expressions dealing with communication (e.g. kinds of messages, verb/noun phrases, etc.). Organise them in a way you prefer to study (e.g. a table with translations or a word map).

WRITING
+ SPEAKING

34 a **Do you find Schulz von Thun's model helpful? Why?/Why not?**

b **Write down four ways the statements below could be interpreted according to the model. Then compare them in pairs and discuss any differences.**

1 You left the lights on.
2 Are you going out in that shirt?
3 That was the last piece of cake you've just eaten.
4 There's something green in this soup you made.
5 Are your friends coming over again this evening?

SPEAKING

35 a *Individual long turn:* **Do this exercise together with a partner. Student A does the individual long turn with the pictures, student B discusses the chart. Give feedback to each other. Throw the dice or a coin to determine who is student A and student B.**

- Compare the different forms of communication in the pictures.
- Comment on young people's language in text messages.
- Outline situations in which you would rather write a letter than a text message.

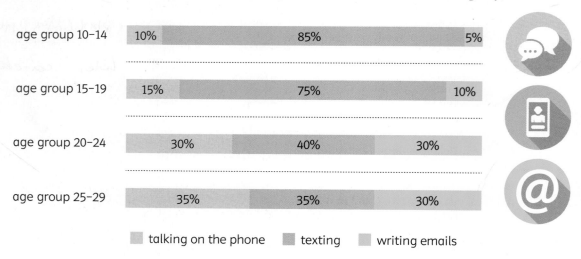

Young people's favourite way of communicating with each other (n = 20 for each group)

	talking on the phone	texting	writing emails
age group 10–14	10%	85%	5%
age group 15–19	15%	75%	10%
age group 20–24	30%	40%	30%
age group 25–29	35%	35%	30%

■ talking on the phone   ■ texting   ■ writing emails

- Present the chart.
- Comment on the popularity of smartphones.
- Outline situations in which talking on the phone might be better than writing text messages.

b **Discuss which of the individual long turns was easier/harder to do. Give reasons for your decision.**

Copy the word map into your notebook and add more ideas and expressions.
Compare in class and with your teacher's model to improve it further.

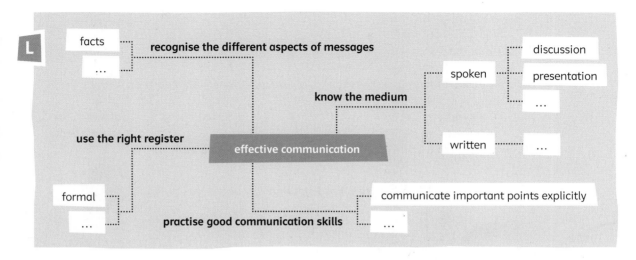

b Write a top 10 list of new expressions related to family from this unit you want to remember.

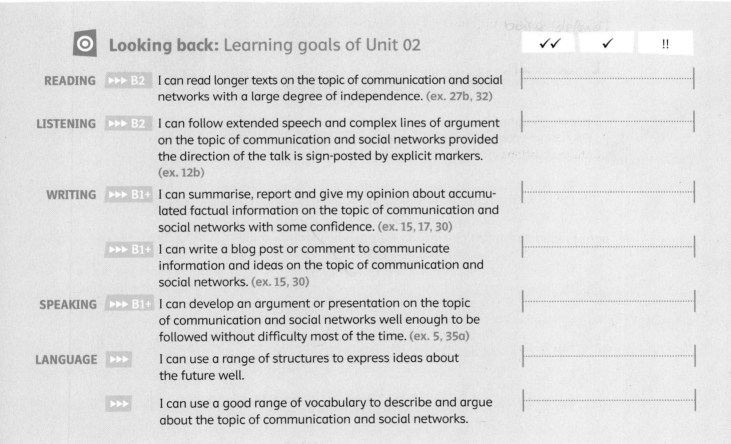

◎ **Looking back:** Learning goals of Unit 02

| | ✓✓ | ✓ | !! |

READING ▶▶▶ B2   I can read longer texts on the topic of communication and social networks with a large degree of independence. (ex. 27b, 32)

LISTENING ▶▶▶ B2   I can follow extended speech and complex lines of argument on the topic of communication and social networks provided the direction of the talk is sign-posted by explicit markers. (ex. 12b)

WRITING ▶▶▶ B1+   I can summarise, report and give my opinion about accumulated factual information on the topic of communication and social networks with some confidence. (ex. 15, 17, 30)

▶▶▶ B1+   I can write a blog post or comment to communicate information and ideas on the topic of communication and social networks. (ex. 15, 30)

SPEAKING ▶▶▶ B1+   I can develop an argument or presentation on the topic of communication and social networks well enough to be followed without difficulty most of the time. (ex. 5, 35a)

LANGUAGE ▶▶▶   I can use a range of structures to express ideas about the future well.

▶▶▶   I can use a good range of vocabulary to describe and argue about the topic of communication and social networks.

The most interesting discussion raised in this unit was ...

A new expression I know I'll use again is ...

The Veldt[1]

by Ray Bradbury

1 **Before you start reading, discuss the following questions with a partner. Then share your ideas with the class.**

1 What are typical issues between parents and their children today?
2 For what reasons might parents not take enough time to look after their children? How might they try to make up for this in other ways?

2 **Now read parts of the short story *The Veldt* and talk about the questions below.**

"George, I wish you'd look at the nursery[2]."
"What's wrong with it?"
"I don't know."
"Well, then."
[...]
"It's just that the nursery is different now than it was."
"All right, let's have a look."
They walked down the hall of their soundproofed Happylife Home, which had cost them thirty thousand dollars installed, this house which clothed and fed and rocked them to sleep and played and sang and was good to them. Their approach sensitized[3] a switch somewhere and the nursery light flicked on when they came within ten feet of it. Similarly, behind them, in the halls, lights went on and off as they left them behind, with a soft automaticity.

"Well," said George Hadley.

They stood on the thatched floor of the nursery. It was forty feet across by forty feet long and thirty feet high; it had cost half again as much as the rest of the house. "But nothing's too good for our children," George had said.

The nursery was silent. It was empty as a jungle glade at hot high noon. The walls were blank and two-dimensional. Now, as George and Lydia Hadley stood in the center of the room, the walls began to purr and recede[4] into crystalline distance, it seemed, and presently an African veldt appeared, in three dimensions, on all sides, in color reproduced to the final pebble and bit of straw. The ceiling above them became a deep sky with a hot yellow sun.

George Hadley felt the perspiration start on his brow.

"Let's get out of this sun," he said. "This is a little too real. But I don't see anything wrong."

"Wait a moment, you'll see," said his wife. [...]

"You see, there are the lions, far over, that way. Now they're on their way to the water hole. They've just been eating. I don't know what."

"Some animal." George Hadley put his hand up to shield off the burning light from his squinted eyes. [...]

What is the nursery like? How does this compare to what a normal nursery would be like?

---

[1] **veldt:** (süd)afrikanische Steppe
[2] **nursery:** *hier:* Kinderzimmer
[3] **sensitize:** *hier:* auslösen
[4] **recede:** zurückweichen, verschwinden

The lions were coming. And again, George Hadley was filled with admiration for the mechanical genius who had conceived this room. A miracle of efficiency selling for an absurdly low price. Every home should have one. Oh, occasionally they frightened you with their clinical accuracy, they startled you, gave you a twinge, but most of the time, what fun for everyone, not only your own son and daughter, but for yourself when you felt like a quick jaunt⁵ to a foreign land, a quick change of scenery. Well, here it was! And here were the lions now, fifteen feet away, so real, so feverishly and startlingly real that you could feel the prickling fur on your hand.

[…]

The lions stood looking at George and Lydia Hadley with terrible green-yellow eyes.

"Watch out!" screamed Lydia.

The lions came running at them. Lydia bolted⁶ and ran. Instinctively, George sprang after her. Outside, in the hall, with the door slammed, he was laughing and she was crying, and they both stood appalled at the other's reaction.

"George!"

"Lydia! Oh, my dear poor sweet Lydia!"

"They almost got us!"

"Walls, Lydia, remember; crystal walls, that's all they are. Oh, they look real, I must admit – Africa in your parlor – but it's all dimensional, super reactionary, supersensitive color film and mental tape film behind glass screens."

[…]

"You've got to tell Wendy and Peter not to read any more on Africa."

"Of course – of course." He patted her.

How is tension created in the reader at this point? What clues does Bradbury give us that something bad is going to happen? (This technique is called 'foreshadowing'.)

3

"And lock the nursery for a few days until I get my nerves settled."

"You know how difficult Peter is about that. When I punished him a month ago by locking the nursery for even a few hours – the tantrum he threw⁷! And Wendy too. They live for the nursery."

"It's got to be locked, that's all there is to it."

"All right." Reluctantly he locked the huge door. "You've been working too hard. You need a rest."

"I don't know – I don't know," she said, blowing her nose, sitting down in a chair that immediately began to rock and comfort her. "Maybe I don't have enough to do. Maybe I have time to think too much. Why don't we shut the whole house off for a few days and take a vacation?"

[…]

Why do you think Lydia wants to shut off the house? At this stage in the story, what do you think will be the children's reaction to this idea? Support your opinion.

As for the nursery, thought George Hadley, it won't hurt for the children to be locked out of it awhile. Too much of anything isn't good for anyone. And it was clearly indicated that the children had been spending a little too much time on Africa. That sun. He could feel it on his neck, still, like a hot paw. And the lions. And the smell of blood. Remarkable how the nursery caught the telepathic emanations⁸ of the children's minds and created life to fill their every desire. The children thought lions, and there were lions. The children thought zebras, and there were zebras. Sun – sun. Giraffes – giraffes. Death and death.

[…]

---

⁵ **jaunt:** Ausflug, Spritztour
⁶ **bolt:** davonstürzen
⁷ **to throw a tantrum:** einen Wutanfall kriegen
⁸ **telepathic emanations:** telepathische Gedankenströme

"Where are you going?" He didn't answer Lydia. Preoccupied, he let the lights glow softly on ahead of him, extinguish behind him as he padded to the nursery door. He listened against it. Far away, a lion roared.

He unlocked the door and opened it. Just before he stepped inside, he heard a faraway scream. And then another roar from the lions, which subsided quickly.

George Hadley stood on the African grassland alone. The lions looked up from their feeding, watching him. The only flaw to the illusion was the open door through which he could see his wife, far down the dark hall, like a framed picture, eating her dinner abstractedly. "Go away," he said to the lions. They did not go. He knew the principle of the room exactly. You sent out your thoughts. Whatever you thought would appear.

[...]

Later, that evening ...

5

"There's no Africa in the nursery," said Peter simply.

"Oh, come now, Peter. We know better."

"I don't remember any Africa," said Peter to Wendy. "Do you?"

"No."

"Run see and come tell." She obeyed.

"Wendy, come back here!" said George Hadley, but she was gone. The house lights followed her like a flock of fireflies. Too late, he realized he had forgotten to lock the nursery door after his last inspection.

"Wendy'll look and come tell us," said Peter.

"She doesn't have to tell me. I've seen it."

"I'm sure you're mistaken, Father."

"I'm not, Peter. Come along now."

But Wendy was back. "It's not Africa," she said breathlessly.

"We'll see about this," said George Hadley, and they all walked down the hall together and opened the nursery door. There was a green, lovely forest, a lovely river, a purple mountain, ... The African veldtland was gone. The lions were gone.

[...]

"I wouldn't want the nursery locked up," said Peter coldly. "Ever."

"Matter of fact, we're thinking of turning the whole house off for about a month. Live sort of a carefree one-for-all existence."

"That sounds dreadful! Would I have to tie my own shoes instead of letting the shoe tier do it? And brush my own teeth and comb my hair and give myself a bath?"

"It would be fun for a change, don't you think?"

[...]

"Will you shut off the house sometime soon?"

"We're considering it."

"I don't think you'd better consider it any more, Father."

"I won't have any threats from my son!"

"Very well." And Peter strolled off to the nursery.

Eventually George Hadley decides to lock up the nursery ...

6

"Don't let them do it!" wailed Peter at the ceiling, as if he was talking to the house, the nursery. "Don't let Father kill everything." He turned to his father. "Oh, I hate you!"

"Insults won't get you anywhere."

"I wish you were dead!"

"We were, for a long while. Now we're going to really start living. Instead of being handled and massaged, we're going to live." Wendy was still crying, and Peter joined her again. "Just a moment, just one moment, just another moment of nursery," they wailed.

"Oh, George," said the wife, "it can't hurt."

"All right – all right, if they'll just shut up. One minute, mind you, and then off forever."

"Daddy, Daddy, Daddy!" sang the children, smiling with wet faces.

"And then we're going on a vacation."

[…]

"I think we'd better get downstairs before those kids get engrossed[9] with those damned beasts again. Just then they heard the children calling, "Daddy, Mommy, come quick – quick!"

They went downstairs in the air flue and ran down the hall. The children were nowhere in sight.

"Wendy? Peter!"

They ran into the nursery. The veldtland was empty save for the lions waiting, looking at them. "Peter, Wendy?"

The door slammed.

"Wendy, Peter!"

George Hadley and his wife whirled and ran back to the door.

"Open the door!" cried George Hadley, trying the knob. "Why, they've locked it from the outside! Peter!" He beat at the door. "Open up!"

He heard Peter's voice outside, against the door.

"Don't let them switch off the nursery and the house," he was saying.

Mr. and Mrs. George Hadley beat at the door. "Now, don't be ridiculous, children. It's time to go."

And then they heard the sounds.

The lions on three sides of them, in the yellow veldt grass, padding through the dry straw, rumbling and roaring in their throats.

The lions.

Mr. Hadley looked at his wife and they turned and looked back at the beasts edging slowly forward crouching, tails stiff.

[…]

What do you think is happening to the parents? Are the children aware of what they have done? Find evidence for your answer.

3 **Discuss these questions about the story in class:**

1 What techniques does Bradbury use to make the story effective and realistic?
Choose a few specific examples from the text that you particularly like and explain why.
2 *The Veldt* was published in 1950. How is the story still relevant today?
3 What is the author's attitude toward technology? What is the story's overall message?
Do you agree with it?

4 **Choose one of these activities to do in class or at home:**

1 Decide what happens next and write an additional page to the story.
2 Write a series of entries for Peter's diary.
3 Complete each of the following seven ideas using the story for
inspiration, then exchange your ideas with other classmates:
This story made me aware that … decide that … wonder about …
see that … believe that … feel that … hope that …
4 Imagine that you have to organise a tour of the house.
Make a recording for an audio guide describing it.

---

[9] **to get engrossed with sth.:** sich von etw. vereinnahmen lassen

Unit 03
Coming home

 4687dx

In this unit you will:

- think about how you'll live after school
- discuss when it's time to move out
- compare living in the city and the country

- improve your summarising skills
- find out how 100 million people are living
- visit a home in Mozambique

SPEAKING 1 Talk about the flatmate advertisements in pairs:

1 What do you learn about the flats and the people who live there?
  What could be fun/terrible/challenging/interesting/etc. about sharing a flat with this person?
2 Who would you like to live with most, and why? Compare your answers in class.

A

YouTuber wants flatmate!

I'm renting out the spare bedroom in my flat, which is also where I keep all my filming equipment. So flatmate must be OK with never locking the bedroom door and sometimes assist me with camera/lighting.

B

Fellow foodie flatmate wanted!

We regularly have barbecues and beer tasting parties on the balcony. Our meat is dry aged in the kitchen cabinet, and we brew beer in the bathtub. Seize your chance for an original gourmet experience.

No vegetarians or vegans, please!

The person in ad A seems …
I'd consider moving in with … (if …)
I think this person is really rude/weird/interesting
  because …
I could/couldn't imagine sharing a flat with … because …
I'd worry about person X's …

C

Flatmate wanted!

Must have a driving license and be willing to drive me to and from work every day. No smokers, no pets, no musical instruments, no whistling.

D

Looking for animal-loving flatmate

You will share the 200-m² flat with me, my 16 well-behaved cats and two robotic vacuum cleaners. While I am on semi-weekly work trips, I would kindly ask you to refill the cat food dispensers daily and empty the cleaners' filters. Please email me for pictures of the cats and/or the flat.

E

Offering free room

Flatmate will be expected to clean, shop and cook for me as I provide rent-free living.

WRITING 2 a Work in pairs. Write your own flatmate ad.

  b Put the ads up in class and read each other's ads. Discuss why you would move in where.

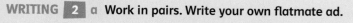

42

Where to live after school

SPEAKING **3** Form small groups and discuss your plans for the future. How do you think your living situation will change once you've finished school? Where will you go? What will you need?

LANGUAGE **4** a Expand your vocabulary: Living arrangements – part 1
Study the expressions in the box below. How many of them can you translate or explain?
Write down what you know already.

b Move around the room and ask your classmates for their ideas on any expressions you don't know.
Can you get all of them? Ask your teacher for any that are left.

L

a	accommodation *a place where you live*	i	homesick *when you miss home*
b	campus *the area where students move around*	j	housework *cleaning house*
c	cleaner *someone who cleans*	k	mess *untidiness*
d	common room _____	l	to move *changing living place*
e	to commute *to go from place to place*	m	on my own *what you do sth. alone by myself*
f	costly *when smth. is pricy*	n	to rent *to borrow flat with money*
g	dorm *a place where students live*	o	studio flat *just one room*
h	flatmate *someone who lives w. you*	p	university *somewhere to study a high level education*

LISTENING **5** ⊙ 06 ⊕ a Listen to some people talking on a radio show about how they live after having finished school.
Take notes on the points below.

- details of their living situation
- what they like about their living situation

b Use the expressions from the box above to write short summaries of each of the four interviews.

SPEAKING **6** a Which of the living situations you heard about would be the most suitable for you? What might be potential upsides and downsides of them? Discuss in small groups.

b Can you think of any other living arrangements for students or people who have finished school and are starting to work?

WRITING **7** One of your friends wants to study at an English university and is looking for inexpensive accommodation. He/She has found flatmate advertisement E on p. 42 in a magazine and has asked you to write an email to the person who posted the advertisement.

In your email you should:

- give your reasons for writing
- comment on your friend's situation
- specify what you need to know

Write around 250 words.

→ See *Writing coach, Formal email*, p. 178.

READING **8** Read the texts on this double page. They are about people who are looking for a place to live (1–4) and people talking about their living experiences (A–C). Which of the texts on the left and right page discuss the same living arrangements? Which text doesn't go with anything?

p. 20

1 **B**

Peter

I wouldn't really enjoy living with other people. I like my privacy and, if I'm honest, a little bit of luxury. I would be an ideal tenant as I'm tidy and wouldn't bother the other residents in the building. Decent facilities in the kitchen including a dishwasher and washing machine would be really important to me. I'm not so keen on doing my own cleaning, so I would need to find someone to do this for me. This would also save me time so I could get on with my studies. Financially I'm quite well off, I can afford to live by myself. It would be great to live on the top floor somewhere as I would really enjoy the view.

2 **C**

Alex

As far as I'm concerned, if you have a roof over your head, it doesn't matter too much what it's like. I definitely don't need luxuries as a student. For me it's most important to have a desk to work at, somewhere to store my books and to be near uni. I really don't want a long commute – the nearer, the better. I'm quite environmentally friendly, so I wouldn't be happy taking a car ride to university – but I couldn't afford a car anyway. I'd need a couple of bookshelves for my books and somewhere to hang a few clothes. An en-suite bathroom would be an advantage, but isn't a necessity because I'm happy to share the facilities with other people. I'd quite like a communal kitchen; this would give me the chance to get to know a few people.

3 **A**

Zahra

I'm going to get a monthly allowance from my parents, and then I can afford a small amount of rent somewhere. Ideally, I'd like to get together with some other students and share a place so I can have a ready-made social life. I'm quite a sociable person and enjoy going out, but I'm also happy to stay home and watch a film. I'm generally a pretty tidy person and don't mind doing a bit of vacuuming, cleaning or doing the laundry now and then, as long as the others aren't too untidy and do their share. Luckily my dad is an electrician. If anything broke, he'd be able to help out and repair things. He could do stuff like install extra sockets so everyone could plug in their devices.

4

Cheryl

I'll be starting my first ever job, which is scary and exciting at the same time. I won't earn that much to begin with, so I won't have much money for rent or furniture. This means I'll need low-cost accommodation that's fully furnished. I grew up in the city near to where the offices of my new job are and my family home's still there. To be honest, I don't really want to bother moving out with all my junk. I get on pretty well with my family, but I also enjoy having my independence and going out for evenings with my mates. I won't be home all that much anyway. I haven't got a car, but fortunately we have access to public transport.

A

In order to make ends meet on a student budget, I decided to share a flat with three other people doing the same university course as me. It's a great way to live! You save money by sharing the rent, utility bills and the home insurance, and you have a lot of fun at the same time. There's always someone to hang out with. The only problem is if one of your flatmates is messy and refuses to do their share of the household chores, like doing the dishes. Also, sometimes things go wrong which you can't fix. Our central heating broke in the middle of the winter. Luckily, the landlady sent a plumber to repair it, but it was freezing cold for a few days.

B

Despite the high cost, I managed to get myself a nice little loft apartment after I had finished school. I work in a well-paid part-time job, so I can afford the rent. I'm really pleased with this place – it's stylish and has all the amenities I need, like a dishwasher, washing machine, dryer and even air conditioning. It's not particularly spacious, but it's in a nice residential area and there's even a housekeeper who comes by every week and cleans the apartment. As soon as the estate agent showed me around, I knew I wanted to live here. It's a cool neighbourhood. The only disadvantage is the construction site next door where they're building new apartments; it's often quite noisy on the balcony.

C

If you ask me, on-campus student accommodation is the only way to live as a student. Of course, you have to be pretty sociable and open-minded – after all, you're sharing a lot of the facilities with others –, but it's worth it. There's a communal bathroom and kitchen, but only for 10 students, which isn't too bad. Living on campus means you don't have to commute to uni, you're already there. That means you can sleep in a bit longer in the mornings! The hall of residence I stayed in was nice and clean. But when I spent a semester in the USA, I shared my dorm room with two students and a family of cockroaches.

LANGUAGE **9** Expand your vocabulary: Living arrangements – part 2

pp. 19+20

Find out the meaning of the green expressions in the vocabulary appendix or a dictionary. Then use them to create 'odd one out' tasks for your classmates. Here's an example:
estate agent – electrician – budget – tenant. **Which word doesn't fit? Why?**

SPEAKING + WRITING **10** **Work with a partner. Write a list of requirements or problems mentioned in the texts. Agree on possible solutions to these problems.**
Example: *little money – get cheap flat, find flatmates, get a job.*

WRITING **11** **Write your own text to go with Cheryl's statement. Include some of the new expressions from exercise 9.**

12 **Create a timeline about how you want to live in the future. How and where will you live when you are 20, 30 or 50 years old? Consider what you will need and how you will finance it.**

13 **You have read the first two sentences of text C in a blog on the advantages of living on campus. Comment on them in around 200 words.**

LANGUAGE 14 a **Expand your vocabulary: Phrasal verbs**

p. 20

Form phrasal verbs with the verbs on the left side and the prepositions on the right, then fill them into the statements below. You can use some of the words more than once.

> L clear ▪ come ▪ get ▪ hang ▪ move ▪ show ▪ sleep
>
> around ▪ away ▪ by ▪ in ▪ on ▪ out ▪ together

1 Student accommodation is a great way for young people to _____ with new people and make friends.

2 When my flatmates _____ here in September, we will split the rent and utility bills.

3 First, we'll finish our household chores and then we can _____ in my room.

4 The first thing Mike wants to do as soon as he has a job is _____ of his parents' house.

5 Rasheed is going to _____ our place later today to drop off some books.

6 Our landlord _____ us _____ the flat and explained how the air conditioning worked.

7 Minnie said she'd rather _____ than have to get up early and commute to university.

8 I don't get much of an allowance, so I won't be able to _____ from home any time soon.

9 If you want the people from housekeeping to clean the bathroom and kitchen, you'll have to _____ all your stuff before next week.

10 It makes flat sharing much more fun when you _____ well with your flatmates.

b **Can you make more phrasal verbs with the verbs from the box? Check how the meaning changes when you use a different preposition.**

15 **Read the statements in 14a again and find situations in which they could be made. (For example, number 2 could be said in a conversation with a friend.)**

SPEAKING 16 *Paired activity:* **Your English language assistant wants to know at what age most young Austrians might want to move out from their family home. Discuss which factors might influence them in their decision. Come up with a suggestion as to when most young Austrians might want to move out.**

▪ relationships
▪ future plans
▪ financial matters
▪ place to live
▪ responsibility

S **Strategies box**

Read the prompt carefully. You are not being asked to agree on a number of aspects, but to make a suggestion. Consider all the factors mentioned carefully: Relationships refer to friends as well as to family, future plans may involve further education as well as a future job or family, etc.

SPEAKING 17 Is it better to live in a (big) city or out in the country? Write down your ideas on why people might prefer to live in either place. Compare in class.

READING 18 a Work with a partner. Person A reads the opinion piece below, person B reads the one on the next page. Take notes on the main points of your article, then tell your partner about it.

p. 18

b Now read your partner's text. Did he/she tell you about its most important points?

The case for living in the country
by Heather Long

Big city glamour? Balderdash. Try big city cost. If you want to live like a king (or at least be your own landlord), move to the country.

It's cheap. You have to actively try to spend more than $20 on a meal, even a good one. A movie still costs single digits. No one has a clue or cares what brand of clothing you're wearing, let alone whether your shoes, purse or belt are this year's season or last. And did I mention housing? You can live in a real house with multiple bedrooms, multiple bathrooms and a garage. Maybe even a pool. And you can own it for under $200,000. Yup, you read that right. I didn't leave off any zeros.

There's space – for you, for your dog, for your kids, between you and your annoying neighbors. An ad on the NY subway sums up: "Raising a baby in an NYC apartment is like growing an oak tree in a thimble." In the city, you live on top of each other. Your kids and your dog barely know what grass is. In the country, you have something called a yard. You run around, kick a football and chase fireflies. You go sledding and build snowmen on fresh snow that hasn't been trodden by hundreds of others. You can actually identify constellations because you see lots of them each night. You are fascinated by a lot more interesting animals than squirrels, and your dog acts like a dog, you don't have to carry around bags for its poop.

There are no billionaires. And frankly, few millionaires. To put it another way, there's a lot less income inequality. Since the cost of living is much lower, even those on the median family income[1] (about $50,000 in the US) can have a decent life. You don't feel poor as you do in big cities, where even those earning six-figures still believe they're "just getting by". In the country, you aren't constantly aware of your socioeconomic status. You worry a lot more about the weather.

You aren't reliant on public transport. You don't have to push your way onto an overcrowded subway car only to find yourself squashed next to someone who smells or elbows you. You aren't late because there's been a delay and some robot-like voice has to tell you about it over and over on the speaker. You can drive yourself where you want, when you want. Even if there's traffic (and there isn't much outside of cities), you can usually find another way to go. You are in control, and there's plenty of (free) parking.

You don't get suspicious when people are nice to you. People say "Hello" and "How are you?" and generally mean it. You go to the grocery store and have a decent chance of seeing at least someone you know. Your doctor actually calls you back the same day you call with a concern. People don't size you up constantly based upon your job, social status or income. Volunteer work isn't something you do for your résumé. You feel a part of a genuine community, not just one person out of millions.

---

[1]**median family income:** *the amount of money a family earns in a year on average*

The case for living in the city

by Jessica Reed

The countryside? It must be nice if you're retired … or dead. If you want to have a semblance of a social life and like to do wild things like, oh, going to the cinema on a Monday night, the city is for you.

Walking. It's a thing. Forget about having to spend a quarter of your paycheck on a car. Forget about feeding your second-hand vehicle loads of earth-destroying gas on a weekly basis. And (unless you live in LA) forget about spending two hours a day stuck in traffic. Living in the city means that walking is often an option. And if it's not, commuting by public transport makes you feel like you're part of the world: you and others are in the same boat, so to speak, taking time to pause and read, or listen to music, before reaching work or going home. And, from London to Paris, Amsterdam to Vancouver, chances are you will also be lucky enough to be able to bike everywhere – making you both fitter and happier.

You will never be the underdog. It sucks to be the odd one out. If you're a goth, head to London's Camden Town, which will love to have you. You like playing in all-female netball teams? You'll find a club. Love mushroom-hunting? Start your own group. In Sydney, where I live, my local park alone is the home to joggers, skateboarders, tai chi lovers and tight-rope walkers. There's something for everyone. And kiss bigotry goodbye, too: if you're gay, you will easily find a welcoming environment. And better dating prospects.

The entire world is (almost) on your doorstep. I don't know about you, but it would be a shame to die on the way to the hospital – or give birth on the side of a road. Which probably won't happen in the city. You can order anything from online stores and – miracle! – receive it the next day. Museums, galleries, libraries are easily accessible, a lot of them free. And food: enough said. Who likes to have the choice only between a grim pub serving dismal burgers or fish-and-chips and the local Subway branch at the back of a derelict mall? Not me.

It teaches you tolerance. The world is a diverse place – and in the city, you learn that fast. There's a reason New Yorkers are

considered to be the most thick-skinned people on earth: nothing fazes them, because no one has time to be fazed and they've seen it all anyway. Someone is rude to you on the subway? Move along. Someone cuts you while queuing in the supermarket? Get ahead and get even. But cities also teach patience and empathy because, after all, you're all in this together. Compromise is in the very fabric of city living. Neighbors complaining about your Saturday party? You have to reach an agreement. People who don't act, think or speak like you do? Kids who annoy you by listening to rap music in the bus? They share your space, too. And you, theirs. It's an imperfect and fragile microcosm, which, despite its many drawbacks, seems to work. Almost like magic.

The countryside is not like living in *Gilmore Girls*. If you think the countryside is like living on the idyllic *Gilmore Girls* set, you're mistaken. True country-living means back-breaking work, including thankless chores performed before dawn. Here in Sydney, I pop to the corner shop to get eggs at midnight if I want. And if you're not a true back-to-the-lander living on a 120-acre farm in the middle of nowhere, you then have to live in a community where everything you do will be scrutinized. Privacy will be hard to maintain. No such thing will happen in the city, where people couldn't care less whether you like to walk around with your pet snake, like to wear miniskirts in sub-freezing weather, or sing idiotic pop songs out loud while on your way to buy a baguette. Short of becoming a hermit, if you're a private individual or an introvert, city life is for you.

Read the statements below. Are they a main point (M), a supporting detail (D) or not mentioned (N) in either article? If they are in a text, do they refer to life in the city or the country?

1 _M_   You have access to many amenities here.   _city_

2 _____   There isn't a lot of space to bring up children in this place.   _____

3 _____   It's less expensive to live here.   _____

4 _____   Living here is less dangerous.   _____

5 _____   You can find a partner here more easily.   _____

6 _____   Living here is like being in a film.   _____

7 _____   You don't always need a means of transport here.   _____

8 _____   People are friendlier here.   _____

9 _____   You can get better food here.   _____

SPEAKING **20**   Work in groups of four. Discuss which of the arguments given in the articles you agree with. Are they true for Austria as well? Agree on three arguments that you think are true and three which you think aren't.

STRATEGIES **21**   Summarising a text

p. 19

Discuss these strategies for summarising a text with a partner. Which of them have you already used? How did they help you? How could the other strategies help you to improve your next summary?

S
1 Read the text carefully to discover its main points. They must be in your summary.
2 Focus on headlines and the start of paragraphs first, they often have the information you need.
3 Make sure you answer relevant *wh*-questions: Who? Where? What? Why? When?
4 Be sure to include the main conclusion of the text.
5 Be concise: do not include examples or other supporting details of the text.
6 Only include what's there: Do not interpret the text or comment on it.
7 Use your own words as much as possible. Never copy complete sentences.

WRITING **22**   Write a summary of one of the two articles in about 100 words.

LANGUAGE **23** a   Word partners: Adjectives and nouns

p. 16

The articles in exercise 18 feature many descriptive adjectives in idiomatic word partnerships. Find the adjectives that go with the following nouns. They are in the order they appear in the texts.

L

a	_____ house	f	_____ chance	k	_____ mall
b	_____ bedrooms	g	_____ community	l	_____ place
c	_____ neighbo(u)rs	h	_____ park	m	_____ people
d	_____ snow	i	_____ environment	n	_____ work
e	_____ subway	j	_____ pub	o	_____ chores

b   Choose one of the adjective-noun combinations above. Paraphrase it to a partner until he/she can guess the correct one. Take turns.

WRITING 24

An international youth magazine has started a series of online articles about where young people would like to live. You have decided to send in an article.

In your article you should:

- present advantages of living in the city **or** country for young people
- outline challenges young people living there might have to face
- recommend ways to deal with these challenges

Write around 400 words. Give your article a title.

S **Strategies box**

In a **400-word writing task** you will have to add **more details/ examples** when dealing with the content points. Also, your **introduction** and **conclusion** might be a bit **longer** than in a 250-word text (see *Writing coach*, p. 183).

SPEAKING 25

Work with a partner. What might people look for in a home at different stages in life? Discuss what the people in the pictures might want and agree on the three most important aspects for each one. The ideas below might help you.

- safety from crime
- recreational facilities
- fresh air

- busy nightlife
- well-paid work opportunities
- parks and green areas

- high-quality schools
- availability of childcare

family with young children

recent university graduate

retired couple

LISTENING + VIEWING + WRITING

02

Watch a news report on something many people enjoy in London. Take notes, then use them to write a summary of the report in about three sentences. Answer as many *wh*-questions as possible. Compare your summaries in class.

1 _____

_____

2 _____

_____

_____

3 _____

_____

_____

p. 17

Expand your vocabulary: Suffix revision

You have already learned many suffixes for changing word classes. Combine the word stems in brackets with the correct suffixes to complete the sentences below.

L | -able ▪ -al ▪ -ed ▪ -er ▪ -ful ▪ -ing ▪ -ity ▪ -less ▪ -ment ▪ -ness ▪ -ion ▪ -y

1 I enjoy spending time in these gardens, it's so _____ here. (peace)

2 Buying a house is a major _____ in the future. (invest)

3 The lawns of these houses look great. The landlords must employ a _____ . (garden)

4 The mornings up here can be quite _____ , but it usually clears up later. (mist)

5 My parents' house is a very _____ home that I always enjoy visiting. (welcome)

6 A flat in an urban _____ can be prohibitively expensive. (locate)

7 Finding a home can be an _____ rather than a rational decision. (emotion)

8 Living in a place you don't like can be a major source of _____ . (unhappy)

9 Many retired people want to live a _____ life in a rural area. (comfort)

10 I was _____ to discover that a flat was available to let just across the road. (thrill)

11 The mansion is decorated with _____ pieces of art from around the world. (price)

12 The _____ of people around the world live in urban areas. (major)

Expand your vocabulary: The suffixes *-ion* and *-ive*

p. 17

Verbs that form nouns ending in *-ion* usually make adjectives ending in *-ive*.
Complete the table below.

	Verb	Noun ending in *-ion*	Adjective ending in *-ive*
L	act	*action*	*active*
	attract		
	create		
	construct		
	extend	*extension*	
	impress		
	negate		
	protect		

b **Write sentences with three of the words. Then cover up or erase the words and leave the paper on your desk. Walk around the class and try to complete each other's sentences.**

Can't go home

SPEAKING 29   Around 100 million people around the world are homeless – they do not legally rent or own a place where they can sleep. Talk in pairs:

1 What might it feel, sound, smell like if you live like in the pictures below?
2 What problems might there be?
3 What could be the reasons why people have to live like this?
4 Read the quote in the box. What do the Human Rights demand from governments?

living on the street (sleeping rough)

living in slums

living in abandoned houses (squatting)

LANGUAGE 30   Expand your vocabulary: Inadequate housing

p. 21

The problems people without a proper home have to face are interconnected in many different ways. Study the expressions and the example below, then try to connect as many of them as you can. Describe how they are connected by labelling the arrows.

L

a poor sanitation	e poverty	i vulnerability to disasters
b little medical help	f spreading of diseases	j no political influence
c poor education	g high unemployment	k no electricity
d lack of clean water	h high crime rate	l high child mortality

young children are especially vulnerable to diseases

spreading of diseases ⟶ **high child mortality**

you can't get a good education while being sick or caring for sick family members

poor education ⟶ **no political influence**

it's very hard to have any political influence if you can't read or write and don't know about politics

READING **31** a **Look up the country of Mozambique and the city of Beira on a map. What do you know about this part of the world?**

b **Read the short description of Mozambique below. What might housing be like there?**

The southeast African country of Mozambique is home to more than 27 million people. In the early 16ᵗʰ century Portugal took over the Arab trading posts along the coast and established a colony dealing in gold and slaves from areas further inland. After gaining its independence from Portugal in 1975, the country descended into civil war, bringing widespread devastation and the death of more than one million of its inhabitants. Since the end of the conflict in 1992, the country has begun to rebuild and establish a multi-party democracy. In 1995 it joined the Commonwealth as the first country that had not been part of the British Empire. Today, it is still one of the world's poorest countries, with a GNI per capita[2] of 420 US\$ in 2017 (Austria: 45,440 US\$).

LISTENING + VIEWING

BBC 03

p. 21

32 a **You are going to watch part of a BBC documentary about a building in Mozambique. Watch the video without sound first. Then describe what you've seen to a partner. What could the video be about?**

b **You are going to watch the video with sound now. First you will have 45 seconds to study the task below, then you will watch the video twice. While watching, answer the questions (1–7) using a maximum of four words. Write your answers in the spaces provided. The first one (0) has been done for you.**

After the second watching, you will have 45 seconds to check your answers.

0	Where in Mozambique is the building located?	Beira
1	When was the building constructed?	
2	What did the building become for a short time?	
3	What effect did the fighting in the country have?	
4	How does the presenter react to the building?	
5	How many occupants does the place have now?	
6	What was the building used as during the wars?	
7	Why do people squat there now?	

33

BBC 04

Now watch the next part of the documentary. What are the problems the people living in the hotel have to face? How are they coping?

SPEAKING **34** **Work in groups of four. Research one of the topics below and present your findings in class.**

- how people in Austria are affected by inadequate housing
- an organisation helping homeless people in Austria

[2] **GNI per capita:** *gross national income per person:* Bruttonationaleinkommen pro Einwohner/in

SPEAKING 35   *Individual long turn:*

- Compare the living situations of the children in the pictures.
- Discuss the impact of housing on young people's growing up.
- Suggest ways to fight poverty.

WRITING 36   **An international think-tank aiming to improve living areas has decided to sponsor a new public park in your neighbourhood. You have been asked to suggest what the park should offer. You have come up with some ideas and carried out a survey among residents of your neighbourhood.**

Residents' preferences for the new park

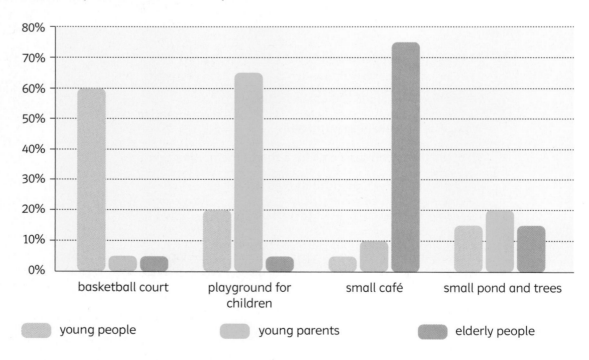

In your report you should:

- give reasons for the ideas you presented to the residents
- explain the results of your survey
- make a suggestion based on your survey

Write around 250 words. Divide your report into sections and give them headings.

→ See *Writing coach, Report*, p. 186.

LANGUAGE **37** a Topic vocabulary: Domestic environment

Expand the word map of pros and cons with ideas from the unit and your own.

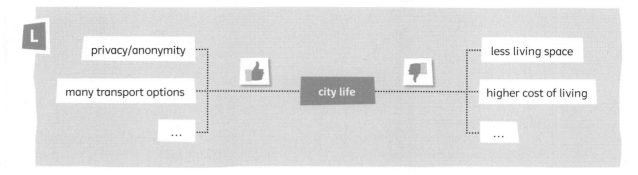

privacy/anonymity		less living space
many transport options	city life	higher cost of living
...		...

b **Choose one of the topics below to design a similar word map. Share the word maps in class.**

- living close to school/university
- living on your own
- staying at home

◉ Looking back: Learning goals of Unit 03   ✓✓ ✓ !!

READING ▶▶▶ B2	I can scan quickly through long and complex texts on the topic of domestic environment, locating relevant details. (ex. 8, 18)
LISTENING ▶▶▶ B2	I can understand most broadcast audio material on the topic of domestic environment delivered in standard dialect. (ex. 26, 32)
WRITING ▶▶▶ B1+	I can summarise, report and give my opinion about accumulated factual information on the topic of domestic environment with some confidence. (ex. 24, 36)
▶▶▶ B1+	I can write a blog post or an email to communicate information and ideas on the topic of domestic environment. (ex. 7, 13)
▶▶▶ B1+	I can write an article to explain a problem somewhat precisely. (ex. 24)
SPEAKING ▶▶▶ B1+	I can maintain a conversation or discussion, compare and contrast alternatives and give brief comments on the views of others. (ex. 1, 6, 16, 20, 25)
▶▶▶ B1+	I can develop an argument or presentation on the topic of domestic environment well enough to be followed without difficulty most of the time. (ex. 34)
LANGUAGE ▶▶▶	I can understand and use a good range of suffixes.
▶▶▶	I can use a good range of phrasal verbs.
▶▶▶	I can use a good range of vocabulary to describe and argue on the topic of domestic environment.

After school, I will live ...   I will help others to have a good home by ...

Unit 04
On the move

 xi77is

In this unit you will:

- find out about an unusual traveller
- perfect your phrasal verbs
- discover why travel makes you happy
- remember to study or studying gerunds
- compare public and private transport
- learn how to take a pooch on a plane

SPEAKING **1** **a** **Look at the cartoon and the excuses for not having a valid ticket:**

1 What does the cartoon tell you about public transport?
2 Which of the excuses do you like best? How would the conductor react?

"I know it's yesterday's ticket! That's when I got on this bloody train!"

G

"I'm working undercover for the train service. I'm here to make sure you're doing your job properly! Looks good – keep it up!"

F

"My bag with my wallet and all my identification cards got stolen, and I'm just on my way to the nearest police station."

E

"I tried to get a ticket from the machine, but it swallowed all my money without printing the ticket. Can I get a refund?"

D

"I would never dodge the fare. Honestly, I've got a ticket. It's on my phone, but the battery's dead and …"

A

"The ticket vending machine is only for left-handed people – I'm right-handed."

B

"I only have a large banknote, and the machine couldn't give me any change."

C

"Pardon! I am Français! Je ne comprends pas what you say. Mon Dieu!"

b **Now make up your own excuse for not having a valid ticket. Then share your excuses in class and vote for the most 'creative' one.**

SPEAKING **2** **a** **Work alone. Think about travelling the world and write down:**

> ✈ three adjectives that come to your mind
> ✈ three nouns that come to your mind
> ✈ three verbs that come to your mind

> ✈ one reason why you would like to travel
> ✈ one reason why you wouldn't like to travel
> ✈ five countries you'd like to see

b **Share your notes with a partner. Do you have the same ideas about travelling?**

3 **Get up and walk around your classroom. Talk to your classmates and find people who share your ideas about travelling. Decide where you would like to go and how you would travel if you had an unlimited budget. Do some research and talk about your destination in a mini-presentation.**

LANGUAGE **4** **a** Expand your vocabulary: Travelling safely
Read the text below and consider the expressions in bold. Then match the phrases in the green box to the ones in the text that have a similar meaning.

> **L**
> **a** embassy
> **b** foreign currency
> **c** hitchhike
> **d** money belt
> **e** non-EU country
> **f** passport

When you travel to a (1) ☐ **country that is not part of the EU**, it's important to consider a few things: First, it would be clever to have some (2) ☐ **dollars, rands, rupees or yen** with you because sometimes you can't pay by credit card. Also, your (3) ☐ **identification or travel document** should be valid, meaning it isn't too old. In order to ensure you don't lose these essential things, you could keep them in a (4) ☐ **bag that you wrap around your waist** or in a hidden pocket of your backpack. Should you lose them anyway, find out where the Austrian (5) ☐ **representative building** is and contact them for help. For safety reasons, learn about the country's laws and culture, stay in contact with other people and don't (6) ☐ **get into strangers' cars to travel**. Then you shouldn't encounter any problems and have a safe trip.

b **What other tips and tricks for travelling safely can you think of? Talk in pairs.**

WRITING **5** **Make a list of five 'dos' and five 'don'ts' for travelling. Compare your list with other students in your class.**
Example: *Do: Find out about customs regulations before entering a particular country. Don't: Don't buy fake designer bags or sunglasses from street pedlars.*

READING `6` Read the short introduction of an English world traveller. What do you think he is like?

Tony Giles is a traveller from the southwest of England. He has been to over 120 countries of the world and has written books about his travels. But he is not like most other travellers you might meet. In fact, he is blind and mostly deaf, which makes backpacking across the world that much more challenging. Nevertheless, having his backpack and cane ready for the next adventure, he has no intention of stopping.

SPEAKING `7` Discuss the following questions with a partner:

1 How do you think Tony manages to travel around strange places without the ability to see?
2 Why do you think he travels the world even though he can't hear or see?

LISTENING `8` You are going to listen to an FM4 interview with Tony Giles. First you will have 45 seconds to study the task below, then you will hear the recording twice. While listening, match the beginnings of the sentences (1–8) with the sentence endings (A–K). There are two extra sentence endings that you should not use. Write your answers in the spaces provided. The first one (0) has been done for you.

radio FM4
◉ 07
🌐
p. 22

After the second listening, you will have 45 seconds to check your answers.

Tony Giles, world traveller

0	Tony Giles first got the idea to travel _____ .	B
1	For Tony, travelling is how he _____ .	
2	The school Tony attended _____ .	
3	Tony started travelling longer distances as he _____ .	
4	Tony encountered difficulties in Paraguay when he _____ .	
5	When Tony was using public transport, someone _____ .	
6	One reason why Tony takes pictures is that he _____ .	
7	Tony chose to go to the USA because the country _____ .	
8	When Tony travels to another country, he _____ .	

A	earns a lot of money	G	was quite like his home
B	from a relative's stories	H	books a room in advance
C	was a long way from home	I	became a student overseas
D	had an accident	J	was becoming a problem
E	finds it amusing	K	took his computer
F	motivates himself to keep going		

1 How did you do in this listening task? How much of the interview did you understand (in percent)?

2 What do you think about Tony Giles' stories? Would you like to accompany him?

LANGUAGE 10 a Expand your vocabulary: Phrasal verbs for movement

📖 p. 23

Read the sentences below and think about the meaning of the phrasal verbs in green.
Match the words from the box (a–i) to the phrasal verbs with a similar meaning.

L	a arrive	c leave	e stay	g talk	i return
	b invent	d meet	f steal	h travel	

1 The train was supposed to get in at 8 a.m., but there was a two-hour delay, so I had to wait at the station to pick up my sister. _____

2 Nick has been to Spain, China and Israel this year – he really gets around! _____

3 I'm off to the coast for a week. See you! _____

4 Did you run into Claire on holiday? She stayed at the hotel next to yours. _____

5 We must catch up after my holiday. Let's meet for coffee! _____

6 There was a traffic jam, so they made us turn back and go in the other direction. _____

7 We stopped over in Bangkok on our flight to Australia. _____

8 I can't believe someone just walked off with my bike. I had locked it! _____

9 Do you think Erica's story about the crocodile is real? Or did she just make it up? _____

b Complete the word map below with the phrasal verbs. You have to put the word 'run' in the correct tense.

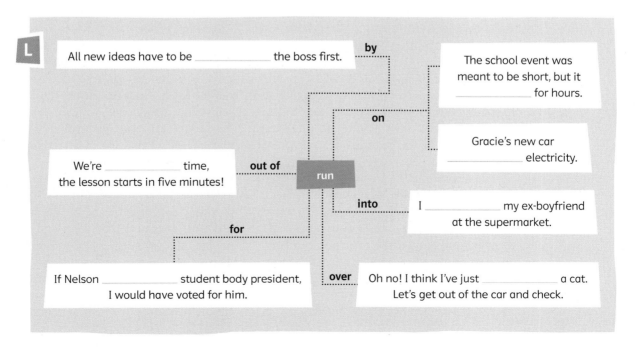

All new ideas have to be _____ the boss first.

The school event was meant to be short, but it _____ for hours.

by

on

out of

run

into

Gracie's new car _____ electricity.

We're _____ time, the lesson starts in five minutes!

I _____ my ex-boyfriend at the supermarket.

for

over

If Nelson _____ student body president, I would have voted for him.

Oh no! I think I've just _____ a cat. Let's get out of the car and check.

READING **11**

a Read the article about reasons why travel might make you happier. Sum up the reasons in a short sentence each.

b Read the text again. First decide whether the statements (1–7) are true (T) or false (F) and put a cross (x) in the correct box. Then identify the sentence in the text which supports your decision. Write the first four words of this sentence in the space provided. There may be more than one correct answer; write down only one. The first one (0) has been done for you.

Why travel makes you a happier person

Travel is beneficial in many ways, but you may not realise it can increase mental well-being. So the next time you find yourself heading out on a shopping spree to lift your mood, why not invest that money in a flight instead? Here are some ways in which travelling can make you happier.

There comes a time when everyone must deal with an unexpected situation that arises when they're on the road. Even if you plan your trip to the letter, things can take a surprise turn. Whatever happens, there is a solution to the problem, and knowing that you can deal with these situations is a huge boost to self-confidence and consequently your happiness.

Travelling proves that absence makes the heart grow fonder. There's nothing like sleeping in your own bed after a long vacation, eating your favourite dish, meeting friends and family to exchange holiday tales or simply noticing the beauty of your own home when you've been absent for some time.

Making new friends is more effortless on the road than it is at home, where people are less inclined to chat to strangers on a bus or strike up a conversation in a bar (at least, that's true of London). When people are away from home, there seem to be fewer boundaries to cross and making friends becomes much easier. Social interactions make us happier, and increasing our social circle means that we're talking more and meeting different, interesting people, which generally means we're learning more too.

The internet has its advantages and disadvantages, but it's healthy for everyone to have a break from it every once in a while. Wi-fi is so prevalent that it's often a challenge to switch off, and far too often you can find yourself tuning out whatever amazing place you're in with your face in your phone, checking Twitter, scrolling through your Facebook feed, checking your emails … stop.

Turn it off. Better yet, find somewhere with no reception and no wi-fi so that you have no alternative. It's liberating and allows you to appreciate the 'here and now', which nicely ties into the following point.

Travelling gives us breathing space that is often lacking in our usual day-to-day existence. Having the opportunity to take advantage of peace and quiet and to simply 'be' allows us to release stress and tension and just value being in the moment – a key focus of meditation and a practice you can take home with you. If you're travelling with a friend or partner, it's a chance to spend time getting to know each other better.

Whether it's acquiring a new skill such as cooking Thai food or learning a new language, travel presents ways in which we can further our knowledge and education. Learning makes our brains more active, which psychologists have found increases our level of happiness – particularly when learning something we consider enjoyable.

For most people, travelling is about the new experiences. I recall with pleasure that moment of awe when I stood watching the sunlight leak out over the rainforest around the ancient temple of Borobudur in Java at sunrise. The sky turned a striking shade of violet: it was one of the most beautiful sights I've ever seen. Recalling memories of happiness can sustain a feeling of contentment long after the moment has passed, and new experiences are memories that can remain with you forever.

Aside from making you happier in the moment, travelling can make you a much more contented, happy and relaxed person in the long run, too. Of course, most travel enthusiasts are constantly planning their next trip, but when we're at home or past a point of being able to jet off whenever we like, past travels leave us with the memories and personal skills, such as confidence, broad-mindedness, friends and a more worldly perspective, that make people happy. And that's why travel makes you a happier person.

	Statements	T	F	First four words
0	The author thinks we should shop less and travel more.	☒	☐	*So the next time*
1	You can't be ready for all eventualities.	☐	☐	
2	Being away makes you appreciate your life at home more.	☐	☐	
3	People are less sociable when they're in unfamiliar surroundings.	☐	☐	
4	You should try to stay online when travelling to keep in touch with family.	☐	☐	
5	Being reflective whilst travelling holds physical benefits.	☐	☐	
6	Expanding our knowledge has a positive influence on our level of contentment.	☐	☐	
7	The beneficial effects of travel such as openness and tolerance soon wear off.	☐	☐	

SPEAKING **12** Discuss with a partner: Are you convinced enough to go travelling now? Why?/Why not?

LANGUAGE **13** Expand your vocabulary: Positive emotions

p. 23

The article features lots of phrases to talk about positive emotions like happiness. Match the phrase halves, which are similar to the ones in the article. For some halves, there is more than one possible match.

L

1 increase your (level of) _____	6 it is _____
2 lift your _____	7 gives you j̶_____
3 give a boost _____	8 let go of _____
4 appreciate _____	9 be in _____
5 have _____	10 find _____

a a break	d mood	g happiness	j̶ ̶b̶r̶e̶a̶t̶h̶i̶n̶g̶ ̶s̶p̶a̶c̶e̶
b stress and tension	e the moment	h moments of awe	k the little things
c liberating	f to self-confidence	i mental well-being	l something enjoyable

WRITING **14** Use the phrases from 13 to write a short advert promoting your favourite leisure activity. Explain why it makes you happy.

SPEAKING 15 *Individual long turn:*

- Compare the different ways of travelling.
- Consider the challenges of travelling alone.
- Discuss whether travelling makes people happy.

> **S** **Strategies box**
>
> **To consider sth.** means **to think about sth. carefully** before making a decision.

WRITING 16 *Young_travellers.com*, an online magazine, is asking young people to send in articles on tips and tricks for travelling safely. The writers of the three best articles will get a free ticket to a destination of their choice. You have decided to send in an article.

In your article you should:

- discuss what makes travelling attractive to young people
- inform your readers about possible risks
- recommend ways of travelling safely

Write around 400 words. Give your article a title.

→ See *Writing coach, Article*, p. 186.

B **By the way: When is the left right?**

The answer to this, of course, is when you're driving in Ireland! Have you ever wondered why the Irish drive on the left? There's a historical reason for this: it's all to do with keeping your sword hand free.

In the Middle Ages you never knew who you were going to encounter when travelling. Most people are right-handed, so if a stranger was passing by on your right side, your right hand would be free to seize your sword if required. Similarly, the staircases in a medieval castle spiral in a clockwise direction going upwards, so the defending soldiers would be able to stab down around the twist, but those ascending the stairs and attacking would not.

Indeed the 'keep to the left' rule goes back even further in time. Although the Romans never invaded Ireland, they did occupy England and Wales. Archaeologists have discovered evidence suggesting that the Romans drove carts and wagons on the left and Roman soldiers always marched on the left. This goes some way to explaining why cars are driven on the left in the UK.

Ireland is largely a rural country, and rural traffic is the norm. Travellers can expect gigantic, slow-moving pieces of farm machinery around every corner. The best option is to adopt the Irish 'sure there's plenty of time' attitude. Also, wildlife and pets may suddenly cross the road, or cows and especially sheep may use the road as a resting place. Even in the capital city Dublin collisions with horses are not unheard of. It's also important to remember that, as a pedestrian, the cars will come from the 'wrong' direction when you're crossing the road, so you need to keep your wits about you!

Find out in which other countries you drive on the left. What do most of them have in common?

SPEAKING 17 **Discuss with a partner:**

1 What kind of public transport is there in your area?
2 What is it like? How often do trains or buses go?
3 Who uses the public transport in the area you live in? For what purposes?

LANGUAGE 18 Expand your vocabulary: Transport

p. 24

Look at the expressions below and discuss with a partner whether they refer to public transport (P) or to cars (C). Which words might refer to both (B)?

L carbon dioxide ▪ carbon footprint ▪ cheap ▪ convenient ▪ delays ▪ environment ▪ insurance ▪ parking space ▪ petrol ▪ quick ▪ relaxing ▪ season ticket ▪ sustainable

READING 19 a **Read the online article and find suitable headlines for the paragraphs.**

p. 25

Public transport – the only way to go!

(1) _____

If you want to do your bit for the environment, getting public transport and leaving the car at home is one of the most straightforward things to do. As you will see below, it can be more convenient, quicker and cheaper to do so. And the green benefits are great too. Car journeys contribute a significant amount of our overall carbon footprint. It's a fact that nearly half of us use a car to drive short journeys, journeys that could otherwise be completed in another, more sustainable way.

(2) _____

The great thing about public transport is that it gets you where you want to be, when you want to be there, particularly in cities and towns. Rather than only being able to drive to a certain point before getting stuck in a one-way system, you can reach your central point directly. Plus, you get the bonus of sitting back, relaxing with a newspaper and letting someone else do the driving.

(3) _____

Despite their tendency to get delayed at times, in the majority of instances your journey from A to B will be quick and often direct as more and more investment is made into new train, tram and bus routes in many European cities.

(4) _____

Contrary to popular belief, nearly all forms of public transport pose less of a cost to the traveller. If you're regularly visiting a place, or planning a trip in advance, you can get season tickets or advance booked tickets for a cheaper price. The cost of running a car goes much further than the mere cost of petrol, which in itself might be very expensive. Getting on public transport means no car insurance and tax costs, plus eliminates the expense of maintaining your car to a high standard.

(5) _____

One of the most frustrating things about driving a car or motorbike is the hunt for a parking space once you arrive at your destination. Parking is often scarce, and usually expensive. The bonus of getting on public transport is being able to hop out and nothing else. Parking can often add extra time to your driving journey.

All things considered, there is no real alternative to public transport.

b **Which of the reasons for using public transport do you find most convincing? Discuss in small groups.**

SPEAKING 20   **Discuss these questions in groups of three or four:**

1   What are some of the disadvantages of public transport?
2   What are some of the most annoying things people might do while using public transport?
    Write a list of the ten most annoying things and compare them with other groups.
    Examples: *listening to loud music, eating, taking off shoes, …*

WRITING 21   **Write a paragraph of around 100 words about the disadvantages of public transport.**
      Start your paragraph with one of these expressions:

If you want to …; The great thing about …;
Despite the low cost of tickets …; Contrary to popular belief …

SPEAKING 22   *Paired activity:* **You and your partner have been invited to take part in an international discussion forum on how convinced car drivers might be persuaded to use public transport instead of their cars. Which of the arguments below would you use? Agree on three.**

Public transport is …

- fast
- cheap
- environmentally friendly
- relaxing
- safe

LISTENING 23   **In many rural communities, getting from one place to another without having a vehicle is often difficult, and getting everything from food to medicine can be a trial in itself. Small towns have the tendency to have some distance between them, and the population densities are low. Thus, public transport is an issue in many areas.**

Look at the picture and discuss the questions in pairs or small groups:

1   What kind of public transport might be available in small villages?
2   Who would need to use public transport the most?
3   What are possible reasons for the lack of good public transport in the country?

24 a   **Listen to the radio feature on transport solutions in a town in County Donegal, Ireland, and note down the answers to the questions above. Compare them to what you've discussed.**

◉ 08
🌐

    b   **Listen to the radio feature again and add the four projects of the town to the list below.**

- safe bike paths to bus/train stops
- affordable taxi service to bus/train stops

- mobile-friendly website with clear info on transit options
- partnerships with neighbouring communities

- _____
- _____

- _____
- _____

SPEAKING 25   **Rank the solutions from the most useful to the least useful one. Discuss the results of your ranking with a partner. Can you add your own suggestions?**

Prepositions

Discuss with a partner how living in rural areas might affect students' chances of education. Then insert the correct preposition into the text below.

L

Many young people living in rural areas can't get to school in a 'reasonable travel time'
(1) _____ public transport or walking, which means their school choices depend
(2) _____ where they can be driven by their parents. According (3) _____
research there are more people with low qualifications (4) _____ rural areas,
but being able to improve their skills and take a step (5) _____ further education
is made difficult because (6) _____ weak transport links. It also shows that the
amount spent on transport (7) _____ rural students is much higher than in urban
areas. Moreover, it's harder (8) _____ young people to get apprenticeships as
there are few big employers to help with work experience. Another obstacle is poor internet
connection in many rural areas. It can be a barrier (9) _____ online learning and
help with homework. It is crucial that policymakers consider how they can help young
people overcome the obstacles (10) _____ them and further education, rather than
creating new barriers.

WRITING 27

Imagine you are spending a semester in a rural area in Ireland and getting to school is difficult and time-consuming. You have decided to write an email to the manager of the local bus service company explaining your situation and suggesting a solution. Write around 250 words.

28

An international forum discussing public transport wants to know what public transport is like in certain areas and how more people can be motivated to use it. You have been asked to hand in a report based on a survey done among users of public transport in your area.

What people like best about public transport (n = 100)

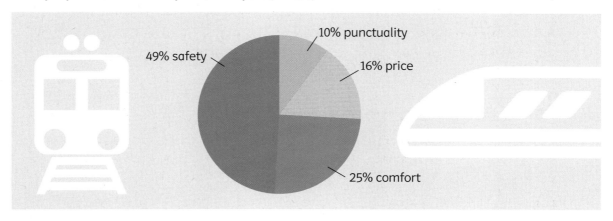

- 10% punctuality
- 49% safety
- 16% price
- 25% comfort

In your report you should:

- describe public transport in your area
- explain the results of the survey
- suggest how more people can be motivated to use public transport

Write around 250 words. Divide your report into sections and give them headings.

→ See *Writing coach, Report*, p. 186.

LANGUAGE **29** Expand your vocabulary: Transporting goods

Not only people, but also goods need to go from one place to another. Use the expressions from the box to discuss the best ways to transport the following goods:

a 25 llamas
b a rhino moving to the zoo
c a famous painting

d 1,000 crystal glasses
e 20,000 frozen pizzas
f an aquarium full of fish

L bike courier ▪ container ▪ delay ▪ delivery ▪ drone ▪ freight train ▪ international ▪ long-haul ▪ lorry ▪ plane ▪ rural ▪ ship ▪ traffic jam ▪ underground ▪ urban

SPEAKING **30** **What kinds of goods or objects might be regularly transported in/from your region? What modes of transport do you often encounter?**

LISTENING **31** a **Watch a video about an unusual mode of transportation in London and take notes.**
+ VIEWING **Then summarise the information in about five sentences. The following questions might help you:**

 05

1 How was this rail network used?
2 What is special about this rail network?

3 What is it like to visit the place?
4 How is it used today?

b **What do you think people might enjoy about visiting this place? Talk in pairs.**

LANGUAGE **32** Infinitive constructions

p. 26

There are a lot of verbs that are always followed by an infinitive. Complete the sentences with a verb from the box in the correct tense, then highlight the infinitive following it.

L agree ▪ decide ▪ encourage ▪ expect ▪ fail ▪ offer ▪ pretend ▪ refuse ▪ warn

1 If you always have your face in your phone, you _____ to appreciate the beauty of your surroundings.

2 When I read travelling makes you happier, I immediately _____ to take some time off for my dream holiday.

3 Don't _____ to be able to pay by credit card in a non-EU country.

4 When I told Mr Giles how much I admire him, he spontaneously _____ to let me accompany him on his next trip.

5 It wasn't easy to persuade her, but now my friend _____ to go to Ireland with me in the summer.

6 The locals _____ him to drive carefully on rural roads in Ireland.

7 The author of the article _____ people to learn a new skill when they're on holiday.

8 If I hadn't trusted the man who stopped for me when I was hitchhiking last summer, I _____ to get into his car.

9 If the conductor asks me for my ticket tomorrow, I _____ to be a tourist.

33 a Complete the sentences below with an infinitive construction so that they are (or could be) true for you.

Example: *On my last holiday, I decided to go scuba diving.*

1 On my last holiday, I decided …
2 It was a tempting offer, but I hesitated …
3 I love travelling, but I can't afford …
4 As soon as I have enough money, I intend …
5 You won't believe this, but I've never managed …
6 On long train rides, I tend …
7 I had planned … on my trip, but then everything went wrong.
8 When I was travelling, I once attempted …
9 For my next holiday, I hope …

b Now compare your sentences in pairs. Did your partner write anything that you find surprising/ interesting? Ask him/her to tell you more about it.

Example: *A: On my last holiday, I decided to go scuba diving. B: Really? Did you enjoy it?*

34 Yesterday a famous traveller came to your school to give a talk, and he had lots of valuable advice for young travellers:

> "Travelling is a wonderful experience for young people. Remember that old saying 'Travelling broadens the mind'? That's absolutely true, and now is the time for you to see the world. Don't miss all the wonderful opportunities for travelling that you have at your age – InterRail Passes, for example. Oh, and don't bring your parents. Get out of your comfort zone and go by yourself! This might seem scary at first, but I'm convinced that you'll love it. When you're famous travellers yourselves, I will come and listen to your talks."

Unfortunately, your friend missed the talk. Tell him/her what the speaker said using the verbs below with an infinitive construction:

advise ▪ encourage ▪ promise ▪ remind ▪ tell ▪ warn

Example: *He advised us to leave our parents at home.*

Language box

Remember how to report what somebody said:

*My friend **advised me to see** Thailand. The police **told them not to get** into strangers' cars.*

LANGUAGE 35 a Gerunds and infinitives

p. 27

With some verbs, the meaning can change depending on whether they are followed by a gerund (verb + *-ing*) or an infinitive. Can you explain the difference in meaning?

He stopped smoking./He stopped to smoke.

→ See *Grammar revisited, Gerunds and infinitives*, p. 174.

b Complete the sentences below using either a gerund or an infinitive.

1 I know I have a bus ticket somewhere in my bag. I clearly remember … (buy) it.
2 You should stop … (waste) your time waiting for the bus. Ride your bike instead!
3 We must remember … (pack) our passports and visas for the trip.
4 Have you tried … (contact) your country's embassy? They should be able to help you.
5 I can't go on … (hitchhike) everywhere, it's too dangerous.
6 I regret … (not travel) more when I was young. What a wasted opportunity!
7 Marty was walking down the street when his phone rang. He stopped … (take) the call.

36 Get together in small groups. Come up with new example sentences for the verbs from the box on the right, using gerunds or infinitives. Write them down as gapped sentences (see exercise 35b). Give your sentences to a different group to fill in and see if they get it right.

go ▪ regret ▪ remember ▪ stop ▪ try

LANGUAGE IN USE **37** a **Read the text about taking pets on a plane. Some words are missing. Choose the correct word (A–O) for each gap (1–12). There are two extra words that you should not use. Write your answers in the boxes provided. The first one (0) has been done for you.**

Where your pets are stored on a plane

Driving with a dog or cat in the car can be a major hassle. What happens if there's a (0) _____ jam? What if Fido needs to go for a walk? What if Mr Bigglesworth coughs up a hairball?

If you've ever (1) _____ such adventures, the idea of taking your pet with you onto an airplane might sound like a (2) _____ at 10,668 meters. However, most airlines allow passengers to travel with their pets. In fact, an (3) _____ two million pets and other animals take to the skies each year in the United States alone.

Pets, however, aren't people. They may be the love of your life, but (4) _____ an airplane, they generally fall into one of three different (5) _____ : carry-on baggage, checked baggage or cargo.

Remember (6) _____ can be a dangerous and stressful undertaking for a pet. Most airlines recommend that a pet be at least eight weeks old before it flies. But even if your pet is a healthy adult, it might not be a good idea to take it on a plane.

If you choose to bring your pet along as checked baggage, it will travel under the same conditions as those shipped as (7) _____ , alone, between bags and suitcases in the hold. In many airplane models, the cargo area takes up the level directly beneath the passenger cabins. While this area is temperature-controlled, other parts of the (8) _____ may not be, so travelling can still be dangerous for pets.

However, if you bring it along as a carry-on baggage, the lucky cat or dog will get to experience the same flying (9) _____ as you do. The only difference is that while you get to sit back in your seat and (10) _____ on peanuts, your furry friend will have to remain inside its carrier box for the whole flight. If your pet happens to bark or meow a lot in small spaces, be prepared to suffer some (11) _____ looks from your fellow passengers.

Of course, for the truly spoiled pet, private planes are always a pricier alternative. Some companies even hope (12) _____ pet-friendly flights in which the animals ride in specially designed passenger cabins. Talk about travelling in style!

A	aboard	D	categories	G	experienced	J	selling	M	to offer
B	airport	E	conditions	H	hateful	K	snack	N	traffic
C	baggage	F	estimated	I	nightmare	L	to fly	O	travelling

0	1	2	3	4	5	6	7	8	9	10	11	12
N												

b **How would you (not) travel long distances with a pet? Are there alternatives to flying? Discuss possible options with a partner, then decide on the best way to get around.**

38 **a** Topic vocabulary: Reasons for travelling/Public transport

Word maps are great for organising arguments into main points and supporting details. Fill in the three main points from the box, then add more main points and details.

gives you time for yourself ▪ helps you make new friends ▪ increases self-confidence

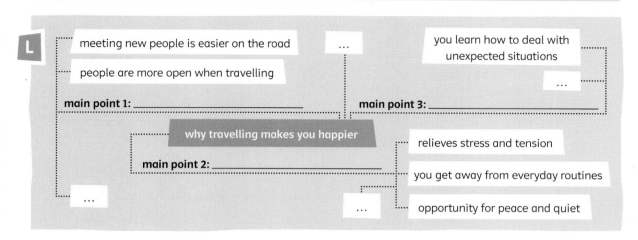

L

meeting new people is easier on the road

...

you learn how to deal with unexpected situations

people are more open when travelling

...

main point 1: _____

main point 3: _____

why travelling makes you happier

main point 2: _____

relieves stress and tension

you get away from everyday routines

...

...

opportunity for peace and quiet

b **Now make a similar word map to organise your arguments for using public transport.**

⊙ **Looking back:** Learning goals of Unit 04

	✓✓	✓	!!

READING ▶▶▶ B2   I can scan quickly through long and complex texts on the topic of transport and tourism, locating relevant details. (ex. 11a/b, 19a)

LISTENING ▶▶▶ B2   I can understand most broadcast audio material on the topic of transport and tourism delivered in standard dialect. (ex. 8, 31a)

WRITING ▶▶▶ B1+   I can write a text to explain a problem somewhat precisely. (ex. 16, 21, 28)

SPEAKING ▶▶▶ B1+   I can maintain a conversation or discussion, compare and contrast alternatives and give brief comments on the views of others. (ex. 1, 7, 12, 17, 20, 22, 26, 31b)

LANGUAGE ▶▶▶   I can use a range of phrasal verbs on the topic of transport and tourism well.

▶▶▶   I can use a range of verbs with gerund and infinitive constructions accurately.

▶▶▶   I can use a good range of vocabulary to describe and argue on the topic of transport and tourism.

To my mind, the best reason to go travelling is . . .

If a blind and deaf person can travel the world, I can be brave enough to . . .

Unit 05
Live and learn

 8a5nm5

In this unit you will:
- consider what makes a good education
- think critically
- find out why you should get a job
- decide how much say parents should have
- read about 'Tiger Moms'
- improve your word formation skills

READING + SPEAKING

1 a Match the eight quotes about education and learning to the statements in the middle.

1 "The foundation of every state is the education of its youth." (*Diogenes, ancient Greek philosopher*)

2 "Education is the passport to the future, for tomorrow belongs to those who prepare for it today." (*Malcolm X, human rights activist*)

3 "The roots[1] of education are bitter, but the fruit is sweet." (*Aristotle, ancient Greek philosopher*)

4 "Intellectual growth should commence[2] at birth and cease only at death." (*Albert Einstein, theoretical physicist*)

5 "The aim of education is the knowledge, not of facts, but of values." (*William S. Burroughs, writer*)

6 "You are always a student, never a master. You have to keep moving forward." (*Conrad Hall, photographer and filmmaker*)

7 "The mark of higher education isn't the knowledge you accumulate[3] in your head. It's the skills you gain about how to learn." (*Adam Grant, psychologist*)

8 "Education is for improving the lives of others and for leaving your community and world better than you found it." (*Marian Wright Edelman, children's rights activist*)

Education is important to every society.

Learning is hard, but worth it.

Learning is about more than just facts.

Education gives you a better future.

Education is never finished.

b Compare your answers in class. Then discuss these questions in pairs:

1 Do you agree that these quotes fit the statements? Why?/Why not?
2 Are these statements true only for school education or also for other things? Give examples.
3 What metaphor/picture is used in quote 3 to describe education? Why?

2 Rank the five statements in the middle (1: most important, 5: least important). Compare your rankings in class.

[1] **roots:** Wurzeln
[2] **to commence:** anfangen, beginnen
[3] **to accumulate sth.:** etw. ansammeln

70

SPEAKING **3** What should schools teach their students? What are the most important things you want to have learned by the time you leave school? Make some notes, then compare your ideas in pairs.

LISTENING **4** **a** You are going to listen to part of a public debate on education. Look at the three goals of education below. Where would your ideas fit?
⊙ 09
⊕

b Listen to the beginning of the debate now. Match the speakers to the three goals of education below and answer the questions.

> **Goal: Preparing for work and daily life**
>
> **Speaker:**
> _____
>
> **What does that mean?**
>
>
> _____
>
> **Why is that so important?**
>
>
>
> _____

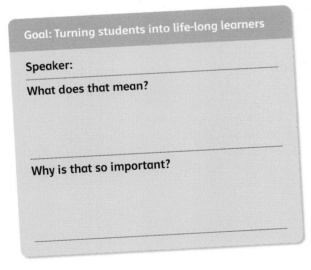

> **Goal: Turning students into life-long learners**
>
> **Speaker:**
> _____
>
> **What does that mean?**
>
>
> _____
>
> **Why is that so important?**
>
>
> _____

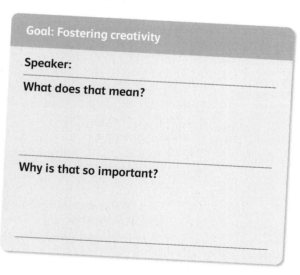

> **Goal: Fostering creativity**
>
> **Speaker:**
> _____
>
> **What does that mean?**
>
>
> _____
>
> **Why is that so important?**
>
>
> _____

c Which of the speakers do you agree with most? Why?

5 What other things should school teach? Change or add to the notes on what schools should teach you've made already. Keep improving your notes as you work through this section.

SPEAKING **6** **a** Get into three groups to prepare for a debate. Your teacher will tell you which of the three opinions to prepare for. Come up with convincing arguments for your position, but also think about what your arguments against the other two points of view could be.

b Now change into groups of three. Every group needs to have one member for each opinion. Debate the issue politely for about 10 minutes.

LANGUAGE IN USE **7** **a** Quickly read the article below. Which of the three definitions of critical thinking comes closest to what is expressed in the text?

 1

If you use 'critical thinking', you only think about the most important (= 'critical') aspects of a problem, without being distracted by small details.

 2

'Critical thinking' means being negative or conservative about new ideas. These new ideas must prove they are better than the old ones before you accept them.

 3

'Critical thinking' is the ability to evaluate ideas by investigating their implications and understanding them, before making an informed decision.

b Read the text about different opinions on critical thinking. Some words are missing. Choose the correct answer (A, B, C or D) for each gap (1–10). Put a cross (☒) in the correct box. The first one (0) has been done for you.

The challenges of critical thinking

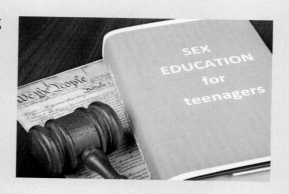

You couldn't make this stuff up! In 2012, a political party in the USA made the following statement about teaching critical thinking skills in schools: "We **(0)** _____ the teaching of critical thinking skills, which have the purpose of challenging the pupil's fixed beliefs and weaken parental authority." Yes, you read that right. The party disapproves of the teaching of critical thinking skills because it believes the **(1)** _____ is to challenge a student's "fixed beliefs" and undermine "parental authority". The party's opinion on sex education in schools, for example, was: "We recognise parental responsibility and authority **(2)** _____ sex education. We oppose any sex education other than abstinence[4] until marriage."

So how do these opinions **(3)** _____ from more common and liberal views on critical thinking? Supporters of critical thinking would post the following on top of all **(4)** _____ smartphones and computers: "Don't accept as true what you're about to read. Some of it is fact; some of it is opinion disguised **(5)** _____; and the rest is liberal, conservative or mainstream propaganda. Make sure you know which is which before choosing to believe it." Can you spot the difference?

(6) _____ critical thinking involves challenging a pupil's fixed beliefs. But that's just the point. Someone with critical thinking skills can understand the links **(7)** _____ ideas, rather than just knowing unconnected facts. They are able to recognise the relevance of arguments and ideas, and can evaluate these. Critical thinkers can identify inconsistencies and errors in reasoning, which would help them to **(8)** _____ 'fake news' and propaganda, for example. They can approach problems in a consistent and systematic way, considering different possibilities and adapting their ideas. They can also **(9)** _____ on the justification of their own values, and it's this part that can (and should) challenge a pupil's fixed beliefs. It is about being an active learner instead of just a passive recipient of information.

Critical thinkers rigorously question ideas and beliefs rather than accepting them at face value. They will always try to discover **(10)** _____ the ideas, arguments and findings represent the entire picture and are open to finding that they do not. Critical thinkers will identify, analyse and solve problems systematically rather than by intuition or instinct. If we want to prepare for a position in 21st-century society and the current workplace, critical thinking is an essential skill.

[4] **abstinence:** Abstinenz, Verzicht auf Sex

0	A oppose	☒	B deny	☐	C support	☐	D forbid	☐
1	A training	☐	B process	☐	C aim	☐	D method	☐
2	A regarding	☐	B demanding	☐	C expecting	☐	D helping	☐
3	A change	☐	B compare	☐	C differ	☐	D contrast	☐
4	A pupil	☐	B pupils	☐	C pupil's	☐	D pupils'	☐
5	A for you	☐	B to help	☐	C from sight	☐	D as fact	☐
6	A Not that	☐	B It's true that	☐	C Therefore,	☐	D Additionally,	☐
7	A among	☐	B by	☐	C for	☐	D between	☐
8	A spot	☐	B understand	☐	C compose	☐	D believe	☐
9	A argue	☐	B reflect	☐	C depend	☐	D think	☐
10	A whether	☐	B why	☐	C when	☐	D how	☐

SPEAKING **8** Discuss the article in small groups and present your findings to the class.

1 Explain what critical thinking means in your own words.
2 Do you agree that critical thinking is the most important goal of education? Why?/Why not?
3 Collect examples of critical thinking exercises in your own education. Are they common?

LANGUAGE **9** Expand your vocabulary: Collocations

p. 28

Complete the phrases with the verbs from the article. Then add more collocations from the article and share them in class.

L

a _____ the links between ideas
b _____ the relevance of arguments and ideas
c _____ inconsistencies and errors in reasoning
d _____ problems in a consistent and systematic way
e _____ different possibilities
f _____ your ideas

STRATEGIES **10** a Boost your learning from multiple choice tasks

There are many ways you can maximise your learning from multiple choice tasks like the one above. For starters, analyse the wrong options and decide why they don't fit the text:

S

1 Start by looking up expressions you don't know. If they are options, you *should* know them!
2 Does the expression fit the text grammatically, but not the context of the text (like **0C**)?
3 Does the expression fit the context, but it doesn't work grammatically (like **3B**)?
4 How would you have to change the text to make the word work? For example, for **3B** to be correct, the sentence would have to read: So how do these opinions (3) _____ **to** more common ...

b Now complete these steps with the task above to improve your learning from it!

WRITING **11** Use your critical thinking skills to write a PEEL paragraph of around 100 words agreeing or disagreeing with the following statement: *Teenagers have too much time on their hands and should get a weekend job.*

LISTENING + VIEWING

⌖ 06
🌐
↗
p. 33

12 **a** Watch a news report on pupils working at weekends and match the statements to the people shown. There are two statements for each person (except for person 1).

1 ___0___   2 _____   3 _____   4 _____   5 _____

a There should be help for young people starting to work.
b It's not hard to combine school and weekend work.
c There is no disadvantage to working as a pupil.
d School should teach pupils the skills they need to find work.
e I'm quite shy, so I can't work at the bar.
f My family helped me to find staff for the bar.
g ~~I want to earn my own money.~~
h Pupils shouldn't let school stop them from working.
i Working on Saturdays helps pupils in their later work life.

b What skills can you develop through jobs like the ones in the video? What other things could work experience be good for? Share your ideas in class.
Examples: *improve time-management skills, develop people skills, …*

c What's your opinion on pupils working at weekends now?

SPEAKING

13 *Paired activity:* Your English language assistant wants to know what kind of Saturday jobs are popular among young Austrians. Discuss the options below with a partner and agree on three.

- babysitting
- tutoring students
- sales assistant
- housekeeping
- your own ideas

S **Strategies box**

'Your own ideas': You are free to come up with any ideas of your own as long as they **fall into the same category** (here: Saturday jobs for teenagers). You discuss arguments for and against and come to a decision.
Examples: *lifeguard, dog walker, …*

WRITING

14 An Irish pub has recently opened in your area. The owner is looking for a waiter/waitress who can speak English fairly well and is prepared to work Saturdays from 2 p.m. to 8 p.m. You are interested in the job and have decided to write an email to the owner.

In your email you should:

- present yourself
- explain why you are interested in the job
- specify what additional information you would need

Write around 250 words.

→ See *Writing coach, Formal email,* p. 178.

Education – a family affair?

SPEAKING **15** **Discuss the following questions with a partner:**

1 There is a saying that "parents are a child's first and most important teacher".
Do you think this is true? Why?/Why not?
2 How far do you think parents should be involved in their child's education, for example checking their homework, rewarding good grades or punishing children for poor grades?
3 Write down three positive and three negative effects of parents being involved in their child's learning. Share your ideas with the class.

LANGUAGE **16** **a** *Expand your vocabulary: Education*

p. 29

Read the following emails from parents to an advice column in a magazine. Choose the correct words to complete the sentences.

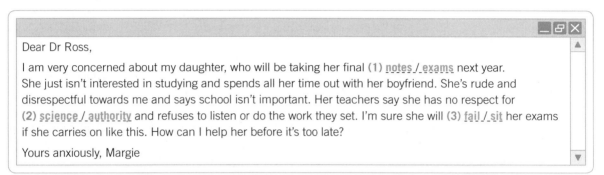

Dear Dr Ross,

I am very concerned about my daughter, who will be taking her final **(1)** notes / exams next year.
She just isn't interested in studying and spends all her time out with her boyfriend. She's rude and disrespectful towards me and says school isn't important. Her teachers say she has no respect for **(2)** science / authority and refuses to listen or do the work they set. I'm sure she will **(3)** fail / sit her exams if she carries on like this. How can I help her before it's too late?

Yours anxiously, Margie

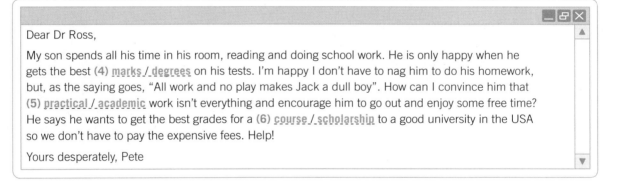

Dear Dr Ross,

My son spends all his time in his room, reading and doing school work. He is only happy when he gets the best **(4)** marks / degrees on his tests. I'm happy I don't have to nag him to do his homework, but, as the saying goes, "All work and no play makes Jack a dull boy". How can I convince him that **(5)** practical / academic work isn't everything and encourage him to go out and enjoy some free time?
He says he wants to get the best grades for a **(6)** course / scholarship to a good university in the USA so we don't have to pay the expensive fees. Help!

Yours desperately, Pete

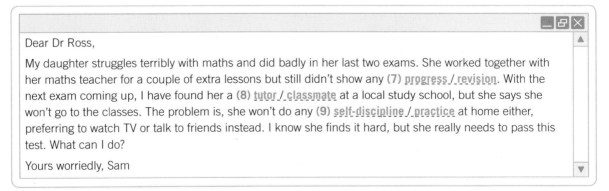

Dear Dr Ross,

My daughter struggles terribly with maths and did badly in her last two exams. She worked together with her maths teacher for a couple of extra lessons but still didn't show any **(7)** progress / revision. With the next exam coming up, I have found her a **(8)** tutor / classmate at a local study school, but she says she won't go to the classes. The problem is, she won't do any **(9)** self-discipline / practice at home either, preferring to watch TV or talk to friends instead. I know she finds it hard, but she really needs to pass this test. What can I do?

Yours worriedly, Sam

b **How many of the words did you already know? Make a note of any new vocabulary.**

17 **Now use six of the green words to write meaningful sentences about education. Try not to use an expression more than once.** Example: *Even a good tutor can't help you if you have no self-discipline.*

p. 30

READING 18 a You are going to read an article about Amy Chua's book *Battle Hymn of the Tiger Mother*, in which Chua writes about how she tried to bring up her two daughters in America according to the strict Chinese parenting methods she herself had experienced. Choose the correct answer (A, B, C or D) for questions 1–7. Put a cross ([X]) in the correct box. The first one (0) has been done for you.

Tough love or cruelty?

It was the 'Little White Donkey' incident that pushed many readers over the edge. That's the name of the piano tune that Amy Chua, Yale law professor and self-described 'tiger mother', forced her seven-year-old daughter Lulu to practise for hours on end – "right through dinner into the night," – with no breaks for water or even the bathroom, until at last Lulu learned to play the piece.

For other readers, it was Chua calling her older daughter Sophia "garbage" after the girl behaved disrespectfully – the same thing Chua had been called as a child by her strict Chinese father.

And for some readers it was the card that young Lulu made for her mother's birthday. "I don't want this," Chua announced, adding that she expected excellence in the form of a drawing that Lulu had "put some thought and effort into." Throwing the card back at her daughter, she told her, "I deserve better than this. So I reject this."

Even before Chua's book *Battle Hymn of the Tiger Mother* was published, her proudly politically incorrect account of raising her children "the Chinese way," her parenting methods were being discussed by many disbelieving, angry people in supermarkets and coffee shops around the USA. A pre-publication excerpt in *The Wall Street Journal* (titled 'Why Chinese Mothers Are Superior') started the buzz. When Chua appeared on *The Today Show* in the US, the usually sunny host Meredith Vieira could hardly contain her dislike as she read aloud a sample of comments that viewers had sent in: "She's a monster;" "The way she raised her kids is outrageous;" "Where is the love, the acceptance?"

Chua's reply was one of defiance: "To be perfectly honest, I know that a lot of Asian parents are secretly shocked and horrified by many aspects of Western parenting and education, including how much time Westerners allow their kids to waste – hours on Facebook and computer games – and in some ways, how poorly they prepare them for the future." She added, "It's a tough world out there."

Chua's account of her authoritarian parenthood is indeed worrying, even shocking. But there's something else behind the intense reaction to *Tiger Mother*, which shot to the top of best-selling book lists despite the fact that it received much criticism. Though Chua was born and raised in the US, her account of what she describes as "traditional Chinese parenting" has hit a national sore spot in America: the fears about losing ground to China and other rising powers, and about adequately preparing children to survive in the global economy. Her stories of never accepting a grade lower than an A, of insisting on obedience and hours of maths and spelling drills and piano and violin practice each day (weekends and vacations included), of not allowing play dates or sleepovers or television or computer games or even school plays, have left many readers outraged but also defensive. The tiger mother's cubs are being raised to rule the world, the book clearly suggests, while the offspring of "weak-willed" and "indulgent" Westerners are growing up ill-equipped to compete in a fierce global marketplace.

Chua's husband makes the occasional appearance in *Tiger Mother*, cast as the tender-hearted opposite to Chua, who is a merciless taskmaster. When her husband protests at Chua's harshness over 'The Little White Donkey', for instance, Chua informs him that their older daughter Sophia could play the piece when she was Lulu's age. Sophia and Lulu are different people, he argues reasonably. "Oh, no, not this," Chua shoots back, adopting a mocking tone. "Everyone is special in their special own way. Even losers are special in their own special way."

0 The name 'tiger mother' was given to Chua by

   A the author's daughter, Lulu. ☐

   B Amy Chua herself. ☒

   C readers of Chua's book. ☐

   D Chua's father. ☐

1 Chua gave the birthday card back to Lulu because she

   A believed, as a bad mother, she didn't deserve it. ☐

   B wanted Lulu to write something in it. ☐

   C felt her daughter hadn't tried hard enough. ☐

   D felt sorry for her daughter. ☐

2 In writing her book, Amy Chua felt

   A she needed to confess what she had done to her daughter. ☐

   B proud of her parenting methods. ☐

   C she should have been more politically correct. ☐

   D embarrassed about her daughter's upbringing. ☐

3 The host of *The Today Show*

   A read out some comments from people watching the show. ☐

   B was usually bad-tempered. ☐

   C agreed with Chua's methods. ☐

   D told Chua she thought she was a monster. ☐

4 Amy Chua's book made people

   A worry American children would be disadvantaged globally. ☐

   B not want to buy it. ☐

   C totally agree with her methods. ☐

   D less worried about their children's place in the global market. ☐

5 Chua's daughter

   A didn't have to play the piano at weekends. ☐

   B sometimes had friends over to play. ☐

   C could play on the computer after piano practice. ☐

   D was never allowed to watch television. ☐

6 Lulu's father

   A supported Chua's parenting methods. ☐

   B was kinder and less strict. ☐

   C features very often in the book. ☐

   D was even harsher on Lulu than Chua. ☐

7 When Chua says, "Everyone is special in their special own way," she is

   A saying that every child is an individual. ☐

   B agreeing with her husband. ☐

   C being sarcastic. ☐

   D making a joke with her husband. ☐

b Now work with a partner and look again at your answers to the questions in exercise 15 on p. 75. Add more points to your list of 'advantages' and 'disadvantages' using what you have read.

ANGUAGE **19 a** Expand your vocabulary: The suffixes *-nce* and *-nt*

pp. 28+32

Look for the missing nouns which appear in the article above and use them to complete the table.

L

Noun	Verb	Adjective
	excel	excellent
	defy	defiant
	obey	obedient
	appear	apparent

b Study the examples in the table carefully. How do the words change when the suffix is added? How does this affect the way you need to study these words?

LANGUAGE **20**   **What are the nouns corresponding to the adjectives in the box? What are the adjectives for the nouns? Use a dictionary to check. Then use the new words to complete the sentences below.**

> absent ▪ confident ▪ convenience ▪ different ▪ distance ▪
> important ▪ independent ▪ violent

1 It may not always be _____ to fit in homework around your social life, but it is essential.

2 You should never underestimate the _____ of a good education.

3 It makes a huge _____ if parents talk about school and learning with their children.

4 Teenagers need some _____ from their parents to grow into responsible adults.

5 Regular or long _____ from school can lead to worse grades or even failing school.

6 Bullying and _____ must never be tolerated at school.

7 Good preparation can lead to improved _____ in your abilities and better exam results.

8 At some point in the _____ future you'll probably look back fondly at your years at school.

WRITING **21**   **Having read the article about Amy Chua's book *Battle Hymn of the Tiger Mother*, you have decided to start a blog on education.**

In your blog post you should:

- ▪ examine why some parents believe in a strict education for their children
- ▪ point out how children might feel about it
- ▪ specify what you would consider an ideal education

Write around 400 words. Give your blog post a title.

→ See *Writing coach, Blog post*, p. 180.

S | **Strategies box**
To examine means to look at something carefully and in detail in order **to find out what it is like** or **to discover something about it.**

SPEAKING **22**   *Individual long turn:* **Give a 4-minute talk on education.**

"Non scholae, sed vitae discimus."

(*Latin for:* We do not learn for school, but for life.)

S | **Strategies box**
When you **discuss a quote**, you **explain** what it means **in your own words**, you illustrate it with **examples**, talk about its **relevance** and give your **opinion** on it.

In your talk you should:

- ▪ discuss the quote
- ▪ explain how school education could prepare young people for their future
- ▪ point out the importance of a good general education for young people today

SPEAKING 23 What are your current plans for further education after you've finished school? Talk to a partner. Ideas you could discuss:

- what and where you would like to study
- your reasons for these choices
- what difficulties you might face
- what alternatives you are thinking about

ANGUAGE 24 a Expand your vocabulary: Tertiary education
Complete the fact sheet with the verbs from the box below.

L				
a attend	c exist	e prepare	g sat
b earn	d pass	f reduce	h submitted

---

fact sheet: universities

Studying in Austria

Federal universities
Austria's federally-funded universities allow you to study a wide range of academic subjects, such as philosophy, psychology or economics. As a student there, you (1) ☐ a range of workshops, seminars and lectures to deepen your understanding of the field. Once you have (2) ☐ all required exams and (3) ☐ your thesis, you are a graduate and hold a degree.

Universities of Applied Sciences (UAS)
In contrast to traditional universities, education at UAS is more focused on practical job training rather than general academic study. Available courses (4) ☐ students for jobs in the medical field, such as physiotherapy, but also management, applied computer science or engineering.

University Colleges of Teacher Education
These specialised institutes train Austria's primary and secondary school teachers. You have to (5) ☐ an entrance exam and go to a personal interview to gain admission. After four years of theoretical and practical instruction, you (6) ☐ a Bachelor's degree and can start teaching at a school while continuing your studies towards a Master's degree and becoming a fully qualified teacher.

Private universities
Private institutions of tertiary education are still quite rare in Austria but do (7) ☐ for medicine, music and business studies, for example. You can expect to pay tuition fees of 15,000 euros or more per year, but you might qualify for a scholarship, which would (8) ☐ the amount. In exchange, you are instructed by lecturers in small groups and might even be supported by a tutor.

---

b Organise the green expressions in a table or word map of your own design.

SPEAKING 25 Use the ideas you've discussed and at least five expressions from the fact sheet above to prepare a 2-minute statement on your plans for further education after school. Talk to a partner, get feedback, and then share your statement in class.

SPEAKING 26   **What are students looking for in a university? Discuss the list of ideas below with a partner and agree on the three most important ones.**

a   diverse community of students
b   focus on academic learning
c   possibility to earn a degree quickly
d   scholarships for students from low-income families
e   self-organised study instead of timetables
f   modern facilities

g   location close to home
h   lectures available online
i   small group sizes
j   in a city with a busy nightlife
k   supportive lecturers, tutors and other staff
l   many extracurricular activities

LISTENING 27   **a**   **Listen to four advertisements for universities. Tick off any ideas from the list above which are mentioned. They are in the order you hear them.**
◎ 10

  b   **You are going to listen to the advertisements again. First, study the task below, then, while listening, match the advertisements with the statements (A–J). There are two extra statements that you should not use. Write your answers in the boxes provided. The first one (0) has been done for you.**

After listening, take some time to check your answers.

University ads

Foxbridge	0	1
Darwin	2	3
Infinity	4	5
Wayward	6	7

A	Participation in university activities in addition to study is encouraged.	F	Meeting people from all walks of life is easily possible here.
B	Studying in small groups makes it easier to get in contact with others.	G	Students of this university can expect to get well-paid jobs after graduation.
C	Everyone can afford to study at this university.	H	The newest equipment is used to improve the education of students.
D	A wide range of study options is available here.	I	This university helps students to study in other countries as well.
E	This university attracts the most intelligent professors and students.	J	Many current world leaders have studied at this university.

0	1	2	3	4	5	6	7
F							

WRITING + SPEAKING 28   **Work in groups. Write a script for a university ad and then perform it for an audio or video recording. Share your recordings in class.**

29 a Modal verbs to express likelihood

Listen to the two conversations and tick the statement which fits best.

The people are …

a making plans for the future together. ☐
b speculating about what is going on/has happened. ☐
c sharing facts they're not sure about. ☐
d misunderstanding each other. ☐

b Listen again and fill in the gaps with the words from the conversations.

1 Someone _____ at them by now.

2 The mailman _____ it to your door as we speak.

3 He _____ his hair.

4 We _____ able to find him.

30 a Read the information on modal verbs and then do the tasks below.

L ▪ **We can use modal verbs to say how likely we think it is that something is true when we have no direct knowledge of the facts.**

Wayward College is a good college. (this is a fact)
*Wayward College **must be** a good college because so many students want to go there.*
(it is likely that this is the case)

▪ **We can speculate about the present and the past in this way:**

*Wayward College **must be** a good university.* (present – general statement)
*They **must have received** thousands of applications last year.* (past)
*They **must be reviewing** this year's applications right now.* (present – right now)

→ See *Grammar revisited, Modal verbs*, p. 175.

Rank the following statements from 1 (most likely) to 4 (least likely):

a He **should** still be at home.   c He **must** still be at home.
b He **may** still be at home.   d He **might** still be at home.

b Now look at the sentences in 29b again and make them sound more likely or less likely.

Example: *Someone **should have looked** at the applications by now.*
             *Someone **must have looked** at the applications by now.* (more likely)
             *Someone **might have looked** at the applications by now.* (less likely)

WRITING **31 a Get into groups of three and prepare conversations about the following situations.**
SPEAKING

1 One of you has been texting with a girl/boy they like and aren't sure about the meaning of a text.
"He/she must be angry with me." – "Or he/she might just be insecure. He/she might be sitting at home right now thinking about you," etc.

2 You can't find an object that is important to you and are wondering where it might be.
"It can't be in my bag because I have already looked there." – "Could you have put it in your locker?"

3 your own idea

b Act out your conversations in class.

B By the way: A fresh(er) start

Most students in the UK move away from home to live on or near to their university campus, so making new pals is a must. Luckily, help is at hand in the form of Freshers' Week. 'Fresher' is the name given to new students in their first year of university life, and Freshers' Week is full of activities organised by the students' union for the newcomers.

It's designed to orientate and integrate the new arrivals, and often students who've been at the uni for a while will volunteer to help out the 'newbies' and point them in the right direction. They frequently wear specially designed T-shirts so that they can be easily recognised. The aim is not only to familiarise students with the basic necessities, such as getting a bank account or finding their way to lectures, but also to encourage them to expand their experience outside the lecture theatres in the way of activities and clubs.

At some point in the week, 'Freshers' Fair' takes place, where the various societies at the university have representatives who present their clubs. Students have the opportunity to sign up to whichever societies take their fancy. From sports clubs to film groups, from choirs to surfing clubs – there's something for everyone at UK universities. Some societies are more serious and cultural, such as the Shakespeare Society or the Economics Society, and keen students can brush up their languages by going to the French or German Societies. However, some clubs take themselves a little less seriously, such as the Disney Society or the Robot Football Society. If students fancy something even more whacky, they can sign up to the Extreme Ironing Society (which involves dragging an ironing board into some remote place and then ironing an item of clothing there), the Custard Wrestling Society or the Competitive Eating Society. There's no excuse for being bored if you're a fresher at a UK university!

Think of one 'serious' society to add to the list above, then add one whacky society. Share your ideas in class and explain why they would be attractive to freshers. Get other students to 'sign up' for one or both of your ideas. See whose ideas are the most popular in class.

LANGUAGE **32** a Topic vocabulary: Brain work

p. 31

Combine the words from the boxes below in meaningful ways and write them down. There are many possible combinations, e.g. *acquire knowledge/facts/skills . . .* or *reflect on beliefs/values/problems*, etc.

L Verbs

acquire ▪ analyse ▪ consider ▪ discover ▪ evaluate ▪ examine ▪ identify ▪ interpret ▪ investigate ▪ justify ▪ question ▪ recall ▪ reflect on ▪ revise ▪ solve ▪ study ▪ tackle ▪ understand

Nouns

accounts ▪ beliefs ▪ concepts ▪ conclusions ▪ errors ▪ facts ▪ ideas ▪ information ▪ issues ▪ knowledge ▪ messages ▪ opinions ▪ possibilities ▪ problems ▪ skills ▪ values

b How and where do you use your brain? Use the phrases you have written down to create a word map similar to the one below. You can add how you feel about these activities as well.

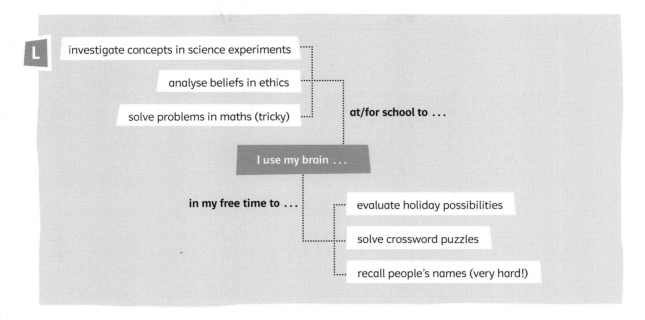

investigate concepts in science experiments

analyse beliefs in ethics

solve problems in maths (tricky)

at/for school to . . .

I use my brain . . .

in my free time to . . .

evaluate holiday possibilities

solve crossword puzzles

recall people's names (very hard!)

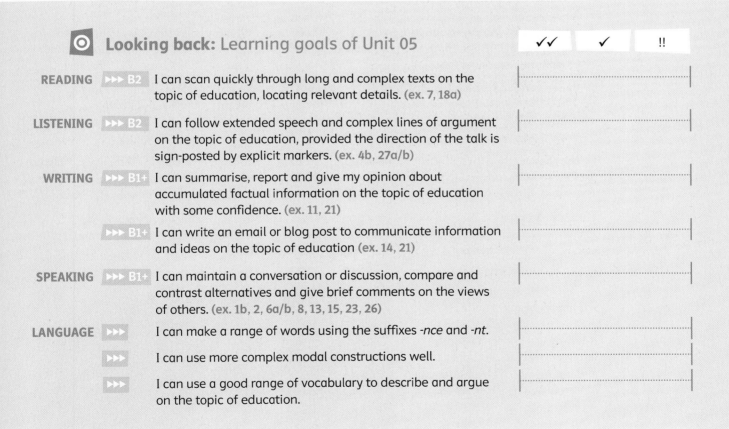

⊙ Looking back: Learning goals of Unit 05

			✓✓	✓	!!
READING ▶▶▶ B2	I can scan quickly through long and complex texts on the topic of education, locating relevant details. (ex. 7, 18a)				
LISTENING ▶▶▶ B2	I can follow extended speech and complex lines of argument on the topic of education, provided the direction of the talk is sign-posted by explicit markers. (ex. 4b, 27a/b)				
WRITING ▶▶▶ B1+	I can summarise, report and give my opinion about accumulated factual information on the topic of education with some confidence. (ex. 11, 21)				
▶▶▶ B1+	I can write an email or blog post to communicate information and ideas on the topic of education (ex. 14, 21)				
SPEAKING ▶▶▶ B1+	I can maintain a conversation or discussion, compare and contrast alternatives and give brief comments on the views of others. (ex. 1b, 2, 6a/b, 8, 13, 15, 23, 26)				
LANGUAGE ▶▶▶	I can make a range of words using the suffixes -nce and -nt.				
▶▶▶	I can use more complex modal constructions well.				
▶▶▶	I can use a good range of vocabulary to describe and argue on the topic of education.				

My number one tip for multiple choice tasks is . . .

The worst possible Saturday job for a teenager would be . . .

Semester check 01

✓✓	✓	!!

LESEN ▶▶▶ **B2** Ich kann längere Texte, auch Berichte und Artikel, zu aktuellen Fragen sowie literarische Texte selbstständig lesen und verstehen.

READING **1** Read the text about a slum in Mumbai, India. First decide whether the statements (1–7) are true (T) or false (F) and put a cross (x) in the correct box. Then identify the sentence in the text which supports your decision. Write <u>the first four words</u> of this sentence in the space provided. There may be more than one correct answer; write down <u>only one</u>. The first one (0) has been done for you.

○ ○ ○

"It feels wonderful": How a Mumbai slum became a riot of colour

When Dedeepya Reddy travelled to work on the Mumbai metro, her spirits would sink at the sight of the slum of Asalpha. Perched on a hilltop, every bit of it was grey, grubby and depressing. Only the blue tarpaulin sheets used to protect the huts from rain provided some colour.

"The metro and the road seemed so developed, and this slum looked so different," says Reddy, 31, co-founder of a digital media agency. "It didn't fit in. I thought of what could be done with minimum resources. Colours make me happy, so I thought, 'Why not paint the homes to brighten them up?'"

Asalpha has an ugliness common to all Mumbai slums. The odd pot plant aside, these areas offer little by way of aesthetic cheer to the 10 million people – more than half the city's total population of 18 million – who live there.

With her partner Terence Ferreira, Reddy got to work on a plan to transform Asalpha. Having persuaded Snowcem Paints to provide 400 litres of paint and brushes, she began an online campaign called 'Chal Rang De' ('Let's Paint It') asking for volunteers to spend a weekend painting the walls.

Before she went to work in earnest, though, she had to find out if the residents liked the idea. "They wanted to know why we wanted to do it. No one had ever done anything for them, so they were suspicious. Others wondered if coloured walls would really change anything in their lives," she says.

Ravindra Sankpal, a 27-year-old construction manager who lives in Asalpha, remembers the scepticism. "Some neighbours refused at first, because they thought it was an evil plan by builders to take over their homes," says Sankpal, whose walls are scarlet.

In December 2017, over three days, a team of roughly 400 volunteers began painting 175 walls. The atmosphere, says Reddy, was electric. The slum hummed with activity, chaos and excitement. The children got involved. Women kept up the supply of tea. At the end of an exhilarating weekend, the slum was alive with colour.

The following weekend, Reddy and Ferreira asked local artists

to paint murals on some of the walls, images that would represent the lives of the residents. One shows a group of women turning steel wool into scouring pads, a source of income for many here. Another, painted for a local boy who said he dreamed of going into space, depicts an astronaut.

When the project was finished, the residents were thrilled at the transformation. "I didn't think paint could cheer me up, but now, when I walk around here, it feels wonderful," says Aparna Chaudar, whose home has flowered walls.

When a policeman walked into the slum last month to meet Sankpal over a local issue, his jaw dropped. He asked Sankpal to turn her brushes to his police station.

Tours of Asalpha will start at the end of February, providing job opportunities for a few young guides. Local women will earn some money by providing meals for tourists.

Reddy has been stunned at the psychological change. "Maybe because of the media coming in or interacting with the volunteers from outside, people are different now. They are proud and confident. Not only is the slum brighter, the people are brighter too. We hadn't expected that at all."

Her favourite part of the slum is an alley that has an arch, niche and bright colours; it could be in Morocco, she says. People have got carried away and compared Asalpha with Positano on the Amalfi coast. The comparison is far-fetched. 'Jolie laide'– French for 'beautiful-ugly' – might be more apt.

Reddy and Ferreira plan to paint the slum on the other side of the road. "I want to brighten up whole neighbourhoods," she says.

	Statements	T	F	First four words
0	Apart from grey, there was only one other colour in the slums.	☒	☐	Only the blue tarpaulin
1	The majority of Mumbai's inhabitants live in inadequate housing.	☐	☐	
2	The supplies needed for the painting project were donated by a company.	☐	☐	
3	Asalpha's residents were immediately on board with painting the walls.	☐	☐	
4	All of Asalpha's buildings were painted in a couple of days.	☐	☐	
5	Numerous people in the slum earn money working with metal.	☐	☐	
6	The project is expected to benefit the local economy.	☐	☐	
7	Asalpha now looks like a famous tourist destination.	☐	☐	

✓✓	✓	!!

HÖREN ▶▶▶ B2

Ich kann längeren Redebeiträgen und komplexer Argumentation folgen, sofern die Thematik einigermaßen vertraut und der Rede- oder Gesprächsverlauf durch explizite Signale gekennzeichnet ist.

LISTENING 2

radio FM4

⊙ 12

🌐

32m3r5

You are going to listen to an FM4 interview with David Lindo, an urban bird watcher from London. First you will have 45 seconds to study the task below, then you will hear the recording twice. While listening, answer the questions (1–7) using a maximum of four words. Write your answers in the spaces provided. The first one (0) has been done for you.

After the second listening, you will have 45 seconds to check your answers.

Birdwatching

0	How does the interviewer feel about their location?	*doubtful*
1	What does Lindo notice first?	
2	How have some woodpeckers changed their behaviour?	
3	What fascinates Lindo about birds?	
4	What is surprising about Lindo's childhood? (Give <u>one</u> answer.)	
5	Which discovery had a huge impact on Lindo's life?	
6	How has Lindo changed nature programmes on TV and radio?	
7	According to Lindo, what does birdwatching teach you about the world?	

SPRECHEN ▶▶▶ **B1+**   Ich kann eine Argumentation, auch in Form einer Präsentation, gut genug ausführen, um die meiste Zeit ohne Schwierigkeiten verstanden zu werden.

▶▶▶ **B1+**   Ich kann ein Gespräch oder eine Diskussion aufrechterhalten und dabei kurz zu den Standpunkten anderer Stellung nehmen, Vergleiche anstellen und verschiedene Möglichkeiten angeben.

SPEAKING **3** **a** <u>Individual long turn (4 minutes)</u>

Prepare for about 10 minutes, then do the task below. Your partner gives you feedback with the checklist in the key.

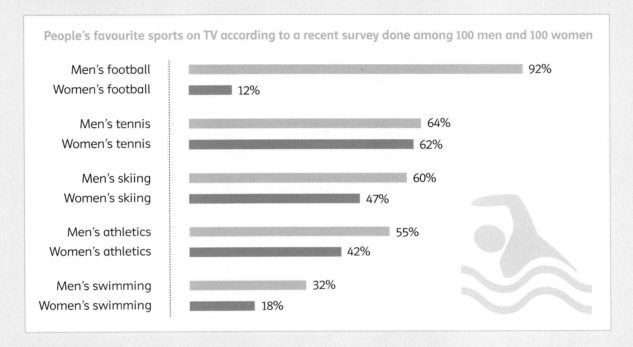

People's favourite sports on TV according to a recent survey done among 100 men and 100 women

Men's football	92%
Women's football	12%
Men's tennis	64%
Women's tennis	62%
Men's skiing	60%
Women's skiing	47%
Men's athletics	55%
Women's athletics	42%
Men's swimming	32%
Women's swimming	18%

- Outline the results of the survey.
- Speculate why people watch men's sports rather than women's sports.
- Suggest ways to make women's sports more attractive.

b <u>Paired activity (8 minutes)</u>

Do the task below in a group of three. Two of you talk, the third person listens and gives you feedback with the checklist in the key.

Your English teacher is planning a language trip for your class to Cambridge in April. Before he/she starts making arrangements, he/she needs to know what you and your classmates consider to be most important so that everybody wants to take part. Discuss the aspects below with a partner and agree on three.

- total costs per student
- number of students per host family
- excursion to London at the weekend
- quality of the language course offered
- length of the language trip

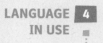
| ✓✓ | ✓ | !! |

**SPRACH-
VERWENDUNG
IM KONTEXT** ▶▶▶ Ich kann ein hinreichend breites Spektrum an sprachlichen
Mitteln korrekt erkennen und anwenden.

LANGUAGE IN USE **4** Read the text about a way of looking at the world. Some words are missing. Choose the correct answer (A, B, C or D) for each gap (1–10). Put a cross (☒) in the correct box. The first one (0) has been done for you.

Do you have a growth mindset?

Let's suppose, just for a moment, that you fail an English test. What would you do? Would you tell yourself that you'll never be able to (0) _____ an English test? Or would you make excuses such as "I would have passed the test if I (1) _____ more time to study"? This could indicate that you have a fixed mindset. (2) _____, if you realise that you need help and seek out new strategies so that you succeed the next time, this is (3) _____ for a growth mindset. So what do these terms mean?

According (4) _____ Carol Dweck, who developed the idea, people with a fixed mindset believe their basic qualities, like their intelligence or talent, are simply unchanging traits. They spend their time showing evidence of these innate qualities (5) _____ developing them. They also believe that talent alone creates success – without effort. Pupils with a growth mindset tend to see struggle as a natural part of getting better at something. When they encounter something they can't yet do, they (6) _____ their effort, try new strategies, and end up learning more.

During her research, Dweck (7) _____ that the distinction between fixed and growth mindsets has potentially far-reaching implications for schools and teachers. This is because the ways in which pupils think about learning, intelligence and their own abilities can have a significant effect on learning progress and academic improvement. If teachers encourage pupils (8) _____ that they can learn more and become smarter if they work hard and practise, Dweck's findings suggest, it is more likely that pupils will in fact learn more, and learn it faster and more thoroughly, than if they are of the opinion that learning is determined by how intelligent or unintelligent they are. Her work has also shown that a 'growth mindset' (9) _____ pupils. If, for example, a teacher is going to intentionally praise a pupil when they excel, they should (10) _____ on effort and perseverance rather than crediting learning achievements to innate qualities or talents, e.g. giving feedback such as "You must have worked very hard," and not "You are so smart."

0	A	pass	☒	B	finish	☐	C	complete	☐	D	manage	☐
1	A	could have	☐	B	might have	☐	C	had had	☐	D	have had	☐
2	A	Therefore	☐	B	Furthermore	☐	C	Despite that	☐	D	Alternatively	☐
3	A	prove	☐	B	a reason	☐	C	sign	☐	D	evidence	☐
4	A	for	☐	B	to	☐	C	in	☐	D	of	☐
5	A	instead of	☐	B	in spite of	☐	C	while	☐	D	before	☐
6	A	make up	☐	B	increase	☐	C	stop	☐	D	decrease	☐
7	A	finds	☐	B	had found	☐	C	found	☐	D	founded	☐
8	A	belief	☐	B	to believe	☐	C	beliefs	☐	D	believing	☐
9	A	might learn	☐	B	may have taught	☐	C	could teach	☐	D	can be taught to	☐
10	A	work	☐	B	depend	☐	C	focus	☐	D	rely	☐

✓✓	✓	!!

SCHREIBEN ▶▶▶ B1+ Ich kann mit einer gewissen Sicherheit größere Mengen von Sachinformationen über vertraute Routineangelegenheiten und über weniger routinemäßige Dinge zusammenfassen, darüber berichten und dazu Stellung nehmen.

WRITING 5

You and your classmates have been talking about moving out after school. You want to discuss this topic with international friends and have decided to start a blog.

In your blog post you should:

- point out disadvantages of living at home with one's family
- specify what makes moving out difficult for young people
- recommend an inexpensive way of starting one's own home

Write around 400 words. Give your blog post a title.

Unit 06
The choice is yours

 y7f747

In this unit you will:
- discuss different lifestyles
- consider the elephant in the room
- visit a dog library
- write your first essay
- read a bit of Shakespeare
- practise the suffix *-ous*

SPEAKING **1** a 'Lifestyle' is the term for the way people live. It refers to the attitudes, behaviour, activities and interests that influence how people spend their time. Compare the pictures below and discuss with a partner what they tell you about the lifestyle of the people shown in the pictures.

how and where people live

what kind of activities people enjoy

what people consider to be a healthy lifestyle

b Choose one of the people and make up a story about why they might have chosen that particular lifestyle. Tell your story to your classmates.

2 Think of more elements of lifestyle and discuss them with your classmates (for example, the kind of music people listen to, their attitude towards work, etc.).

SPEAKING **3** **a** Read through the topics below and decide which ones you would find in the lifestyle section of a newspaper. Discuss your choices with a partner.

> Animals ▪ Books ▪ Cartoons ▪ Cricket ▪ Fashion ▪ Family ▪ Food ▪ Games ▪
> Global development ▪ Health & fitness ▪ Home & garden ▪ Love & sex ▪ Men ▪
> Money ▪ Opinion ▪ Sport ▪ Travel ▪ Women

b What other topics would you like to find in a lifestyle section?

LISTENING **4** **a** Listen to the editorial meeting of a magazine for young adult readers and answer the questions in note form.

⊙ 13
🌐

1 Why does the lifestyle section have to be done differently?
2 What is the first suggestion that is made?
3 How does the team define 'lifestyle'?
4 What unusual lifestyles are mentioned?
5 Why do they decide to take things a little more slowly?
6 How are they going to start their new lifestyle section?

b Do you agree with what they think will appeal to young people? Why?/Why not?

LANGUAGE **5** **a** Expand your vocabulary: Describing lifestyle

p. 35

Look at the adjectives in the boxes below and check them in a dictionary (if necessary). Match them to form as many opposing pairs as possible.

> **L** active ▪ extravagant ▪ fast ▪ glamorous ▪ healthy ▪ mainstream ▪ minimal ▪
> slow ▪ traditional

> affluent ▪ alternative ▪ busy ▪ comfortable ▪ expensive ▪ fast-paced ▪ hectic ▪
> lavish ▪ mindful ▪ modern ▪ nomadic ▪ ordinary ▪ relaxed ▪ sedentary ▪ simple ▪
> spiritual ▪ sustainable ▪ toxic ▪ unhealthy

b Check your pairs with a partner.

c Think of three different lifestyles and describe them to someone using as many adjectives from 5a as possible. Can your partner guess what your lifestyle is?

WRITING **6** Imagine you've made your lifestyle choice and you want to become active in your community. Write the teaser for a website advocating your lifestyle. It shouldn't be longer than 50 words.

SPEAKING **7**   Are people who prefer dogs different from people who like cats better? Together with a partner, come up with three characteristics you think are typical of dog people and cat people.

LANGUAGE **8**
IN USE

p. 36

Read the text on the differences between animal owners. Some words are missing. Change the word in brackets to form the missing word for each gap (1–9). Write your answers in the spaces provided. The first one (0) has been done for you.

Cat and dog owners – the purrplexing[1] differences surveyed
by Louis Baragona

We often separate people into categories of dog owners vs. cat owners, but what (0) _____ (exact) is the difference between the two?

It's an age-old debate, a tale as old as time, a common icebreaker on first dates. "Are you a cat person or a dog person?" But in the past, it's never really been clear just how much someone's choice of pet actually says about their (1) _____ (person) or their lifestyle. Now, a recent survey of 1,000 dog owners vs. 1,000 cat owners is providing more concrete (2) _____ (prove) as to the differences between cat and dog people. It turns out that your (3) _____ (prefer) pet actually might say much more about you than a curious blind date ever anticipated.

According to the survey, dog owners tend to be more affluent. This is good because they also spend an estimated 33% more on clothes or accessories for their pets, as well as 26% more on (4) _____ (entertain) than cat owners. Luckily, dog owners are able to handle the expenses and plan their spending because they're (5) _____ (two) as likely to work in finance, according to the survey.

Meanwhile, cat owners are (6) _____ (appear) more creative than dog owners. They're more likely to enjoy a sedentary lifestyle, spending more time on documentaries, (7) _____ (music), books and gardening than dog people, who prefer action movies and travelling as well as activities like running, yoga and dancing.

The difference in (8) _____ (active) levels could be explained by the fact that 45% of dog owners said that their lives are improved through exercise with their pets. Conversely, cat owners cherish the (9) _____ (depend) of their pets and that they can tell their pets their thoughts and secrets, which in turn may be why more cat owners credit their pets for reducing their stress.

0	exactly	5	
1		6	
2		7	
3		8	
4		9	

[1] **perplexing:** verblüffend; **to purr:** schnurren

WRITING **9** Work with a partner to do the tasks below:
SPEAKING

1 Draw up a list of differences between cat and dog owners according to the survey.
2 Discuss the findings of the survey. Do you think they are accurate? Why?/Why not?
3 What are people like who keep spiders or ride horses? Make up your own description of an 'animal person'. You can choose any kind of animal or also people who like all or no animals. Share in class and comment on each other's descriptions.

LANGUAGE **10** a Expand your vocabulary: Animal idioms

p. 35

There are countless idioms involving animals in English. Here are some common ones.
Work with a partner to guess what they could mean, then check with your teacher.

L	a the elephant in the room	d be a one-trick pony	g get the lion's share
	b go on a wild goose chase	e like a fish out of water	h be a guinea pig
	c be a cold fish	f let the cat out of the bag	i let sleeping dogs lie

b **Use five of the idioms to make sentences or a short dialogue. Share in class.**

B **By the way: Famous dogs**

As the oldest domesticated animal, dogs in human society have a long and interesting history full of strange stories.

Dedication for life (or even beyond)

Greyfriars Bobby was a Skye Terrier who lived in Edinburgh in the late 19th century. His fame comes from the fact that he is said to have guarded his master's grave for fourteen years before dying himself. A statue erected in his honour and his nearby gravestone have become popular tourist attractions. The gravestone reads: "Let his loyalty and devotion be a lesson to us all."

An award for bravery

The Dickin Medal was created in 1943 in the UK by a woman called Maria Dickin to recognise the work done by animals in the military. So far, the medal has been awarded 69 times, with most of the awards going to dogs (pigeons coming in as a close second). One of the most famous recipients is Bing, a UK army dog who parachuted over enemy territory twice during the Second World War. A book about his life was published in 2012.

Dog's Got Talent

The popular UK talent show *Britain's Got Talent* has actually been won by dogs not just once, but twice, in both 2012 and 2015. The 2012 winner Pudsey was called "one of the best dancing dogs I've ever seen" by one of the judges. The triumph of Matisse in 2015 caused some controversy as it was later revealed that one of the tricks in the final act was actually performed by a different dog of the same trainer.

Do some research on one of the stories above to find out more about it and share your findings in class.

LISTENING 11 a The British Kennel Club has a whole library entirely dedicated to books about dogs. What kinds of books would you expect to find there? Who do you think would go to a library like that? Write down a few ideas, then compare them with a partner.

radio
FM4

◉ 14
🌐
↗
p. 34

b You are going to listen to an FM4 interview with Ciara Farrell, librarian of the Kennel Club Library. First you will have 45 seconds to study the task below, then you will hear the recording twice. While listening, choose the correct answer (A, B, C or D) for each question (1–7). Put a cross (x) in the correct box. The first one (0) has been done for you.

After the second listening, you will have 45 seconds to check your answers.

0 The interviewer asks

A what the oldest books are. ☐

B who visits the library. ☒

C how many books the library has. ☐

D what happened in the 15th century. ☐

1 At the library, people can

A learn about different breeds of dogs. ☐

B find out where to buy a dog. ☐

C sign up for dog sports. ☐

D borrow dog-related books. ☐

2 One visitor of the library

A had lost his family in 1920. ☐

B was a fan of a rare dog breed. ☐

C was addicted to dog shows. ☐

D wanted to learn about a relative. ☐

3 When another visitor found a photograph of herself in the library, she

A felt very proud. ☐

B started crying. ☐

C was embarrassed. ☐

D asked if she could keep it. ☐

4 The interviewer was surprised that

A so many visitors come to the library. ☐

B a dog lives in the library. ☐

C there are pictures of champion dogs. ☐

D a visitor was named after the family's dog. ☐

5 Dogs like Louis used to

A do a range of jobs for their owners. ☐

B be very popular. ☐

C be a sign of wealth. ☐

D keep poor people warm. ☐

6 The book *British Dogs*

A explains what dogs had to do. ☐

B is the library's oldest book. ☐

C tells owners how to care for their dogs. ☐

D was written in the 16th century. ☐

7 According to the book, sheep dogs can

A work without humans as well. ☐

B run long distances easily. ☐

C understand difficult instructions well. ☐

D live outside in any weather conditions. ☐

SPEAKING 12 Imagine you are the lady who visited one day. Tell a partner about your visit to the library. You could start like this: *"So, last week I finally managed to go to the Kennel Club Library. You won't believe …"*

LANGUAGE 13 Expand your vocabulary: Dog language
Complete the phrases from the interview with the missing words, then define them.

L a her family's <u>champion</u> dog   *a dog that has won lots of competitions*

b he's a Chinese crested dog – he came **from** r_____

c it describes the **working** f_____ of them

d they can work at a long distance from **their m**_____

e they can o_____ really complex **commands**

f any of the sheep **dog** b_____ today

SPEAKING **14** a Do you think teenagers should be encouraged to keep a pet at home? Discuss this question with a partner and draw up a list of reasons for and against.

b Now get together in small groups and compare your ideas. Collect your pros and cons in a table or a word map and present it to the class.

READING **15** Study the task, then read the title and the first paragraph of the essay below to find out what the author thinks about teenagers and pets. Then read the rest of the essay.

Your English class is discussing whether teenagers should be encouraged to keep a pet at home or not. You have been asked to give your opinion on this question in an essay.

In your essay you should:

- outline the impact of keeping a pet on family life
- consider the costs of keeping a pet
- discuss if teenagers are responsible enough to keep a pet

Write around 400 words. Give your essay a title.

Why teenagers should not have pets

Many young people like animals, so they dream of having a pet of their own. Being a pet owner, however, comes with a lot of responsibilities. As animals in the home might disrupt the family, cost a lot of money and tax teenagers' sense of responsibility, teenagers should not be given pets.

Although it is often said that a pet is a member of the family, they can also cause problems in the household. There may be arguments between teenagers and their parents about whose turn it is to walk the dog or clean out the guinea pig's cage. Unless everyone does their part in caring for the pet, stressful situations may occur. Besides, going on holiday might be a challenge as many animals are not suited to travel, and holiday destinations are often reluctant to accept pets. Disagreements about what to do with the pet will certainly have a negative effect on the family.

Owning a pet will also involve costs that could exceed teenagers' monthly allowance. Apart from the original cost of buying a pet, they need food, which can become very pricey as it has to be provided every day. No matter what type of animal it is, it will require expensive equipment or create other costs. Smaller pets need cages or tanks with plants and filters; dogs require leads and collars and might need professional training to learn to obey their owners. Additionally, owners will be faced with veterinary bills for regular check-ups and vaccinations or treatment in case the pet becomes ill.

Furthermore, many young people lack maturity and are just not responsible enough to look after another living being. They are generally too busy with their own needs and responsibilities to worry about a pet, whether they are socialising with friends or studying for school. They might not be able to spend time with the pet and may forget to feed it or take it for a walk. Dogs, for instance, need to go outside several times a day and teenagers are frequently out of the house for longer periods so that the dog's needs would not be met.

Consequently, most teenagers are not suited to owning pets due to the high cost in time and money. Pets can cause family arguments, and many teenagers are not mature enough to take responsibility for animals as they are still concerned with their own needs. In the interest of teenagers and animals, pets should only be owned by responsible adults.

STRATEGIES **16** **a** Discovering the essay

p. 38

Look at the characteristics of different text types below and highlight the ones which apply to the essay.

S

1 Who is most likely to read the text? Who is the text written for?

| a | It is usually written for a broad audience, often published in a (school) magazine. | b | It is written for a teacher, possibly for a jury, or as part of an exam. |

2 Why is it written? What is its function/purpose?

| a | It is written to discuss an issue, to inform the readers, or to convince them of the writer's opinion. | b | It is written to engage and entertain the readers, or to persuade them to take action. |

3 What should the title be like?

| a | The title should be catchy and should attract a wide audience. | b | The title should be factual, stating the topic. |

4 How should the text be organised? What is the purpose of the first paragraph?

| a | The first paragraph introduces the topic and ends with the thesis statement, which expresses the author's opinion on the topic. | b | The first paragraph should pull the readers right in from the beginning by arousing their interest in the topic. |

5 How are the bullet points (content points) dealt with?

| a | Each of the following paragraphs has a topic sentence and supporting details including examples and reasons. | b | Each of the following paragraphs has a heading so that the readers know what the paragraph is about. |

6 What should the conclusion (last paragraph) be about?

| a | The concluding paragraph should summarise and paraphrase the author's opinion. It should not introduce a new argument. | b | The concluding paragraph should encourage the readers to take action. |

7 What register and style are required?

| a | The text can be neutral, semi-formal or informal, the reader is directly addressed by (rhetorical) questions, contractions (*you've, it's* …) are quite common. | b | The text should be neutral or formal, the reader is not addressed, there are no contractions. |

b In pairs, go through the essay on p. 95 again and comment in the margin where you can find the typical features of the essay: thesis statement, topic sentences, relevant supporting details (evidence, examples, reasons) and conclusion.

WRITING **17**

p. 37

Look at the essay task on p. 95 again and write an essay arguing that teenagers should be encouraged to keep a pet.

→ See *Writing coach, Essay*, p. 184.

To thine own self be true[2]

LISTENING **18** **a** **Listen to a parent and teenager arguing and tick the phrases you hear:**

⊙ 15

a I'm out of here!

b Please, I'll do anything!

c You're just like your brother.

d I'm not a child anymore!

e As long as you live under my roof, I will make the rules!

f Calm down.

g You're such a stupid $#%!& !

h That's how we've always done it!

i Because I say so, that's why!

b **Which of these phrases do you think are (not) helpful in a discussion between parents and teenagers?**

c **What could the argument have been about? List a few topics that they might be arguing about.**

LANGUAGE **19** **a** Expand your vocabulary: Approval and disapproval

Read the text below and consider the expressions in bold. Then match the phrases from the box to the expressions in bold that have a similar meaning.

L

a are unwilling to

b denying

c disapprove of

d judge

e reluctant

f speak their mind

When teenagers and parents talk, it should be accepted for everyone to (1) ☐ **say what they think.** When parents, for example, (2) ☐ **don't agree with** their child's choice of friends or use of free time, they must be allowed to say so. Likewise, if children clearly (3) ☐ **don't want to** do something, their viewpoint should be taken seriously, too. It is never helpful to (4) ☐ **express a negative opinion about** the other person in an argument. Although teenagers can be (5) ☐ **hesitant and slow** to follow their parents' advice, (6) ☐ **not giving** them their say will always result in resistance instead of results.

b **What are helpful tips for a discussion between teenagers and parents? Talk in groups.**

WRITING **20** **Write a story about the argument you listened to. What could have happened?**

SPEAKING **21** **Family conflict is an ever-present topic in literature and films. Do you know the names of these famous stories? Compare your results in class.**

1

Two Italian families have been feuding each other for generations. This conflict often results in physical violence. When members of the feuding families fall in love, things get out of hand.

2

An eight-year-old boy mis-behaves and is sent to the attic. When his family leaves for a Christmas holiday the next day, they forget him. He is alone in the house when two burglars arrive.

3

A nobleman's son, (apparently) born out of wedlock, leaves his troubled family to join the 'Night's Watch', a military organisation. But his new-found family is heading for dangerous times, as winter is coming.

[2]**to thine own self be true:** sei dir selber treu (*Hamlet*, erster Akt, dritte Szene)

READING 22 Read the chronological events from Shakespeare's tragedy *Romeo and Juliet*. Consider the phrases in bold and make sure you know what they mean.

1
Romeo Montague and Juliet Capulet come from (1) **very wealthy** families in Verona who have been feuding for as long as anyone can remember. Recently there have been three street fights!

2
Juliet's father throws an (2) **awesome** masked ball. Romeo and his friends gatecrash the party. Romeo falls in love at first sight with (3) **beautiful** Juliet. She feels the same. Then they become (4) **aware** that they come from opposing families. Uh-oh!

3
A (5) **daring** Romeo climbs over the walls into Juliet's family garden. He is (6) **extremely brave** risking being killed if caught. This is the balcony scene! He and Juliet declare their love for one another. They decide to get married the next day.

4
The couple are married by Friar Lawrence, who hopes Romeo and Juliet's marriage will bring peace. They have to be (7) **careful** as their parents know nothing about it. It would cause a (8) **huge** fuss! Besides, Juliet's father is trying to marry her to a rich young nobleman, Paris.

5
Juliet's cruel, aggressive cousin Tybalt is (9) **very angry**. He thinks it was (10) **disgraceful** of Romeo to go to the party and wants to fight him. He ends up killing Romeo's friend Mercutio instead. This is (11) **terrible** as Romeo then kills Tybalt and is banished from Verona. Romeo and Juliet spend one night together. Then Romeo has to leave.

6
Juliet's father tells her she has to marry Paris. A (12) **defiant** Juliet refuses. Friar Lawrence tries to help, giving Juliet a drink which removes any (13) **clear** signs of life. She drinks it, goes to sleep, but looks dead. Her family believe she's dead and bury her in the family tomb. She's meant to wake up hours later, then run away with Romeo, but Romeo doesn't get the letter telling him she's not really dead. Poor Romeo!

7
Romeo arrives at Juliet's grave, takes an extremely (14) **harmful** drink and dies. Minutes too late, she is suddenly (15) **awake**, finds her beloved Romeo dead and kills herself with a dagger. Everyone arrives at the tomb to find the tragic scene. The heartbroken families decide to forget their feud and live peacefully.

SPEAKING 23 With a partner, discuss whether you think Romeo and Juliet did the right thing by keeping their relationship a secret. At which points in the plot could they have handled their situation differently so that the story had a happy ending?

LANGUAGE 24 a Expand your vocabulary: The suffix *-ous*
Now look at the expressions in bold again. Find a word with a similar meaning for each one among the options ending in *-ous* below.

L					
	a adventurous	d conscious of	g enormous	j gorgeous	m poisonous
	b cautious	e courageous	h fabulous	k obvious	n prosperous
	c conscious	f disastrous	i furious	l outrageous	o rebellious

b Choose five of the words above and write a sentence with each.

c You can make nouns from most of the words above. Make a list. Example: *adventurous – adventure*

Now try out your Shakespearean English! Take it in turns to read out the quotes from the original play below and match them with five of the summaries on the previous page. There are two summaries you won't need.

Romeo: With love's light wings did I o'erperch these walls,
For stony limits cannot hold love out,
And what love can do, that dares love attempt.
Therefore thy kinsmen are no let to me.
Juliet: If they do see thee, they will murder thee.

A ☐

B ☐

Prince: Let Romeo hence in haste,
Else, when he is found, that hour is his last.
Bear hence this body, and attend our will.
Mercy but murders, pardoning those that kill.

C ☐

Romeo: Thou desperate pilot, now at once run on
The dashing rocks thy seasick weary bark!
Here's to my love! *[Drinks.]* O true apothecary!
Thy drugs are quick. Thus with a kiss I die.

Nurse: His name is Romeo, and a Montague,
The only son of your great enemy.
Juliet: My only love, sprung from my only hate!
Too early seen unknown, and known too late!
Prodigious birth of love it is to me
That I must love a loathed enemy.

E ☐

Prince: Three civil brawls, bred of an airy word
By thee, old Capulet, and Montague,
Have thrice disturb'd the quiet of our streets
And made Verona's ancient citizens
Cast by their grave beseeming ornaments
To wield old partisans, in hands as old,
Cank'red with peace, to part your cank'red hate.

D ☐

LISTENING `26`
⊙ 16
🌐

Listen to and enjoy a performance of the excerpts on this page.

LANGUAGE `27` a **Expand your vocabulary: Elizabethan English**
Shakespeare wrote most of his works in the 'Elizabethan era', named after Queen Elizabeth I, who reigned in England from 1558 to 1603. The English used during this time was somewhat different from the Modern English we use today and is called 'Early Modern English' or 'Elizabethan English'.

Go through the excerpts from *Romeo and Juliet* on this page and find expressions with a similar meaning to the ones below.

a If they see you	d have three times upset
b your drugs	e Romeo should hurry away
c your relatives	f caused by a meaningless comment

b **Summarise the differences between Elizabethan English and Modern English that you found here.**

READING 28 **a** **Before reading the article below, write in your notebook three ways in which reading classic literature such as Shakespeare benefits your education, and three ways in which it doesn't help your education.**
Example: *Reading challenging texts expands my vocabulary and benefits my education,*
but old-fashioned language can't be used, so doesn't benefit my education.

p. 39

b **Read the text about how relevant Shakespeare is. First decide whether the statements (1–6) are true (T) or false (F) and put a cross (x) in the correct box. Then identify the sentence in the text which supports your decision. Write <u>the first four words</u> of this sentence in the space provided. There may be more than one correct answer; write down <u>only one</u>. The first one (0) has been done for you.**

Why Shakespeare still matters

Shakespeare would be amused at how famous he is nowadays. Before anything else, he was a businessman: an actor, a shareholder in his company as well as a playwright whose priority was to sell tickets. Half of his plays weren't even published during his lifetime. Now his legacy is all around us, from *The Simpsons* and *Doctor Who* to films such as *Shakespeare in Love*. Too bad he didn't live to see the royalties.

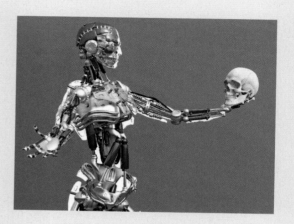

You don't have to live in England to see Shakespeare's influence everywhere you look. Shakespeare is embedded in our history. His plays were performed consistently throughout the 19th and 20th centuries and remain some of the most frequently adapted stories in Hollywood. But why should we continue to see Shakespeare's plays and to read his work? For some, the beauty of his language and the relatable characters he created is enough. His fellow playwright and friend Ben Jonson described Shakespeare as "not of an age, but for all time." When we think of romance, we think of *Romeo and Juliet*. When we think of the dangers of ambition or of ruthlessness in politics, we think of *Macbeth* and *Richard III*. When a comical mix-up takes place, we still refer to *The Comedy of Errors* with its confusion of not just one set of twins, but two.

Arguably what makes Shakespeare's work so enduring is that he doesn't provide easy answers. He does not tell us what to think; he teaches us how to think. His characters and the situations they find themselves in are complex; complex enough to require continued investigation four centuries later. Were Romeo and Juliet's parents cruel, or were they being responsible and pragmatic in looking after their children's long-term interests? Should Hamlet have trusted his instinct and acted decisively, or was he wise to delay until he thought he had proof? Or, as King Lear's decision to divide his land but retain the crown prompts us to consider, does power reside in a title or in actions?

There has never been a better time to enjoy Shakespeare. The Bard's enduring popularity proves that even four centuries after his death, he can teach us much about dealing with humanity's great questions. The questions of identity, race, terror, sex, violence, religion and gender raised by Shakespeare's plays continue to be hotly debated in contemporary culture, though rarely with the subtlety and intelligence found in Shakespeare. In wrestling with the provocative questions and scenarios Shakespeare created, we question our own assumptions and beliefs, clarify our own thoughts, and become better thinkers. And as the vast diversity of film and stage performances suggests, we continue to have fun in the process.

	Statements	T	F	First four words
0	Shakespeare sold many of his collected works before he died.	☐	☒	*Half of his plays*
1	The impact of Shakespeare's plays can be seen around the world.	☐	☐	
2	Shakespeare's works have often been made into films.	☐	☐	
3	Reading or seeing Shakespeare's plays means we'll get the answers to our problems.	☐	☐	
4	Shakespeare shows that there are often two sides to an issue.	☐	☐	
5	Shakespeare confirms that our ideas and beliefs are correct.	☐	☐	
6	The author feels that Shakespeare's work is still amusing and entertaining.	☐	☐	

SPEAKING 29 Now work in pairs. Decide with your partner how you would encourage other students to read Shakespeare. Speak for 1 minute to convince the class.

WRITING 30 Imagine Shakespeare travelling through time to the present. Would he think that the issues he wrote about (e.g. identity, race, terror, gender) still affect people today? Write an inner monologue of Shakespeare as he spends one day in the present outlining the things he sees and hears. How might he feel about these? Write about 150 words.
Example: *It seems that no one is getting married at 14 anymore. I wonder why they wait so long?*

SPEAKING 31 *Individual long turn:* **Prepare for 10 minutes and talk for 5 minutes about conflicts within the family.**

In your talk you should:

- compare the situations shown in the pictures
- outline common reasons for conflicts within the family
- advise teenagers on how to avoid conflicts with their parents

SPEAKING **a** **Shakespeare's themes in _Romeo and Juliet_ include feuds, where families fight for generations in the name of honour passing on senseless hate, arranged marriage, where young people marry a partner of their parents' choosing, and disapproval of relationships between individuals from opposing groups. But such things could never happen today, right? As a class, talk about possible situations in the world today that fit these themes. Discuss how these problems could be resolved.**

b **Here are some first-hand accounts of such conflicts still going on today. Discuss in pairs what you think about the issues and what practical solutions you would suggest. Share your ideas with another pair.**

A

"I'm a so-called 'blood child', which means I can be killed for a crime which was committed many years ago, but I don't even know what it was. No one will tell me. I have to live with my grandparents and I'm in danger every time I go outside. I have a special teacher who comes to my home to teach me because I can't go to school."
(_Saban, 16, Albania_)

B

"My parents had an arranged marriage. They got lucky and have been very happy, but I definitely didn't want them choosing a partner for me. So I was devastated when my father told me he'd found the 'perfect husband'. I refused to marry a person who was practically a stranger. My parents threw me out and no longer speak to me." (_Myra, 20, India_)

C

"I met the love of my life in a café, but the problem is I'm Catholic and he's Protestant. Although the 'troubles' have been over for a long time, there is still some stigma about 'marrying out' as it is called. My family is strict and would never accept him. We had to end the relationship."
(_Eileen, 19, Northern Ireland_)

WRITING **Your English language assistant is involved in a project called 'Teaching Shakespeare'. Pamela Brady, the head of this project, is interested in young Austrians' opinions on Shakespeare. Your English language assistant has asked you to send her an email.**

In your email you should:

- inform Ms Brady about your experience with Shakespeare
- outline a scene you have read
- explain what you liked or disliked about this scene

Write around 250 words.

→ See _Writing coach_, Formal email, p. 178.

SPEAKING _Paired activity:_ **Your English language assistant has been asked to work on _Romeo and Juliet_ with your class. He/She wants to get ideas on how to go about it. In pairs, look at the ideas below and agree on one that you would like to suggest to the assistant.**

- act out some important scenes in English
- read some important scenes in German and compare them to the English version
- read a summary of the play in English and watch the film in English
- watch two different versions of the film and compare them
- see the play in German at the theatre and then read some important scenes in English

35 **a** Topic vocabulary: Animal ownership/Lifestyles

Use the ideas from the box to start a word map on animal ownership. You need to find the categories yourself. Compare it with your teacher's word map, then add more expressions.

> breeder ▪ cause arguments ▪ champion dog ▪ dog from rescue ▪ expenses ▪
> make demands on your time ▪ master ▪ owner ▪ reason for exercise ▪ reduce stress ▪
> service dog ▪ sheep dog breed ▪ teach responsibility ▪ trainer ▪ working dog

b Pick a lifestyle choice you are interested in and collect related expressions for this way of life in categories like *people*, *items*, *advantages* or *disadvantages*. Create a word map and present it in class.

◎ Looking back: Learning goals of Unit 06

		✓✓	✓	!!

READING ▶▶▶ B2 — I can read texts on the topic of traditions and trends in which the writers adopt particular attitudes or viewpoints. (ex. 15, 28b)

LISTENING ▶▶▶ B2 — I can understand the main ideas and specific details of propositionally and linguistically complex speech on the topic of traditions and trends delivered in a standard dialect. (ex. 4, 11b)

WRITING ▶▶▶ B2 — I can write clear, detailed descriptions on the topic of traditions and trends. (ex. 9, 17, 33)

▶▶▶ B2 — I can write an essay which develops an argument, gives reasons in support of or against a particular point of view and explains the advantages and disadvantages of various options. (ex. 17)

SPEAKING ▶▶▶ B2 — I can take an active part in informal discussion on the topic of traditions and trends, commenting, putting my point of view clearly, evaluating alternative proposals and making and responding to hypotheses. (ex. 1, 9, 14a, 23, 34)

▶▶▶ B2 — I can give clear, detailed descriptions on the topic of traditions and trends, expanding and supporting ideas with subsidiary points and relevant examples. (ex. 12, 14b, 31)

LANGUAGE ▶▶▶ — I can use a good range of vocabulary to describe and argue on the topic of traditions and trends.

▶▶▶ — I can make and use a range of adjectives ending in -ous.

> **Without looking back in the book, the animal idioms I can remember are . . .**

> **Three things I've learned about writing essays are . . .**

Unit 07
You be the judge

8aq8ks

In this unit you will:

- compare different kinds of crime
- think about how to stop burglars
- consider ways to protect schools
- speculate about an imaginary past
- discover the role of an interlocutor
- discuss rules that need to be broken

SPEAKING 1   **Look at the WANTED posters and match the crimes to the people.**

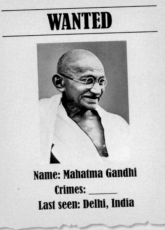

WANTED

Name: Mahatma Gandhi
Crimes: _____
Last seen: Delhi, India

1

multiple robberies, murder of civilians and police officers

2

theft, poaching, murder

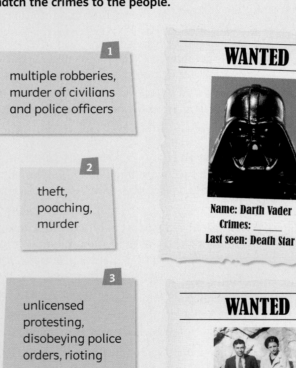

WANTED

Name: Darth Vader
Crimes: _____
Last seen: Death Star

3

unlicensed protesting, disobeying police orders, rioting

WANTED

Name: Robin Hood
Crimes: _____
Last seen: Sherwood Forest, England

4

burglary, kidnapping, torture, murder, genocide

WANTED

Name: Bonnie and Clyde
Crimes: _____
Last seen: Sowers, Texas, USA

2   **Discuss in small groups:**

1 What else do you know about the people shown in the posters? Are they all the same kind of 'criminal'?
2 What other famous criminals from history or fiction do you know? Do they have anything in common with the people in the posters?
3 Why do you think people find real and fictional crime stories so fascinating?

SPEAKING **3**
Should there be a law against doing the following activities, or should they be allowed? Discuss your ideas with a partner. Support your opinions.

a riding bikes on the pavement
b drinking alcohol in public
c smoking in restaurants
d cheating on a test

LISTENING **4**
VIEWING
WRITING
⌕ 07
🌐

Watch the news report about local laws affecting skateboarders in British towns and take notes. Then summarise the information in about five sentences. The following questions might help you.

1 What does the local council want to do?
2 Why do they want to do it?
3 What do the skateboarders think about it?
4 What does the report suggest the skateboarders should do?

LANGUAGE **5** a Expand your vocabulary: Dealing with offences
Match the expressions from the news report to the correct definitions.

L		
1 an unwelcome sight	a to be banned	
2 to cause trouble	b to charge sb. an amount of money as punishment for a crime	
3 to be outlawed		
4 to deal with a nuisance	c to solve sth. annoying or troubling	
5 an offence	d sth. people don't want to see	
6 loitering	e staying in a public place for a long time, looking as if you are going to do sth. illegal	
7 to issue a fine		
8 a justified measure	f to create problems such as arguments or violence	
	g dealing with a problem for a good reason	
	h an illegal act	

b Watch the news report again. Use the expressions to make sentences about its content.
Examples: *Many residents consider skateboarders an unwelcome sight in cities.*
The skateboarders don't want to cause trouble, they only …

SPEAKING **6**
What's your opinion on the conflict described in the video? Have there been any similar cases in your area? Discuss in class.

WRITING **7**
Imagine your local council wants to ban teenagers from a park or other public space. Write an email of about 150 words to your mayor to protest against this change.

LANGUAGE **8** **a** Expand your vocabulary: Types of crime

p. 40

Look at the different types of crime in the box and make sure you know what they mean.

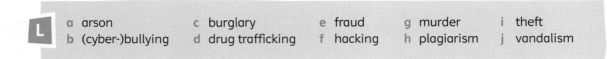

L	**a** arson	**c** burglary	**e** fraud	**g** murder	**i** theft
	b (cyber-)bullying	**d** drug trafficking	**f** hacking	**h** plagiarism	**j** vandalism

b **Use the verbs in the word field below to write definitions of each crime.**

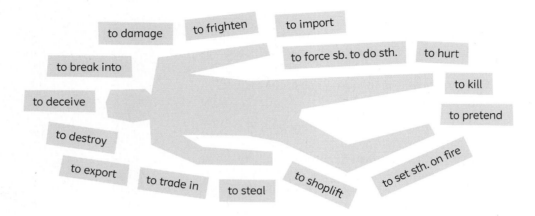

to damage   to frighten   to import

to break into   to force sb. to do sth.   to hurt

to deceive   to kill

to destroy   to pretend

to export   to trade in   to steal   to shoplift   to set sth. on fire

c **Now work in pairs and add any other crimes you know to the list above.**

SPEAKING **9** **Work in small groups:**

1 Discuss which of the crimes you consider major or severe, and which minor or petty offences.
2 Find categories such as 'crimes against people' or 'should be punished with a prison sentence' to put the offences into different groups.
3 Agree on the three worst crimes.

WRITING **10** **Remember Tony Giles, the blind traveller from Unit 04, who mentions that his camera was stolen? What do you think happened to it? Was it:**

- sold?   - stolen again?   - given away as a gift?   - left somewhere?   - used by the thief?
- transplanted into outer space to watch over Tony?

Decide on one option and write the camera's story. You could start like this: *One minute I was in Tony's hand and he was asking a man to take a picture with me, the next minute this thief ran out of the church with me. Oh dear, I thought, what will happen to me …*

11 **Browsing young people's street art blogs, you have come across the blog post on the right.**

You have decided to comment on the blog post. In your blog comment you should:

- discuss if you consider spray painting to be art
- explain how you feel about punishing spray painters
- give an example of a crime that you consider worse than spray painting

Write around 250 words.

→ See *Writing coach, Blog comment*, p. 182.

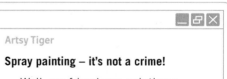

Artsy Tiger

Spray painting – it's not a crime!

… Well, my friend was painting a dream world on this ugly wall in this poor area. He only wanted to give the people something beautiful, something to enjoy, simply a piece of art. Anyway, he was caught and got arrested for it! Do you think that's fair?

reply

Burglary is among the most common crimes people fear. Read the tips on how people can protect themselves, which were published on a UK police website, and match them to the explanations. There is one explanation you won't need.

How to prevent burglaries

When trying to improve security around your home, the best way to approach it is to look at your home as if you were the offender. Identify the weak spots and vulnerable areas and prioritise the areas for improvement.

1 Make sure your property looks well cared for. ☐
2 Make sure that a potential target is out of view. ☐
3 Remove items that may help commit a crime. ☐
4 Reduce the profit the criminal could make from the offence. ☐
5 Improve surveillance around your home. ☐

a Don't leave valuables (laptops, phones, keys, bags) visible through the window.
b Make sure domestic or commercial waste is cleared up.
c Mark your property in such a way that others will not want to buy it from the thief.
d Upgrade the locks on your doors and windows.
e Remove high fences at the front of your home that allow an offender to remain unseen. Ask neighbours to be watchful.
f Don't leave ladders in the garden, and keep wheelie bins out of reach as they may be a climbing aid or help transport stolen goods.

SPEAKING `13` *Paired activity:* **Together with a partner, discuss the five tips about the prevention of burglaries and rank them from 1 to 5 according to their usefulness.**

`14` *Individual long turn:* **You have been asked to give a 5-minute talk on crime.**

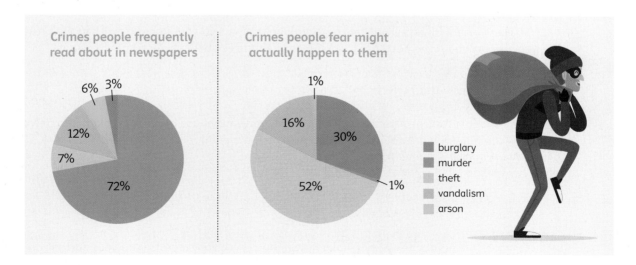

Crimes people frequently read about in newspapers

6% 3%
12%
7%
72%

Crimes people fear might actually happen to them

1%
16%
30%
52% 1%

- burglary
- murder
- theft
- vandalism
- arson

In your talk you should:

- compare the charts
- suggest how some of these crimes can be prevented
- discuss if the job of police officer might be attractive for young people

LANGUAGE **15** a Mixed conditionals (or: talking about imaginary past and present situations)

p. 45

We often imagine what *would have happened* or what our lives *would be like* now if something had happened differently in the past. Read the information and do the task below.

L

Imaginary past situation . . .	. . . influences the past.
If Bonnie and Clyde **had** not **lived** such colourful lives,	they **would** not **have become** legends.
Imaginary past situation . . .	**. . . influences the present.**
If Bonnie and Clyde **had** not **become** legends,	there **would** not still **be** a special Bonnie and Clyde Festival every year.

→ See *Grammar revisited, Mixed conditionals*, p. 176.

Look at the verbs in bold in the text below. Do they refer to the past or the present?

The first *Star Wars* film, which introduced Darth Vader as the main villain, was very successful. If the first *Star Wars* film had not been so successful, the director **would not have gone on** to make several more *Star Wars* films, and there **would not be** a whole fictional *Star Wars* universe today.

b **Using the information above, write similar texts about these two situations:**

1 **Mahatma Gandhi** went on the Salt March in 1930 to protest against British rule in India. He became world-famous for non-violent resistance and inspired Martin Luther King and Nelson Mandela. Gandhi's story still gives hope to oppressed people today.
If Mahatma Gandhi had not gone on the Salt March …

2 **Robin Hood** was famous for stealing from the rich and giving to the poor. He inspired many legends. Today, his story is one of the best-known English folk tales, and he still appears in many books and films. *If Robin Hood hadn't been so famous …*

LANGUAGE **16** Regrets and wishes

p. 45

You can use *I wish* and *If only* to complain about things you are unhappy with in the present or things you regret about the past. Are the following sentences about the present or the past?

1 I wish/If only there hadn't been a burglary.   present / past
2 I wish/If only I had insurance.   present / past

17 **You have just returned from a holiday abroad, and your house has been broken into. Tell your partner how unhappy you are about the situation using *I wish* and *If only*.** Example: *My home is a crime scene now. → If only my home wasn't a crime scene!*

1 I don't have insurance.
2 The place is such a mess!
3 I must find a new flat now.
4 I left my valuables on display through the window.
5 I did not upgrade the locks on my doors and windows.
6 I forgot to keep my wheelie bins out of reach of intruders.

18 **Consider the points below and make notes, then share your regrets with your partner.**

1 a useless thing you bought
2 a holiday destination you hated
3 a stupid thing you said
4 sth. you don't like about your timetable
5 sth. you hate doing at home
6 sth. you don't like about your school building

Examples: *If only I hadn't bought a phone that doesn't work well.*
        I wish our school had a bigger cafeteria.

Do guns keep us safe?

LISTENING **19** **a** Write down any ideas that you associate with the expressions in the box below. Compare your ideas with other students in class. How do your lists differ?

> gun laws ▪ the American Constitution ▪ mass shootings

⊙ 17
🌐

b Listen to a reporter talking about a debate in the US Congress and answer the questions below.

1 What does the Second Amendment to the Constitution protect?
2 When was it introduced?
3 Which argument against gun control does the reporter mention?
4 What do people in favour of gun control say?

20

⊙ 18
🌐

Some people say there are as many reasons for keeping the right to bear arms as there are for stricter gun laws. Listen to the reporter interviewing people on the streets of Washington and take notes on the most important points. Compare your notes in class.

LANGUAGE **21** Expand your vocabulary: Gun laws and safety
Use your notes to complete the words in these summaries of the individual statements.

1

The majority in the US agrees with st_____ c_____ of gun ownership. Young people in particular favour gun ownership r_____s. The NRA[1] spends a lot of money persuading politicians that guns will k_____ pe_____ f_____ harm and are needed as s_____ devices.

2

Changing the Second Amendment of our constitution takes away every American's right to p_____ th_____ if they are in d_____. Gun ownership is the only way to gua_____ sa_____, so it needs to be beyond go_____ control. Control is just one more step to mo_____ every m_____ of US citizens.

3

For people who feel at r_____, owning a gun is a way of fe_____ s_____ and pr_____ c_____. CCTV can also improve the se_____ of se_____ of these groups through recording sus_____ be_____, as long as no da_____ pr_____ laws are violated.

SPEAKING **22** **a** Do some research on the internet to collect more arguments for or against gun control.

b Get together in groups of three and roll the dice to determine who is student A, B, or C. Student A argues in favour of gun control, student B argues against it. Student C functions as an interlocutor, making sure that each speaker has about the same speaking time, encouraging the speakers to support their arguments with details and helping out with polite questions if one of the speakers does not know how to continue.

---
[1]**NRA:** (*abbr. for*) National Rifle Association

READING 23 a The question of how to keep schools safe against gun crime causes widespread disagreement. Before reading the text below, work in pairs and come up with three ways in which schools could be protected from gun crime. Share your ideas with the class.

p. 43

b Now read the texts about five different approaches to school safety. Choose the correct texts (A–E) for each question (1–10). You can use a text more than once. Write your answers in the boxes provided. The first one (0) has been done for you.

Making schools a safe place

A **Lock it**

The answer to school safety may lie in keeping out the perpetrators in the first place. Keeping all exterior doors, except the main entrance to each building, locked throughout schools and requiring staff, students and parents to wear and display photo ID badges could help. However, as some offenders have been students themselves, the ID system may not be enough. A functioning public address system would enable a 'lockdown' in which classrooms with students in are locked from the inside for protection. Additionally, schools can buy bullet-resistant Kevlar[2] panels which are mounted over the classroom door to protect them, and steel barricade locks are also available for extra-secure doors.

B **Security staff in schools**

Many schools have security guards to ensure the safety of the children learning there. These guards need to be properly trained so they can take the necessary steps at the right time and safeguard the children and school. They can vacate the school quickly without causing chaos and panic among the students or call for a lockdown if necessary. One other advantage of a regular security officer is that they will be familiar with the teachers, pupils and parents and should be able to quickly spot anyone who doesn't belong in the school building. It is also possible that an armed security guard may act as a deterrent discouraging any potential attackers.

C **Armed, but not dangerous?**

There have been calls to arm teachers in schools so that they can protect the pupils in their care. Already more than a dozen US states have trained teachers who now carry a gun in school. It is cheaper for schools to arm teachers than to hire more security staff. Furthermore, there are schools in the countryside where the police may take longer to respond to emergency calls, and having armed teachers would cut down response time. However, teachers have expressed concern that they may be mistaken for the shooter if they are seen with a gun by police in the event of a school shooting.

D **The power of education**

Many educators feel that preventing violence in school starts with teaching young people how to control their emotions, recognize others' feelings and to negotiate. We learn social skills from everyday interactions with each other, but frequent social media use and a decrease in free leisure time has reduced young people's opportunities to learn these basic social skills. However, social and emotional skills can – and should – be taught in school as a way to prevent student violence. Students with more fluent social skills connect better with others and may be more able to recognize troubled peers who need help. To prevent school shootings, schools should also address key risks for violence, such as bullying, harassment, and a hostile school climate.

---

[2]**Kevlar:** *Markenname für ein sehr zug- und reißfestes synthetisches Material*

E Rucksacks as lifesavers

Some companies that make tactical gear for military and law enforcement officers have developed bullet-resistant backpacks for school children. The backpacks are made with either a metal insert or whole panels constructed with Kevlar, a material used in bulletproof vests. The companies say that these panels provide children and parents with peace of mind, but schools argue that children may be falsely confident about the effectiveness of the panels, which do not stop more powerful assault rifle bullets. They believe that children may not follow their teachers' instructions to stay safe. Additionally, the rucksacks cost between $200 and $300, which many parents cannot afford.

According to the descriptions, which safety solution(s) . . .

could result in high costs for families?	0	
could be more dangerous for teachers in an emergency situation?	1	
involves changing young people's mindsets to stop school gun crime from happening?	2	
involve teaching adults special skills?	3	4
do schools fear may cause students more harm than good?	5	
may stop anyone daring to attack a school?	6	
involves personal identification?	7	
involves students assisting one another?	8	
could make a profit for companies producing special materials?	9	10

0	1	2	3	4	5	6	7	8	9	10
E										

SPEAKING 24 Work with a partner and consider the five safety solutions above. Discuss how you would feel if each of these safety measures were used in a school you were attending. Would you feel more/less secure? Rate the solutions in order of most (1) to least effective (5) in your opinion. Share your conclusions with the class.

WRITING 25 Your English class is discussing whether CCTV cameras inside the school building would improve safety in schools. You have been asked to write an essay on this question.

In your essay you should discuss:

- whether students would feel more secure
- the effect of CCTV cameras on students' privacy
- if hiring security staff might be more effective

Write around 400 words. Give your essay a title.

→ See *Writing coach, Essay*, p. 184.

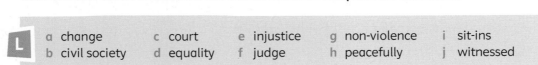

Civil disobedience

SPEAKING 26 **Look at the picture and discuss:**

1 What could the people be protesting against or demonstrating for?
2 Why would they do this?

LANGUAGE 27 **Expand your vocabulary: Civil disobedience**
Read the text below and choose the correct words to complete the sentences.

> **L**
> a change   c court   e injustice   g non-violence   i sit-ins
> b civil society   d equality   f judge   h peacefully   j witnessed

Throughout history, people have fought **(1)** ☐ for the right to vote, for freedom, **(2)** ☐ , and, more recently, they are protesting against companies which pollute our environment. Based on the principle of **(3)** ☐ , an act of civil disobedience involves deliberately refusing to obey unjust laws to initiate political, social or economic **(4)** ☐ .

Clearly, protests of this kind will lead to clashes between the authorities (e.g. the police) and those protesting, with the authorities claiming that the **(5)** ☐ , camp-ins, blockades, marches or hunger strikes are a threat to public safety and need to be banned. Most protesters are trained in how to peacefully resist if the police use water jets, mace, dogs, clubs and violent methods of arrest. They are prepared to get beaten, arrested, taken before a **(6)** ☐ and thrown into jail. Often, larger organisations support the protesters by paying lawyers who defend them in **(7)** ☐ .

Civil disobedience is an effective tool to fight **(8)** ☐ by drawing attention to important issues that would otherwise go unnoticed. Social media has created new possibilities to strengthen **(9)** ☐ . During the Arab spring, for example, people used Facebook and Twitter to communicate and report with/to each other and YouTube to document what they **(10)** ☐ and experienced. As Mahatma Gandhi very correctly said, "Non-violence is the greatest force at the disposal of mankind. It is mightier than the mightiest weapon of destruction devised by the ingenuity of man."

SPEAKING 28 **Discuss with a partner:**

1 Do you think non-violent protests are an effective way to reach the protesters' aims? Why?/Why not?
2 Have you ever taken part in such a protest? What was it about? What was it like?
3 Which of these forms of peaceful protest are most effective, and why?
   - sit-ins
   - hunger strikes
   - flash mobs
   - boycotts
   - protest marches or demonstrations
   - signing (online) petitions
4 What do you think about people who use violence to achieve their aims?

29 **Work in groups and choose one of the activists below or another civil rights activist you want to know more about. Research their lives on the internet and prepare a poster for class.**

   - Nelson Mandela
   - Malala Yousafzai
   - Rosa Parks
   - Mahatma Gandhi
   - Martin Luther King
   - Emmeline Pankhurst

Things you could include: when and where they were/have been active, their reasons for protesting, their achievements, anything else you find remarkable.

30 **a** Expand your vocabulary: Using prefixes to make antonyms

📎
p. 44

You already know you can use the prefixes dis-, im-, in- and un- to make opposites (antonyms).
Complete the table using the words from the box.

| advantage ▪ agree ▪ convenient ▪ experienced ▪ ethical ▪ fit ▪ formal ▪ |
| likely ▪ lock ▪ moral ▪ obedience ▪ polite ▪ possible ▪ satisfaction |

L

dis-	im-	in-	un-
disadvantage			

b Study the words in the im- column carefully. What do they have in common? Try pronouncing them with an in- prefix instead. What's the problem?

31 Depending on how the base word starts, opposites are sometimes formed with il-, im-, in- or ir-.
Try pronouncing the words below with all four prefixes and then decide which one fits best.
Can you find a rule?

| ability ▪ credible ▪ expensive ▪ legal ▪ literate ▪ logical ▪ |
| patient ▪ perfect ▪ personal ▪ regular ▪ relevant ▪ responsible |

L

il-	im-	in-	ir-
illegal			

32 **Use words from this page to complete the sentences below.**

1 If something is _____, there is a law that states you must not do it.

2 Some crimes aren't just against the law, they are also considered to be _____.

3 Forgetting to _____ your bike makes it very easy for someone to steal it.

4 Civil disobedience might seem _____ to achieve anything, but it has worked in the past.

5 Teenagers can be _____ and sometimes take great risks without a good reason.

6 The 1968 Olympic Games were the _____ moment for Tommie Smith to protest.

7 It's _____ if you don't say 'please' and 'thank you'.

8 There have been protests due to widespread _____ with the police.

SPEAKING 33 **Get into pairs and talk about the picture showing the construction of an oil pipeline.**

1 Why might people oppose the construction of a pipeline?
2 What function does a pipeline have?
3 Why could it be dangerous?
4 What other ways to transport oil do you know and how safe are they?
5 What (other) protests concerning environmental issues have you heard of?

READING 34 **Read the story of a recent civic protest in the US and put the paragraphs into the correct order.**

p. 42

The youth group that launched a movement at Standing Rock

A ☐ At the start, the camp seemed like a hopeless undertaking. Lakota culture is run by the old – traditionally young people are supposed to apologize before they even speak in front of elders –, so for the youths to lead a movement was a radical act. The tribal council agreed to the camp but offered little support. In early April 2016, with snow still on the ground, One Mind Youth moved into tepees on the Standing Rock Sioux Reservation. They called the prayer camp 'Sacred Stone' and lit the sacred fire. Life was lived 'in ceremony', a religious mindset in which all things are done with the intention of maintaining purity. Days began with a water ceremony; the sacred fire had to be regularly fed; meals began with prayer and a 'spirit plate' served for the ancestors; alcohol and drugs were strictly forbidden.

B ☐ To gain more recognition, the young leaders decided to organize first a 500-mile relay run from the Sacred Stone Camp to deliver a letter to the Army Corps of Engineers in Omaha, asking it to deny the Dakota Access Pipeline permission to cross the Missouri River and later, a 2000-mile relay run to the Army Corps Headquarters in Washington, D.C. The run inspired the belief that a group of lost people from scattered nations could still find kinship. At every reservation, the runners met with reservation youths, telling them about the old ways and the camp at Standing Rock, where those ways were being revived.

C ☐ On December 4, 2016, the Department of the Army announced its decision to deny an easement[3] for the Dakota Access Pipeline route. The decision was an unexpected triumph. That night, as a blizzard descended on the camp, the reservation's official tribal government held a ceremony around the main fire to thank the youths. "We all came here to stand for something greater than whatever we did at home," a spokesman told the crowd as people lined up to shake the hands of the runners. The camp emptied out with winter bearing down, but most of the young people reunited in January for mass protests against Donald Trump. They were still in Washington when the news came that Trump had signed executive orders allowing the Dakota Access Pipeline construction to continue.

D ☐ Despite their failure to stop the pipeline, all believe their work should continue because the movement had connected, as one activist says, "youths who would otherwise never have had much interaction." He offers a practical reason as well: In December he got a call from a young person on the verge of suicide. He felt helpless, but he stayed on the phone, "listening to hear, not listening to respond. All I could do was say, 'You are loved, someone

---

[3] An easement will grant persons who don't own a property some right to it, for example, to walk across a piece of land. In this case, it would have granted the company building the pipeline the right to build it on land belonging to the reservation.

cares about you … in your community at Standing Rock. Even if you feel no one loves you, no one cares about you, I love you, I care about you. I want to pray with you again. And if you kill yourself now, I won't be able to do that.'" He pauses. "And my brother is still alive today."

E ☐ As one of the leaders of One Mind Youth, Jasilyn Charger, explains, they were hoping the religious activities would teach children the skills to survive threats like drug abuse and bullying. The One Mind Youth leaders had been exposed to ideas and training that linked the pipeline fights to larger struggles in their society. Pipelines, for example, are linked to the prophecy of the black snake, a figure out of Lakota myth. It symbolizes a darkness, a sickness, and its only intention is to create dysfunction and loss of life in native communities. The message was clear: The struggle against the pipeline was part of the struggle against alcoholism, suicide and abuse so frequent on Native American reservations. But what could they do to get their message out?

F ☐ In November 2015, the company Energy Transfer Partners was trying to build the Dakota Access Pipeline, which would move half a million barrels of oil a day beneath the Missouri River, the main source of drinking water for the Standing Rock Sioux and other downstream Sioux reservations. A group of young Sioux activists, called 'One Mind Youth', came to believe that the Dakota pipeline was not only a threat to their drinking water but also a sign of the environmental crisis their generation would inherit. For this reason, they helped establish a tiny 'prayer camp' just off the Dakota Access route. Over the next six months that camp grew into a movement that united conservative farmers with the American Indian Movement and urban environmentalists with the traditional chiefs of Native American tribes. But barely noticed at the time was the unlikely start of the movement: a tight-knit group of youths, most younger than 25.

G ☐ One factor that helped increase nationwide support even more was the growing violence by the police. The images of campers being maced or attacked by dogs spread anger across the country. Part of the prophecy that underlies the movement is the idea that should the Sioux resort to violence, they could be wiped out. There were strict rules that the protest would have to be done in 'peace and prayer'. The youths took this seriously, even as they found themselves under physical threat. Twenty-six-year-old Eryn Wise had moved to the camp in late August 2016. She remembers watching on Facebook Live as her sister was maced. Furious, she raced to the scene and threw herself at the police. Suddenly there were six hands on her shoulders, pulling her back. Others were praying for the police and keeping the protest peaceful, their faces white with what looked like war paint but was in fact tear gas.

WRITING **35** **a** Work with a partner to write seven questions about the article using each of these question words
SPEAKING once: *who, which, what, when, where, how, why.*

b Swap your questions with another pair and answer theirs.

c Now work in groups of four to discuss your answers.

LANGUAGE **36** Expand your vocabulary: Collocations
Read through the article again and underline expressions that mean:

a to not give a lot of encouragement
b to be shown admiration and respect
c to refuse to allow something
d to make an official statement about a choice

e to perform a set of traditional or religious acts
f to be given the opportunity to learn about sth.
g to use actions that are intended to hurt people
h to consider sth. worth your respect

SPEAKING 37   **Work in groups:**

1 Reconstruct the timeline of the protests.
2 Why were the protests so important to young Native Americans?
3 Do you know of a project in your region where tradition and technology clash in a similar way? What's your stand on it?

LISTENING 38   **a**   **You are going to listen to an FM4 interview with Eryn Wise, one of the leaders of Sacred Stone Camp. Write down three questions that you would like to ask her.**

radio
FM4

⊙ 19
🌐
🗗

p. 41

b   **Now listen to the interview with Eryn. First you will have 45 seconds to study the task below, then you will hear the recording twice. While listening, complete the sentences (1–8) using a maximum of four words. Write your answers in the spaces provided. The first one (0) has been done for you.**

After the second listening, you will have 45 seconds to check your answers.

Standing Rock protests

0	Eryn thinks the pipeline is an important issue as it will _____ .	*affect many people*
1	The pipeline is badly made because _____ .	
2	Eryn is unhappy with the traditional image _____ .	
3	She stresses that Native Americans are _____ .	
4	One of Eryn's relatives was _____ .	
5	During the protests, Eryn saw a lot of _____ .	
6	The police complained that the protests were _____ .	
7	The young Native Americans brought the policemen _____ .	
8	The police were afraid that what they received _____ .	

c   **Did the interview answer all your questions? If not, discuss possible answers in small groups, or do some internet research to find out more.**

WRITING 39   **Use what you know about the protests at Standing Rock to do one of the following tasks.**

1 Write ten tweets (280 characters or less per tweet) that could have been posted by one of the protesters.
2 Write an email to One Mind Youth asking whether you can join the movement.
   In your email you should:

   ▪ explain why you would want to join the movement
   ▪ emphasise the importance of such movements
   ▪ specify what you need to know about the movement

Write around 250 words.

→ See *Writing coach, Formal email*, p. 178.

S   **Strategies box**

To emphasise sth. means **to highlight the importance of sth.**, to say that sth. is worth giving attention to.

40 **a** Topic vocabulary: Crime/Public safety

Word families. **Complete the table of word families on crime. Then add more words from the unit and your ideas.**

Noun (idea)	Noun (person)	Verb	Adjective
		burgle	—
legalisation	—		
		offend	
murder			
		criminalise	
	hacker		
law		outlaw	

b **Create a word map containing the arguments for and against a safety measure like gun ownership or CCTV cameras. Get feedback on it, then share it in class.**

◎ **Looking back:** Learning goals of Unit 07 | ✓✓ | ✓ | !! |

READING ▶▶▶ B2	I can understand the main ideas of complex texts on the topic of rules and regulations. (ex. 23b, 34)	
LISTENING ▶▶▶ B2	I can understand the main ideas and specific details of propositionally and linguistically complex speech on the topic of rules and regulations delivered in a standard dialect. (ex. 19b, 20, 38b)	
WRITING ▶▶▶ B2	I can write an essay or blog comment which develops an argument, gives reasons in support of or against a particular point of view and explains the advantages and disadvantages of various options. (ex. 11, 25)	
SPEAKING ▶▶▶ B2	I can take an active part in informal discussion on the topic of rules and regulations, commenting, putting my point of view clearly, evaluating alternative proposals and making and responding to hypotheses. (ex. 2, 3, 9, 13, 22b, 24, 26)	
LANGUAGE ▶▶▶	I can use a good range of prefixes to make antonyms.	
▶▶▶	I can use a range of complex conditional constructions to express wishes and regrets.	
▶▶▶	I can use a good range of vocabulary to describe and argue on the topic of rules and regulations.	

Something I would protest for is . . .

I believe guns should be . . .

Literature along the way

Getting to know Oscar Wilde

1 Oscar Wilde (1854–1900) was a popular Anglo-Irish author and playwright in late Victorian England[1] known for his brilliant wit and extravagant style. To the present day he is remembered for his novel *The Picture of Dorian Gray*, his plays, with *The Importance of Being Earnest* (1894) being the most famous one, and his well-known quotes.

Discuss the following quotes together with a partner. Which one do you like best? Why? Are his words still relevant today?

A "If one cannot enjoy reading a book over and over again, there is no use in reading it at all."

B "I can resist everything but temptation."

C "If you want to tell people the truth, make them laugh, otherwise they'll kill you."

H "We live in an age when unnecessary things are our only necessities."

D "Nowadays people know the price of everything and the value of nothing."

G "There is only one thing in the world worse than being talked about, and that is not being talked about."

F "It takes great deal of courage to see the world in all its tainted glory, and still to love it."

E "Education is an admirable thing, but it is well to remember from time to time that nothing that is worth knowing can be taught."

Meeting Lady Bracknell

2 Lady Bracknell is probably one of the most popular characters in Oscar Wilde's comedy *The Importance of Being Earnest*. She represents Victorian aristocracy with all its conventions and at the same time satirises it with her witty and pointed remarks.

In the following scene Jack Worthing has asked Gwendolen, Lady Bracknell's daughter, to marry him, and she is willing to accept his proposal. The young lovers are interrupted by Lady Bracknell, who has decided to question Jack as a potential husband for her daughter before giving her consent.

Make a list of possible questions Lady Bracknell might be asking Jack Worthing. Then read and listen to the scene.

 20

---

[1] Victoria was Queen of Great Britain and Ireland from 1837 to 1901

Gwendolen. I am engaged to Mr. Worthing, mamma.

Lady Bracknell. Pardon me, you are not engaged to anyone. When you do become engaged to someone, I, or your father, should his health permit him, will inform you of the fact. An engagement should come on a young girl as a surprise, pleasant or unpleasant, as the case may be. It is hardly a matter that she could be allowed to arrange for herself … And now I have a few questions to put to you, Mr. Worthing. While I am making these inquiries, you, Gwendolen, will wait for me below in the carriage.

[…]

Lady Bracknell. [Sitting down.] You can take a seat, Mr. Worthing. [Looks in her pocket for note-book and pencil.]

Jack. Thank you, Lady Bracknell, I prefer standing.

Lady Bracknell. [Pencil and note-book in hand.] I feel bound to tell you that you are not down on my list of eligible[2] young men, although I have the same list as the dear Duchess of Bolton has. We work together, in fact. However, I am quite ready to enter your name, should your answers be what a really affectionate mother requires. Do you smoke?

Jack. Well, yes, I must admit I smoke.

Lady Bracknell. I am glad to hear it. A man should always have an occupation of some kind. There are far too many idle men in London as it is. How old are you?

Jack. Twenty-nine.

Lady Bracknell. A very good age to be married at. I have always been of opinion that a man who desires to get married should know either everything or nothing. Which do you know?

Jack. [After some hesitation.] I know nothing, Lady Bracknell.

Lady Bracknell. I am pleased to hear it. I do not approve of anything that tampers with natural ignorance. Ignorance is like a delicate exotic fruit; touch it and the bloom is gone. The whole theory of modern education is radically unsound. Fortunately, in England, at any rate, education produces no effect whatsoever. If it did, it would prove a serious danger to the upper classes, and probably lead to acts of violence in Grosvenor Square[3]. What is your income?

Jack. Between seven and eight thousand a year.

Lady Bracknell. [Makes a note in her book.] In land, or in investments?

Jack. In investments, chiefly.

---

[2] **eligible:** geeignet
[3] **Grosvenor Square:** *a famous park reserved for the rich people living in extravagant houses surrounding it*

Lady Bracknell. That is satisfactory. [...] You have a town house, I hope? A girl with a simple, unspoiled nature, like Gwendolen, could hardly be expected to reside in the country.

Jack. Well, I own a house in Belgrave Square, but it is let⁴ by the year to Lady Bloxham. Of course, I can get it back whenever I like, at six months' notice.

Lady Bracknell. Lady Bloxham? I don't know her.

Jack. Oh, she goes about very little. She is a lady considerably advanced in years.

Lady Bracknell. Ah, nowadays that is no guarantee of respectability of character. What number in Belgrave Square?

Jack. 149.

Lady Bracknell. [Shaking her head.] The unfashionable side. I thought there was something. However, that could easily be altered.

Jack. Do you mean the fashion, or the side?

Lady Bracknell. [Sternly.] Both, if necessary, I presume. What are your politics?

Jack. Well, I am afraid I really have none. I am a Liberal Unionist.

Lady Bracknell. Oh, they count as Tories. They dine with us. Or come in the evening, at any rate. Now to minor matters. Are your parents living?

Jack. I have lost both my parents.

Lady Bracknell. To lose one parent, Mr. Worthing, may be regarded as a misfortune; to lose both looks like carelessness. Who was your father? He was evidently a man of some wealth. Was he born in what the Radical papers call the purple of commerce⁵, or did he rise from the ranks of the aristocracy?

Jack. I am afraid I really don't know. The fact is, Lady Bracknell, I said I had lost my parents. It would be nearer the truth to say that my parents seem to have lost me ... I don't actually know who I am by birth. I was ... well, I was found.

Lady Bracknell. Found!

Jack. The late Mr. Thomas Cardew, an old gentleman of a very charitable and kindly disposition, found me, and gave me the name of Worthing, because he happened to have a first-class ticket for Worthing in his pocket at the time. Worthing is a place in Sussex. It is a seaside resort.

Lady Bracknell. Where did the charitable gentleman who had a first-class ticket for this seaside resort find you?

Jack. [Gravely.] In a hand-bag.

Lady Bracknell. A hand-bag?

Jack. [Very seriously.] Yes, Lady Bracknell. I was in a hand-bag – a somewhat large, black leather hand-bag, with handles to it – an ordinary hand-bag in fact.

---

⁴ **let:** vermietet
⁵ **the purple of commerce:** *people who might have become rich only recently and were looked down on by the aristocracy*

Lady Bracknell. In what locality did this Mr. James, or Thomas, Cardew come across this ordinary hand-bag?

Jack. In the cloak-room at Victoria Station. It was given to him in mistake for his own.

Lady Bracknell. The cloak-room at Victoria Station?

Jack. Yes. The Brighton line.

Lady Bracknell. The line is immaterial. Mr. Worthing, I confess I feel somewhat bewildered[6] by what you have just told me. To be born, or at any rate bred, in a hand-bag, whether it had handles or not, seems to me to display a contempt[7] for the ordinary decencies of family life. [...]

Jack. May I ask you then what you would advise me to do? I need hardly say I would do anything in the world to ensure Gwendolen's happiness.

Lady Bracknell. I would strongly advise you, Mr. Worthing, to try and acquire some relations as soon as possible, and to make a definite effort to produce at any rate one parent, of either sex, before the season is quite over.

Jack. Well, I don't see how I could possibly manage to do that. I can produce the hand-bag at any moment. It is in my dressing-room at home. I really think that should satisfy you, Lady Bracknell.

Lady Bracknell. Me, sir! What has it to do with me? You can hardly imagine that I and Lord Bracknell would dream of allowing our only daughter – a girl brought up with the utmost care – to marry into a cloak-room, and form an alliance with a parcel? Good morning, Mr. Worthing!

[Lady Bracknell sweeps out in majestic indignation.]

3 **a** Compare your list of possible questions to what Lady Bracknell actually wanted to know from Jack. Discuss the differences.

b Underline examples of Lady Bracknell's witty and pointed remarks and compare them with a partner. Has your partner decided on the same examples?

c How is humour created in the scene? (E.g. Lady Bracknell approves of Jack smoking.)

d What does the scene tell you about Victorian society?

4 Choose one of these activities to do in class or at home:

1 Change the setting. Write a dialogue between a strict father and a prospective husband for the daughter today.
2 Write a WhatsApp conversation between Jack and his fiancée Gwendolen after the scene with Lady Bracknell.
3 Do some research on Oscar Wilde and/or the play and discover the significance of its title.

---

[6] **bewildered:** verwirrt, bestürzt
[7] **contempt:** Verachtung

Unit 08
Culture vulture

 qh45cg

In this unit you will:

- discuss what's high and what's not
- read about loos in Shakespeare's theatre
- learn to use more formal language
- discover who you can tell to 'break a leg'
- hear about a famously unknown author
- read about a boy raised by ghosts

SPEAKING **1** **a** **Discuss the cartoon below in small groups:**

1 What does it say about (modern) art?
2 How is register used to create humour?
3 What might the blonde woman be thinking in panels three and five?

b **Talk in pairs. Have you ever been to an art exhibition? What was it like? Did you enjoy it? Who went with you?**

c **What was the last concert/performance you went to? Talk about it using the questions in 1b.**

[1] **haunting rumination on:** eindringliches Nachdenken über
[2] **total futility:** völlige Sinnlosigkeit

'High' and 'low' culture

p. 51

ISTENING **2** **a** **What do you think the terms 'high culture' and 'low culture' mean? Discuss your ideas with a partner.**

b **You are going to listen to a conversation between the artist Antonia Morris and a radio presenter. Before you listen, read through the statements below and guess who says what. Put an A next to what Antonia says and an R next to what you think the reporter says.**

1 … the tour received rave reviews …
2 … artists often have to fight against stereotypes …
3 … people's ideas about artists changed through the tour …
4 … there is a division between high culture and popular culture …
5 … art is about exploration and experience …
6 … art doesn't have to be expensive …
7 … money isn't important for creating art …

 21

c **Now listen to the conversation. Were your guesses correct?**

3 **Answer the questions below as well as you can before listening again to check and improve your answers.**

1 What is Antonia's profession?
  What else do you learn about her?
2 What was special about the tour? Describe it.
3 What is her idea of art?

ANGUAGE **4** Expand your vocabulary: Art and culture
The following expressions are taken from the conversation. Decide whether you can use them to talk about the tour (A), the picture of the artist in society (B), art (C), or art and money (D). Some expressions can be used more than once.

1 artistic endeavour	11 high culture	21 to participate in
2 audience	12 iconic	22 to perform
3 classical music	13 inspiration	23 performance
4 commercial	14 instrument	24 poetry
5 crossover	15 to interpret	25 popular music
6 division (between)	16 joint experience	26 the public's perception of artists
7 electronic amplification	17 journey of exploration	27 rave reviews
8 entertainer	18 low culture	28 rehearsal
9 expensive	19 my inner self	29 to sell out
10 expression of	20 painting	30 stereotype of

SPEAKING **5** **a** **Say what you think about each of the topics A–D in exercise 4 using as many expressions from the box as possible.**

b **Discuss the statement on the right with a partner. Do you agree? Why?/Why not?**

c **Who should decide what is high and what is low culture? Give reasons for your answer.**

> "Art brings out the 'poetry' in everyone, and that can be through music, through painting or through language, and it doesn't have to cost much."

WRITING **6** **Do you agree that art is important in our lives? Write a paragraph of around 100 words.**

READING **7** **a** Skim the article below and underline any facts that you find strange or surprising.
With a partner, try to agree on the two most surprising facts.

p. 46 ■ **b** Now read the text closely. Answer the questions (1–8) using a maximum of four words.
Write your answers in the spaces provided. The first one (0) has been done for you.

When Shakespeare was low culture

What are you doing this evening? If you tell people you are going to the theatre to see a performance of a Shakespeare play, they may think you are into high culture. So it might surprise you to know that Shakespeare and his contemporaries such as Christopher Marlowe and Ben Jonson have not always been seen in this light. Read on to find out why.

What did people in the 1600s do for fun? After all, there was no TV, no social media and not even radio. The answer is they went to the theatre – not just the rich, but everybody. However, at that time the theatre did not have a good reputation. London authorities refused to allow theatres within the city, so they opened across the Thames in Southwark (pronounced 'suthuck'), outside the city boundaries. The city of London disapproved of theatre because public performances were thought to be a breeding ground for the plague and for indecent behaviour. The theatre often served as a place for prostitutes to find their customers, and many people disliked the fact that the theatre allowed several different social groups to mix together. Also, since theatre performances took place in the middle of the day, they took workers away from their jobs, which employers were unhappy about.

The first proper theatre as we know it was *The Theatre*, built in Shoreditch in 1576. Before this time, plays used to be performed in the courtyard of inns, or, sometimes, in the houses of noblemen. A nobleman had to be careful about which play he allowed to be performed within his home, however. Anything that was too political or seemed disloyal was likely to get him in trouble with the Queen or King, and this could lead to imprisonment or even execution!

The most famous playhouse was *The Globe*, built in 1599 by the company in which Shakespeare had invested money. In 1613, a cannon fired during a performance of *Henry VIII* set the roof on fire, and unfortunately *The Globe* burned to the ground. The site of the theatre was rediscovered in the 20th century and a reconstruction built near the spot, by which time, of course, Shakespeare's work was very much high culture.

These theatres could hold several thousand people, most standing in the open pit before the stage, though rich nobles could watch the play from a chair set on the side of the stage itself. Theatre performances were held in the afternoon because there was no artificial lighting. Women attended plays, though no women were allowed to perform in them. Female roles were generally performed by young boys. The theatres were very unhealthy as there were no toilet facilities and people relieved themselves outside. Sewage was buried in pits or disposed of in the River Thames. This improper sanitation could have been responsible for outbreaks of the plague.

As you can see, there were many practical reasons why performances in the city were unacceptable to the London authorities and how theatre was seen as low culture. Furthermore, there was an ethical drawback: At certain times in history, the Church considered actors and dancers immoral and refused to marry or bury them. Even the famous French playwright Molière was refused a church burial.

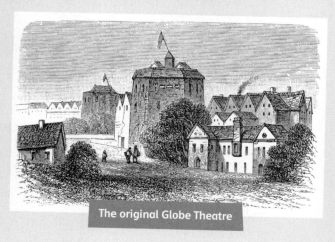
The original Globe Theatre

However, some years after Shakespeare's death, the large open-air theatres became smaller indoor theatres that catered exclusively to aristocrats who could afford high-priced tickets. For poor workers it was impossible to pay these prices. Thus, Shakespeare's plays became exclusive, high culture.

Shakespeare's high culture influence has endured through the ages. For instance, classical music giants Tchaikovsky, Liszt and Chopin all wrote instrumental pieces based on the play *Hamlet*. At least 25 operas have been inspired by the story. Two of the world-famous poet TS Eliot's most celebrated poems, *The Waste Land* and *The Love Song of J. Alfred Prufrock* quote Shakespeare's words directly. *Hamlet* even gets a mention in *A Christmas Carol*, written by that other iconic figure of English words, Charles Dickens.

So we can see that almost everything that is now 'high' culture was 'low' culture (or popular culture) once. Who knows, 100 years from now, maybe the punk movement or reality TV shows will be regarded 'high' culture too.

0	How is Shakespeare's work considered nowadays?	*as high culture*
1	Why were the theatres built in Southwark? (Give <u>one</u> answer.)	
2	What did noblemen have to be careful about?	
3	Why did people go to the theatre in the daytime?	
4	Why were no women seen on the stage?	
5	Why were the theatres such health risks?	
6	Why did the Church refuse to give actors certain religious rites?	
7	Why were poor people no longer able to see plays easily?	
8	What can be said about Shakespeare's influence on other famous musicians and writers?	

SPEAKING 8 **Discuss the following questions with a partner and share your answers with the class.**

1 Do you think going to the theatre is an activity for the rich or something everyone can enjoy nowadays?
2 Does visiting the theatre in the 1600s sound like more fun than nowadays? Why?/Why not?
3 Predict which of today's low culture activities might be seen as high culture 100 years from now. Give a reason why this might be.

LANGUAGE 9 Expand your vocabulary: Antonyms

p. 48

Read through the article again and underline 11 words which have prefixes that create antonyms. The first one is highlighted for you. Make a list of the words in your notebook and write their opposites next to them.
Example: *disapprove(d) – approve(d)*

SPEAKING 10 a **Read the short text by Charles Bukowski. Would you say it is high or low culture? Give reasons for your answer.**

b **Work in groups.**

1 Decide on the main message of the text.
2 Discuss how you could use the text as a stimulus to create a piece of art (e.g. a painting, sculpture, video or song) and what this piece of art could look or sound like.
3 Plan an exhibition around the piece of art you have 'created'. What other exhibits would you want there? How would you advertise the exhibition? Who would you invite to the opening night?
4 Share your ideas in class in a short presentation. Each group member talks for 2 minutes.

> We are here
> to laugh
> at the odds
> and live our lives
> so well that
> death
> will tremble
> to take us.

LANGUAGE 11 a Expand your vocabulary: Language in formal writing

p. 49

Together with a partner, discuss what you remember about formal and informal language. If you need help, go back to p. 31.

b **Which text types need to be written in formal language? Give reasons for your choices. Then read the tips on formal writing below.**

L

1 Don't use contractions like *don't, won't* or *can't*. Instead, write *do not, will not* or *cannot*.
2 Avoid addressing the reader, e.g. *You can see*. Write *It can be seen* instead.
3 When expressing your opinion, avoid phrases like *I think going to the theatre is a great idea*. Instead just write *Going to the theatre is a great idea*, because this is in fact your opinion. Support your opinion with relevant details (reasons, examples).
4 Use passive structures if appropriate. Instead of *Young people still read Shakespeare* write *Shakespeare is still widely read by a young audience*.
5 Use formal linking devices[3], such as *moreover, furthermore, another point, not only – but also, however, in comparison, yet, in spite of, although, whereas, in addition, as well as, nevertheless, provided that, therefore, thus, consequently*, etc.
6 Avoid using phrasal verbs and simple words if possible. Instead, use more formal expressions that have the same or a similar meaning. Be careful: Only use the more formal expressions if you are sure what they mean. For instance, *big* could be replaced with *enormous, immense, large, huge, great* or *massive*, but each of these adjectives collocates with different nouns.

c **Below you can find some examples of simple expressions and possible replacements with more formal expressions. Match them.**

Phrasal verbs	
1 to ask for	a to consider
2 to call off	b to tolerate
3 to pick up	c to postpone
4 to think about	d to request
5 to talk about	e to discover
6 to find out	f to discuss
7 to put off	g to collect
8 to put up with	h to cancel

Simple words	
1 to tell	a pleased
2 cheap	b amusing
3 big	c to obtain
4 happy	d sufficient
5 enough	e enormous
6 to buy	f to inform
7 to get	g to purchase
8 funny	h inexpensive

[3]For more examples, see *way2go!* 6, pp. 119 and 123.

WRITING **12** Write some sentences about going to the theatre or streaming a recording of a play using the suggested linking devices and some of the more formal expressions in the table. Share your sentences.

Examples: *Streaming a play is **inexpensive in comparison** to seeing it in the theatre./**Another point** is that students would have to purchase **expensive** tickets.*

S **Strategies box**

To argue means **to give reasons** for your opinion with the aim of **convincing others** of your view.

13 See a classical play in a theatre or stream its film adaptation? Your English teacher wants to know what young people prefer. He/She has asked you to write an essay to answer this question.

In your essay you should:

- argue why **or** why not the live performance might offer the better quality
- consider the effect of the atmosphere in a theatre
- discuss the costs

Write around 400 words. Give your essay a title.

→ See *Writing coach*, Essay, p. 184.

SPEAKING **14** Every culture has superstitions. In England walking under a ladder brings bad luck, in Austria pigs bring good luck for the New Year. Discuss why you think people believe these superstitions. Are there any that you believe?

LANGUAGE IN USE **15** Read the article about theatre superstitions. In most lines (1–16) there is a word that should not be there. Write these words in the spaces provided. 2–4 lines are correct. Make a ✓ in the space if the line is correct. There are two examples (0, 00) at the beginning.

p. 50

Theatre superstitions

You wouldn't normally tell someone to 'break a leg' if you were wishing | ✓ | (0)

them good luck, would you do? But actors believe that saying 'good luck' | do | (00)

brings up bad luck in the theatre! Actors are often a superstitious bunch, so | _____ | (1)

there are a few other things you should make bear in mind if you are in a | _____ | (2)

theatre. The name of the play *Macbeth* did by Shakespeare must not be | _____ | (3)

spoken by actors in the theatre; they have to call it 'The Scottish Play' instead. | _____ | (4)

Peacock feathers are very beautiful, but they must ever never be brought | _____ | (5)

onto stage as the pattern is said to look like an 'evil eye', which bringing a | _____ | (6)

curse to the performance. Mirrors are also being banned from the stage, but | _____ | (7)

this is probably because they reflect the stage of lights and cause problems. | _____ | (8)

Superstitious people often believe in ghosts, and actors are too no exception. | _____ | (9)

To keep ghosts away from the stage, they make sure a single normally light | _____ | (10)

is left on in the middle of the stage which is that known as the 'ghost light'. | _____ | (11)

Of course, this light also helps people avoid falling over things on the dark | _____ | (12)

stage! Lastly, no way whistling is allowed backstage. This also has a good | _____ | (13)

reason as stage workers would message each other between by whistling. | _____ | (14)

An unsuspecting person could whistle and get heavy a piece of scenery | _____ | (15)

dropped on them by accident! So, next time you to visit the theatre, take care! | _____ | (16)

WRITING + SPEAKING **16** Now make a list of the superstitions mentioned in the text and note down which ones have a logical explanation. For those with no explanation, make up reasons why they might exist.
Example: *mirrors: reflect light and cause problems.*

17 a What other superstitions do you know of? Tell a partner about two superstitions, then present your information to the class.

b Create a new superstition of your own. Come up with a good explanation for it.
Example: *Stepping on the cracks in the pavement brings bad luck. Reason: you could fall over the uneven pavement.*

B ## By the way: Tap your toes in Ireland

Pubs and traditional music in Ireland are like Tarzan and Jane, cheese and onion or yin and yang. On their own they're grand, but together … together, they create a magical partnership. Enter a pub playing live trad (traditional) music and it's lively banter and foot-tapping entertainment that borders on iconic. It's local culture and you'll find it pretty much everywhere in Ireland. Traditional Irish music is a full-body experience: The beats compel you to dance a jig, clap your hands and join in. And that's what trad music is all about, joining in and having the craic (pronounced 'crack'), meaning fun.

So where does this tradition come from? Back when music and storytelling were the only forms of entertainment on the island, villagers would crowd together into their local pub to share a warm fire, hear stories and listen to music played by the local musicians. Of course, there was usually dancing too, which is where traditional Irish dancing originates from.

A trad music seisún (pronounced 'seh-shoon') can best be described as an informal gathering of musicians. Often, it'll kick off with just a guitar, but before long you've got a whole group of musicians. It's hard to predict just what instruments you might hear, but there's usually at least one fiddle, often accompanied by guitar, banjo, mandolin, and if you're extra lucky, flute, bodhrán (a special drum), uilleann pipes (the bagpipe of Ireland), or concertina (a small accordion-like instrument). Many musicians in Ireland are skilled on more than one instrument, sometimes as many as six or seven, so you'll often see them passing instruments around or choosing a different one for each song.

When it comes to trad music, few places offer a better selection than Dublin City. Many people head straight for Temple Bar in the city centre. This is the city's cultural quarter, where the streets are lined with medieval cobble stones. It's here that Dublin comes to party. The trad music begins in the early afternoon and doesn't stop until closing. Many Irish pubs serve good, hearty Irish food, so you can tick two authentic Irish experiences off your list in one night.

Get into groups of three. Each group member picks one of the following topics: a typical Irish musical instrument, the history of pubs, Irish dancing. Research it online and present your findings to the rest of the group in a few minutes.

SPEAKING **18** **a** Who is your favourite author? Take about 10 minutes to prepare a 2-minute presentation on him/her for your classmates. You could talk about:

- what you know about the author's life
- the genre of his/her writing
- the language of the books (e.g. easy to read, serious/humorous, a lot of metaphors, etc.)
- your favourite book by the author
- what makes the book special to you

b Get into small groups to give your presentations to each other.

READING **19** Read the following short biography of the British author Neil Gaiman.
Summarise it in three sentences, then compare your summary with a partner and in class.

Neil Gaiman

Neil Gaiman was born in Hampshire, England, in 1960 and has been living in the United States since 1992, currently residing near Minneapolis.

Following the publication of his groundbreaking series *Sandman* (1989–1996), he has become established as one of the creators of modern comics, as well as an author whose work crosses genres and reaches audiences of all ages. He is listed in the *Dictionary of Literary Biography* as one of the top ten living post-modern writers and is a prolific creator of works of prose, poetry, film, journalism, comics, song lyrics and drama. His most recent work for TV includes serialisations of his books *American Gods* and *Good Omens*.

He is also an established writer for children. His most famous work

The Graveyard Book, published in 2008, won several prizes and awards including the Newbery Medal, the highest honour given in US children's literature. In addition to that, Gaiman was awarded the UK Carnegie Medal in 2010, which makes him the first author ever to win both the Newbery Medal and the Carnegie Medal with the same book.

Interestingly enough, as one of the world's most famous cult writers, Gaiman actually has a paradoxical kind of fame. As the *Telegraph* has observed, "You're either a Gaiman fan, in which case you know absolutely everything about him, or you've never heard of him." Pointing to the same quirk of the modern literary world, the London *Times* referred to him as "the most famous writer you've never heard of."

LANGUAGE **20** Expand your vocabulary: Talking about literature
Find expressions in the biography above that mean the following:

a the act of making a story or other information available
b to be accepted or successful in a position
c to have features of different kinds of text styles
d to be popular with young and old readers
e a very productive author
f a reward or title showing great respect
g an author very popular with a group of people
h the state of being well-known

LISTENING **21** a You are going to listen to a lecture about Neil Gaiman. First you
⊙ 22 will have 45 seconds to study the task below, then you will hear
🌐 the recording twice. While listening, answer the questions (1–8)
using a maximum of four words. Write your answers in the spaces
provided. The first one (0) has been done for you.

After the second listening, you will have 45 seconds to check your
answers.

Neil Gaiman

0	Why do people in the audience nod their heads?	because they recognise Gaiman
1	How many collections of Gaiman's stories have been published?	
2	What kind of book features supernatural beings?	
3	What is a central plot element of Gaiman's stories?	
4	How does Gaiman feel about not being popular with everyone?	
5	Where do Gaiman's stories typically take place? (Give one answer.)	
6	Why is *The Graveyard Book* an easier read than some of Gaiman's other stories?	
7	What served as a model for *The Graveyard Book*?	
8	How does the structure of *The Graveyard Book* differ from other novels?	

b **The lecturer is showing five different slides while presenting the section you've heard. Listen again, then write short descriptions of what you think might be on those slides. Compare in class.**
Example: *First slide: a picture of Neil Gaiman, second slide: ...*

SPEAKING **22** In interviews, Gaiman has often used the quote on the right to explain why he is so fascinated by dark stories. Discuss with a partner how it relates to the features of dark fiction you've heard about.

> "Where there is a monster, there is a miracle."
> (*Ogden Nash, US poet*)

WRITING **23** Following one of your favourite English authors on Twitter, you have found out that he/she intends to visit Austria to read from one of his/her famous novels for a charity event. As there is no further information, you have decided to write an email to his/her agent.

In your email you should:

- explain why you are interested in this event
- point out what you like about the author's books
- ask about further information concerning the event

Write around 250 words.

→ See *Writing coach, Formal email*, p. 178.

Individual long turn: Do this task in pairs. Student A discusses the quote, student B compares the pictures. Throw the dice to determine who is A and who is B. Give feedback to each other. Then discuss which task was easier to do.

<u>Student A:</u> You have been asked to give a 5-minute talk on reading books.

> "In old days books were written by men of letters[4] and read by the public. Nowadays books are written by the public and read by nobody." (*Oscar Wilde*)

In your talk you should:

- discuss the quote
- outline the reading habits of people your age
- specify what makes a book a 'good book'

<u>Student B:</u> You have been asked to give a 5-minute talk on popular culture.

In your talk you should:

- compare the pictures
- comment on the popularity of rock concerts
- suggest how to get young people interested in the theatre

25 *Paired activity:* A British language school for students from abroad wants to know what kind of books suitable for your age group you could recommend. Consider the books you have read and discuss with a partner which one(s) you want to suggest to the language school. In your discussion focus on the following aspects:

- level of difficulty
- topics
- characters
- entertainment value
- educational value

---

[4] **men of letters:** Gelehrte

READING **26**

Read the extract from *The Graveyard Book*. First decide whether the statements (1–7) are true (T) or false (F) and put a cross (x) in the correct box. Then identify the sentence in the text which supports your decision. Write <u>the first four words</u> of this sentence in the space provided. There may be more than one correct answer; write down <u>only one</u>. The first one (0) has been done for you.

THERE WAS A WITCH buried at the edge of the graveyard, it was common knowledge. Bod had been told to keep away from that corner of the world by Mrs. Owens as far back as he could remember.

"Why?" he asked.

"T'aint healthy for a living body," said Mrs. Owens.

"There's damp down that end of things. It's practically a marsh. You'll catch your death."

Mr. Owens himself was more evasive and less imaginative. "It's not a good place," was all he said.

The graveyard proper ended at the bottom of the west side of the hill, beneath the old apple tree, with a fence of rust-brown iron railings, each topped with a small, rusting spearhead, but there was a wasteland beyond that, a mass of nettles and weeds, of brambles and autumnal rubbish, and Bod, who was, on the whole, obedient, did not push between the railings, but he went down there and looked through. He knew he wasn't being told the whole story, and it irritated him.

Bod went back up the hill, to the little chapel near the entrance to the graveyard, and he waited until it got dark. As twilight edged from grey to purple there was a noise in the spire, like a fluttering of heavy velvet, and Silas left his resting place in the belfry and clambered headfirst down the spire.

"What's in the far corner of the graveyard?" asked Bod. "Past Harrison Westwood, Baker of this Parish, and his wives, Marion and Joan?"

"Why do you ask?" said his guardian, brushing the dust from his black suit with ivory fingers. Bod shrugged. "Just wondered."

"It's unconsecrated ground," said Silas. "Do you know what that means?"

"Not really," said Bod.

Silas walked across the path without disturbing a fallen leaf, and sat down on the bench beside Bod. "There are those," he said, in his silken voice, "who believe that all land is sacred. That it is sacred before we come to it, and sacred after. But here, in your land, they blessed the churches and the ground they set aside to bury people in, to make it holy. But they left land unconsecrated beside the sacred ground, Potter's Fields to bury the criminals and the suicides or those who were not of the faith."

"So the people buried in the ground on the other side of the fence are bad people?" Silas raised one perfect eyebrow. "Mm? Oh, not at all. Let's see, it's been a while since I've been down that way. But I don't remember anyone particularly evil. Remember, in days gone by you could be hanged for stealing a shilling. And there are always people who find their lives have become so unsupportable they believe the best thing they could do would be to hasten their transition to another plane of existence."

"They kill themselves, you mean?" said Bod. He was about eight years old, wide-eyed and inquisitive, and he was not stupid.

"Indeed."

"Does it work? Are they happier dead?"

"Sometimes. Mostly, no. It's like the people who believe they'll be happy if they go and live somewhere else, but who learn it doesn't work that way. Wherever you go, you take yourself with you. If you see what I mean."

"Sort of," said Bod.

Silas reached down and ruffled the boy's hair.

Bod said, "What about the witch?"

"Yes. Exactly," said Silas. "Suicides, criminals, and witches. Those who died unshriven." He stood up, a midnight shadow in the twilight. "All this talking," he said, "and I have not even had my breakfast. While you will be late for lessons." In the twilight of the graveyard there was a silent implosion, a flutter of velvet darkness, and Silas was gone.

The moon had begun to rise by the time Bod reached Mr. Pennyworth's mausoleum, and Thomes Pennyworth (*here he lyes in the certainty of the most glorious resurrection*) was already waiting, and he was not in the best of moods.

"You are late," he said.

	Statements	T	F	First four words
0	Bod was warned not to visit a certain part of the graveyard by Mrs Owens.	[x]	[ ]	*Bod had been told*
1	Bod disliked others keeping secrets from him.	[ ]	[ ]	
2	Silas lived at the top of a small church near the gate of the graveyard.	[ ]	[ ]	
3	Not everyone was allowed to be buried in the graveyard near the church.	[ ]	[ ]	
4	The people buried beyond the fence were evil and dangerous.	[ ]	[ ]	
5	Moving to a different place can solve problems you might have.	[ ]	[ ]	
6	Silas wanted to leave because he was hungry.	[ ]	[ ]	
7	Mr Pennyworth was delighted at the sight of Bod.	[ ]	[ ]	

27 **Take notes on the following questions, then compare your results in class.**

1 How is Silas described in this passage of the book? What kind of (dark fiction) being does this make him sound like? He comes out after sunset …

2 Which examples of the following typical elements of dark fiction can you find in the text?
- spooky places
- signs of age and decay
- questions of morality
- supernatural elements

3 Does the extract make you want to read more of the book? Why?/Why not?

4 Would you consider writing like this to be art? Give reasons.

WRITING **28** **Choose one of the ideas below to write a creative text (e.g. a story, poem or conversation) of about 200 words. Try to include some typical elements of dark fiction in your text.**

1 how Bod came to live in the graveyard

2 the first meeting of Bod and the witch

3 Mr Pennyworth's lesson for Bod

LANGUAGE **29**   Topic vocabulary: High and low culture
**Study the word map below and complete it with examples and characteristics of low culture.
Then add more of your own ideas (to both high and low culture).**

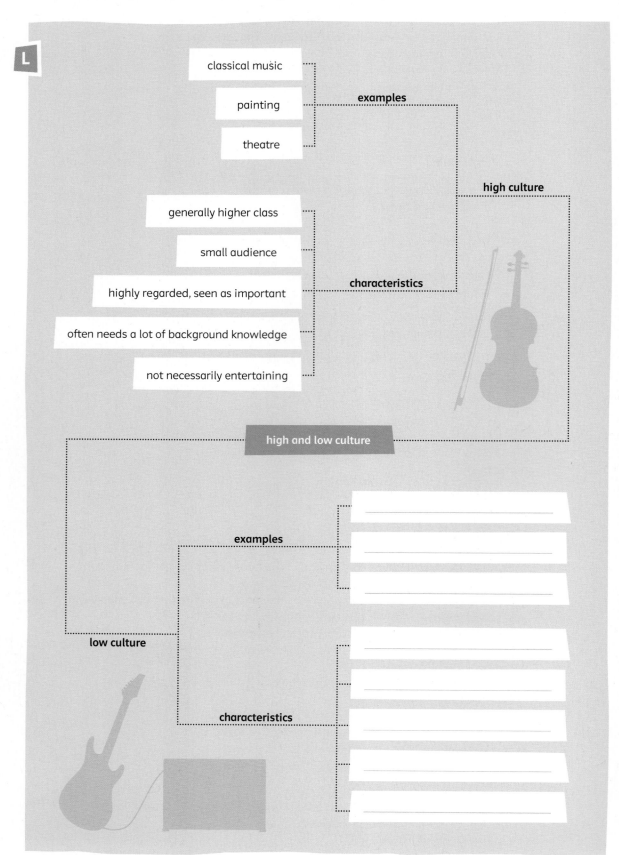

L

classical music

painting

theatre

examples

high culture

generally higher class

small audience

highly regarded, seen as important

often needs a lot of background knowledge

not necessarily entertaining

characteristics

high and low culture

examples

low culture

characteristics

LANGUAGE **30** **a** Topic vocabulary: Adjective-noun collocations

Form pairs of adjectives and nouns that collocate well. Sometimes more than one combination is possible. Write the pairs down and use them in a sentence.

p. 47

1 daily
2 common
3 highest
4 established
5 good
6 fallen
7 groundbreaking
8 artificial

a reputation
b series
c leaf
d lighting
e routine
f knowledge
g honour
h writer

b **Find at least five more adjective-noun collocations in the texts of this unit.**

⊙ Looking back: Learning goals of Unit 08

		✓✓	✓	!!

READING ▶▶▶ B2 I can understand the main ideas of complex texts (including literary texts) on the topic of art and culture. (ex. 7b, 26)

LISTENING ▶▶▶ B2 I can understand the main ideas and specific details of propositionally and linguistically complex speech on the topic of art and culture delivered in a standard dialect. (ex. 2b/c, 21a/b)

WRITING ▶▶▶ B2 I can write an essay which develops an argument, gives reasons in support of or against a particular point of view and explains the advantages and disadvantages of various options. (ex. 13)

SPEAKING ▶▶▶ B2 I can take an active part in informal discussion on the topic of art and culture, commenting, putting my point of view clearly, evaluating alternative proposals and making and responding to hypotheses. (ex. 1, 5, 8, 10a/b, 14, 22, 25)

▶▶▶ B2 I can give clear, detailed descriptions on the topic of art and culture, expanding and supporting ideas with subsidiary points and relevant examples. (ex. 17, 18b, 24)

LANGUAGE ▶▶▶ I can use prefixes to make antonyms well.

▶▶▶ I can use a good range of formal language to describe and argue in writing.

▶▶▶ I can use a good range of vocabulary to describe and argue on the topic of art and culture.

Living in a graveyard would be . . . because . . .

The craziest superstition I heard about was . . .

Unit 09
Someone's watching

 8z8g2z

In this unit you will:
- discover bias and fake news
- think about what (not) to share online
- read a comic
- consider the importance of free media
- learn about the dangers of being a journalist
- find out who's interested in your feelings

SPEAKING **1** **a** Which six of the headlines below are true and which four of them have just been made up? Discuss in small groups.

b Find the correct answers on p. 143. Try to come up with explanations why they might be untrue.

1 UN unveils design for floating city for 10,000 people

2 MISSING WOMAN UNWITTINGLY JOINS SEARCH PARTY LOOKING FOR HERSELF

3 SHOCKED 'OUR PLANET' VIEWERS WATCH AS DAVID ATTENBOROUGH ENTERS SCENE TO BREAK NECK OF STARVING POLAR BEAR

4 Cat has been mayor of Alaska town for 15 years

5 CHINESE ASTRONOMERS INFORM BEIJING RESIDENTS SKY WILL BE VISIBLE FOR RARE 2-MINUTE WINDOW TOMORROW MORNING

6 Mother renames son after tattooist makes spelling error

7 MAN FRIES EGGS ON HIS BALD HEAD

8 FISH LEAPS FROM RIVER, KNOCKS FLORIDA TEEN UNCONSCIOUS

9 Investigators trace cause of NOTRE DAME FIRE to cathedral's outdated 12th-century electrical system

10 ARIZONA FIGHTS HIGHWAY DUST STORMS WITH HAIKU

WRITING **2** Do some research and find another funny or bizarre headline that is true. Then make up one yourself and let your classmates guess which one is true and which one isn't.

World news and you

SPEAKING **3** Make notes on the questions below. Compare your answers with a partner, then share them in small groups.

1 What media do you use to learn about recent events taking place in the world?
2 How do you know you can believe what these media are telling you?
3 Have you ever read or seen any news that you later discovered to be wrong? Give examples.

LANGUAGE **4 a** Expand your vocabulary: The media

Write down as many expressions connected with media as you can in 5 minutes (e.g. *journalism, journalist, publish, ...*). Who in class can find the most?

b Share the expressions you've found in class. Collect all expressions in a way that helps you to study them, such as a word map, a word cloud or a table.

> **!**
>
> **Uncountable nouns**
> The news **is** …
> Some information **is** …

READING **5** Read the extract from a brochure on media literacy.
Which of the activities it describes do you already do?
What more could you do?

pp. 52+54

Being smart about media

In today's online world of uncountable media outlets providing nearly limitless information, knowing how to deal with the flood of news is more important than ever. Media literacy refers to a combination of critical thinking skills and knowledge of media that allows you to have an undistorted view of the world. By reading and watching news from a variety of sources and thinking about them critically, you can spot fake news, misleading articles or sensationalist reporting in any media.

It's also important to know about personal beliefs that might affect you, the journalists or other people reporting on an event. In general, a bias is an unfair support of a person or idea caused by personal opinions influencing your judgement. You can be knowingly biased, such as when you're a fan of a sports team, but also without realising it. An example of the latter is confirmation bias: a tendency humans have to look for and believe in information that supports their already existing beliefs or expectations.

How can you deal with these problems in understanding the world? Here are some suggestions:

– Start out by asking: Is this true? It's the first step towards becoming a critical reader.
– Check the source of information: How trustworthy is it? Why is it putting out this information?
– Producing news costs money: If you're not paying for them, you should know who does and why.
– Reading and watching news stories from a variety of sources helps you to verify their truthfulness.
– Evaluate what you've read, question the objectivity of the reporting. Take both your own as well as your sources' biases into account.

LANGUAGE **6 a** Expand your vocabulary: Media literacy

Study the green expressions in the text above. Copy them into your notebook with an explanation in your own words.

p. 54

b Read your explanations to a partner and let him/her guess the correct expression.

LISTENING **7** Listen to four news reports on the same event. How are they different? Which ones would you consider biased, which ones neutral? Why?

⊙ 23

SPEAKING **8** What do you think of the idea of journalists publishing news in the form of comics instead of articles? Discuss possible pros and cons with a partner.

LISTENING **9** **a** You are going to listen to an FM4 interview with comic journalist Sarah Glidden. First you will have 45 seconds to study the task below, then you will hear the recording twice. While listening, choose the correct answer (A, B, C or D) for each question (1–7). Put a cross (x) in the correct box. The first one (0) has been done for you.

radio
FM4

⊙ 24
🌐
🗄
p. 53

After the second listening, you will have 45 seconds to check your answers.

Sarah Glidden, comic journalist

0 The book deals with a journey to

- A a rural part of Turkey. ☐
- B Middle Eastern countries. ☒
- C regions attacked by the US. ☐
- D a country where wars took place. ☐

1 Joe Sacco was one of the first journalists to

- A report from the Middle East. ☐
- B draw pictures about his experiences. ☐
- C tell stories about local inhabitants. ☐
- D use comics as a medium. ☐

2 Drawing a picture of a person

- A makes it easier to talk to them. ☐
- B helps you to understand them. ☐
- C allows you to look at them closely. ☐
- D makes them feel better. ☐

3 There is a belief that comic books

- A cannot be taken seriously. ☐
- B are old-fashioned. ☐
- C harm young readers. ☐
- D have become too popular. ☐

4 Sarah Glidden believes comic journalists

- A show reality very accurately. ☐
- B work harder than other journalists. ☐
- C have a duty to work carefully. ☐
- D sometimes invent their stories. ☐

5 If comic journalists do their job well,

- A they can make the world better. ☐
- B people might still doubt their work. ☐
- C they can influence people's opinions. ☐
- D their books will find an audience. ☐

6 Sarah Glidden hopes her readers

- A will want to find out more. ☐
- B aren't afraid of difficult topics. ☐
- C like the characters in her book. ☐
- D believe what she is telling them. ☐

7 According to Sarah Glidden, journalism

- A means showing people's feelings. ☐
- B can never be completely objective. ☐
- C needs to communicate opinions. ☐
- D must always consider the reader. ☐

b Are you more interested in fictional or journalistic comics? Give reasons for your answer.

READING + SPEAKING **10** **a** Read the page taken from Sarah Glidden's book *Rolling Blackouts* on the right. Do the tasks below with a partner and take notes.

1 Describe what the comic looks like. Consider how this influences your understanding of events.
2 Explain what the journalists consider "the hard part about journalism" in your own words.
3 Find possible answers to the journalist's question in the last panel.

b Use your notes to prepare a short oral statement summarising your findings. Share your statements in small groups, then decide on the best ones to share with the rest of the class.

WRITING **11** Write an email to Sarah Glidden expressing your opinion on comic journalism.

This is the hard part about journalism from a moral standpoint.

You have to go around taking people's stories... They spend a lot of time telling you how they feel and what happened to them.

And you can't guarantee that it's going to go anywhere.

And that's the crappy end of our job: marketing. You have to figure out how to market these stories so people will be interested.

We could publish the transcript of that interview but nobody's going to read the whole thing.

Would you say you already have a picture painted and you're going to arrange those soundbites to fit the picture?

Or you're going to let the refugee paint their own picture?

I mean, are you already trying to market the story a certain way before you hear it?

We're trying to let the story tell itself, but that doesn't mean the marketing angle is out of the picture.

What I'm always aware of is the friend test: I think of my peers back home. They're super busy, they're self-involved, they might spend fifteen minutes a day to consume something outside of their own lives.

So how do you make sure your story becomes that fifteen minutes?

66

Silencing the voices

READING + SPEAKING **12** **a** Read the statements below. Underline what you think are the two most important pieces of information in each statement.

b In pairs, talk about what you have chosen as being most important and what it means to you.

c Now work with your partner to discuss these questions: What is freedom of the press? Why is it important?

"Our journalism is free from commercial bias and not influenced by billionaire owners, politicians or shareholders. [...] This is important as it enables us to give a voice to those less heard, challenge the powerful and hold them to account. It's what makes us different to so many others in the media, at a time when factual, honest reporting is critical." (*Online editorial statement of* The Guardian)

"An independent press ensures that citizens stay informed about public affairs and the actions of their government, creating a forum for debate and the open exchange of ideas." (*Trevor Timm, US free press advocate*)

"... [T]he only reason the full story came out at all was down to a free press. ... [W]hat these reporters did – examine evidence; accumulate facts; ask questions; cultivate sources; look at documents; talk to people who were involved; win trust; ignore threats; verify information; report accurately – is as good an illustration as you could have for the importance of a free press." (*Alan Rusbridger, editor of* The Guardian *from 1995 to 2015*)

SPEAKING **13** You are going to read an article on freedom of the press. Work with a partner and make a list of countries that you think will be mentioned in the article in a positive or negative way. Compare your list with another pair. What made you choose these countries?

READING **14** Read the article about the annual World Press Freedom Index released by *Reporters Without Borders* (*RWB*). Complete the sentences (1–8) using a maximum of four words. Write your answers in the spaces provided. The first one (0) has been done for you.

p. 56

Press freedom slides as journalists face growing threats around the world

Hostility towards the media is spreading from dictatorships to democracies. This is encouraged by US president Donald Trump's attacks on the press and his hatred of reporters that leads to physical aggression, according to the latest World Press Freedom Index. The Index is produced by *Reporters without Borders*, which measures media freedom in 180 countries.

The worst decline in freedom was in Europe, though the region is still the world's safest for reporters. Two murders helped drive the decline in the last couple of years. Daphne Caruana Galizia, a prominent Maltese journalist who examined corruption by the country's elites, was assassinated in a car bomb. In Slovakia, 27-year-old investigative reporter Ján Kuciak and his fiancée Martina Kušnírová were shot to death during Kuciak's investigation of ties between Slovakian officials and the Mafia.

Both murders were a shake-up. Kuciak's lead to massive popular protests that ended the regime of Prime Minister Robert Fico. The killings also made other journalists carry on the work of their late colleagues and continue their efforts to expose illegal actions and cover-ups. Investigative reporters now collaborate, sharing data and documents and helping one another to stay informed. These networks of collaboration keep stories alive even when a reporter is harassed or killed. Yet Saudi columnist Jamal Khashoggi's gruesome murder in the Saudi consulate in Istanbul sent another chilling message to journalists.

Another troubling trend noted in the World Press Freedom Index is increasing efforts to intimidate the factual reporting in countries with traditions of democracy. US president Donald Trump's attacks on 'fake news' to denounce unfavourable coverage have been adopted by authoritarian leaders in nations such as Turkey and Cambodia. As studies show strong correlations between independent media, stable democracies and limited corruption, hatred towards journalists is one of the worst threats to democracies.

Reporters Without Borders also noted a substantial decline in press freedom in the Asia-Pacific region, where China is taking censorship and surveillance to new heights, and Vietnam, Cambodia and Singapore ranking increasingly close to China. These nations have been adopting China's model of fighting dissent through strict control of mass and social media.

Norway tops the list of countries where journalists have most freedom, followed by Sweden, the Netherlands, Finland and Switzerland, based on pluralism and media independence. North Korea finished last at 180, with Eritrea, Turkmenistan, Syria and China completing the bottom five. Overall, the 2019 report concludes, journalists around the world faced more hostility towards their work in 2018 than they did in previous years.

0	*Reporters without Borders* monitors _____ .	*press freedom worldwide*
1	Europe is still _____ .	
2	However, in Malta a journalist was killed because _____ .	
3	In Slovakia, another murder of a journalist caused _____ .	
4	Journalists work together to _____ .	
5	Authoritarian leaders are encouraged by President Trump's _____ .	
6	Strong independent media are _____ .	
7	For authoritarian governments, it is also important to _____ .	
8	Northern European countries are champions of _____ .	

SPEAKING **15** How many of your guesses from exercise 13 were correct? Are you surprised by (some of) the countries mentioned in the article? Why?/Why not? Discuss in small groups.

LANGUAGE **16** a Expand your vocabulary: Adjectives describing critical journalism and its opponents
Write definitions of the words below based on their meaning in the text.

a authoritarian	c independent	e investigative	g substantial
b factual	d informed	f limited	h unfavourable

b Mix your definitions and pass them on to someone else to match to the correct word.

LANGUAGE **17** **a** Expand your vocabulary: Describing hostility
Read the article again and make a list of all the words that describe hostile activity towards journalists. Use a dictionary to find words that collocate with them.
Example: *attack – to attack somebody – to launch an attack – a physical attack – to be attacked for sth.*

b Compare your list with a partner.

18 You are going to listen to a radio report on the dangers of investigative journalism. Before you listen, write down five sentences about dangers that journalists might face today using the expressions from 17a. Compare your sentences in pairs.

LISTENING **19** **a** Listen to the first part of the radio report and label the diagrams.
⊚ 25

Threats to journalists

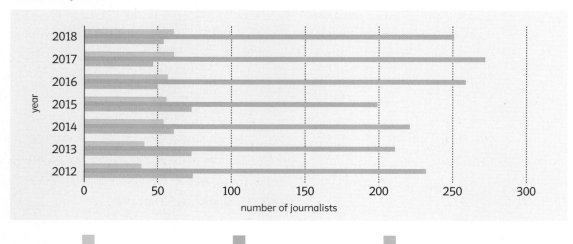

■ _____ ■ _____ ■ _____

Freedom of the press worldwide

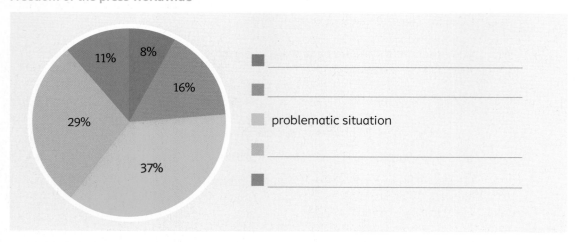

■ _____
■ _____
■ problematic situation
■ _____
■ _____

b Now listen to the second part of the radio report and take notes. Which of your ideas from exercise 18 are mentioned?
⊚ 26

SPEAKING **20** **a** Has the situation improved or deteriorated further? Work in groups to research the current status, update the charts and compare your results in class.

b What can you find out about the situation in Austria?

21 How might press freedom come into conflict with other needs and priorities of society? Discuss in groups.

Read this extract from a statement by the chairman of the *International Center for Journalists* made to the US Congress about a journalist and how he is treated by his country. Complete it using the words from the box.

L

a books	d jail	g newspapers	j sentence
b correspondent	e journalist	h raid	k security
c family	f media	i report on	l suffer

"For our (1) _____ colleagues, the prison sentences are catastrophic. Yehia Maghem, his country's most prominent foreign (2) _____, is in perhaps the worst situation. His two-year (3) _____ was not suspended, which means he will go to (4) _____ if he returns home, so he can never again (5) _____ what he knows best. Yehia has not seen his (6) _____ in more than a year. His distinguished career in the (7) _____ is over. He is now looking for a job in one of the smaller (8) _____ . While he has been in the US, his family has continued to (9) _____ harassment, including three raids on their home by (10) _____ officials looking for him, confiscating the (11) _____ he left behind. The most recent (12) _____ happened last Sunday night."

SPEAKING **23**

Work in small groups. Go online to find the latest map of press freedom worldwide from *Reporters without Borders*. Imagine living in a red or black country, with one of your parents being a journalist. Think about at least five things in your life that would be different from now. Present your ideas in class.

WRITING **24**

Write one of these texts about one of the situations you have brainstormed.

a a diary entry
b a blog post
c an email to an international organisation asking for help

25

In your English class you are discussing whether being a foreign correspondent might be an attractive job for young people. Your English teacher wants to get your opinion on this and has asked you to write an essay.

In your essay you should discuss:

- whether the opportunity to travel the world makes this job attractive
- if foreign correspondents need special skills
- possible dangers foreign correspondents might face

Write around 400 words. Give your essay a title.

→ See *Writing coach, Essay*, p. 184.

Answers to ex. 1, p. 136: Not true: 1, 3, 5, 9

Big data – big business

SPEAKING **26** **a** Collecting personal data on the internet has become a big business. Get together with a partner and discuss what that means. What is your personal data? Who is collecting it? Why would someone be interested in your data?

b Make a list of all the things you have done online (on a computer, on your phone, . . .) over the last 24 hours. Compare with a partner.

c What can a company learn about you by observing your online activity? What could they do with this information? Discuss in class.

LANGUAGE **27** **a** Expand your vocabulary: Online advertising
Read the fact sheet and circle the correct options. Check with your teacher.

p. 57

L

What is online advertising?

Online advertising is everywhere in the digital world, from simple (1) banners / email spam on web pages to (2) video ads / commercials on streaming sites.

There are many reasons for its continuing popularity: It is relatively inexpensive to (3) advertise / reach a wide audience, success or failure of ads can be (4) aimed / tracked easily and, most of all, it is possible to select and (5) personalise / block the ads for a (6) target / general audience. With the collected (7) customer / costumer data from online shops, social media sites and search engines, marketing firms can now use (8) algorithms / surveys to calculate who the users are and then choose who gets to see which ads.

The possibilities of online advertising are constantly growing and evolving. (9) Pop-up / Classified ads were once state-of the-art, but now more modern forms such as (10) brochures / advertorials and (11) influencer / flyer marketing are becoming popular.

What hasn't changed are the aims of advertising. Companies are still trying to (12) create a trademark / demand for their products or services by making them look and sound (13) appalling / appealing to customers. But using these (14) contemporary / viral forms of marketing, they can be more effective than ever.

b Find reasons why the wrong options don't fit the text and compare your ideas with a partner.
Example: *You can only get email spam in an email account, but not on a website.*

c Use five of the wrong options in meaningful sentences.

WRITING **28** Write an entertaining blog post about your experiences with online advertising. Using some expressions and ideas from the previous exercises will help you.

a Speculate about the topic of the task below with a partner: What is 'predictive advertising'? What are 'data hunters'? What is 'data mining'?

b You are going to watch a BBC video on predictive advertising. First you will have 45 seconds to study the task below, then you will watch the video twice. While watching, match the beginnings of the sentences (1–7) with the sentence endings (A–J). There are two extra sentence endings that you should not use. Write your answers in the spaces provided. The first one (0) has been done for you.

After the second watching, you will have 45 seconds to check your answers.

Data hunters

0	By using smart devices for a range of activities, people are _____ .	E
1	It's possible to predict what people will do by _____ .	
2	Companies are interested in _____ .	
3	Finding mathematical models for data analysis was _____ .	
4	Baker could solve a problem he had by _____ .	
5	A computer system is used for _____ .	
6	Customers show what they are interested in by _____ .	
7	Refusing data analysis means _____ .	

A	proving to be difficult	F	sending relevant ads to customers
B	becoming very expensive	G	analysing large amounts of data
C	relating to possible customers	H	making ads less targeted
D	doing the same actions repeatedly	I	searching for help
E	creating large amounts of information	J	not seeing ads anymore

WRITING 30 Summarise the content of the video in two to three sentences, then comment on it.

SPEAKING 31 *Paired activity:* In your English class you are discussing different forms of advertising that might be successful with young people. Discuss the options below with a partner and agree on three.

- TV commercials
- online advertising
- pre-video advertisements
- advertisements in print media
- billboards

LANGUAGE **32** a **Expand your vocabulary: Verb-noun collocations**
Match the verbs on the left to fitting nouns on the right.
There may be more than one correct answer.

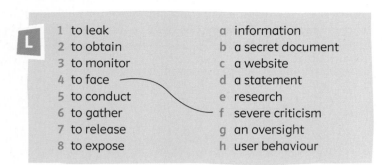

L
1 to leak	a	information
2 to obtain	b	a secret document
3 to monitor	c	a website
4 to face	d	a statement
5 to conduct	e	research
6 to gather	f	severe criticism
7 to release	g	an oversight
8 to expose	h	user behaviour

b **Complete the sentences below using some of the verbs or nouns from above. Make sure to use the correct form if necessary.**

1 _____ reliable information is the first step in producing a news story.

2 After the scandal, the president released a dramatic _____ .

3 Research into climate change _____ for years, but there are still people who believe it to be fake.

4 The journalists exposed a critical _____ in the government's plans.

5 A government official _____ secret agents' private details to the press.

c **Write five similar gapped sentences for the collocations and share them in class.**

WRITING **33** Your English language assistant wants to do a project on advertising with two seventh-grade classes at your school. He/She has suggested a number of projects and wants to know which ones the classes are interested in. You have been asked to write a report based on a survey you have done among the students of the two classes and to outline your ideas for the project.

Advertising project students of classes 7a and 7b are interested in (n = 40)

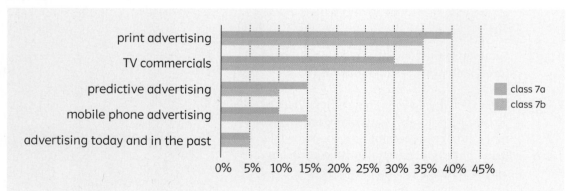

In your report you should:

- present the results of your survey
- give reasons for the results
- outline your ideas for the project

Write around 400 words. Divide your report into sections and give them headings.

→ See *Writing coach, Report*, p. 186.

34 a **Read the text about Facebook and its advertisers. Some words are missing. Choose the correct word (A–N) for each gap (1–11). There are two extra words that you should not use. Write your answers in the boxes provided. The first one (0) has been done for you.**

Facebook told advertisers it can identify teens feeling "insecure" and "worthless"

Facebook showed advertisers how it has the ability to identify when teenagers feel "insecure", "worthless" and "need a confidence boost", according to a leaked document based (0) _____ research quietly conducted by the social network.

The internal report produced by Facebook executives (1) _____ obtained by *The Australian* and made public. It states that the company can monitor posts and photos in real time to determine when young (2) _____ feel "stressed", "defeated", "anxious", "nervous", "stupid", "silly", "useless" and a "failure". It describes how the social network gathers psychological insights on 1.9 million high schoolers, 1.5 million tertiary students and 3 million young workers in Australia and New Zealand.

In response to the report, the company released rather contradictory[1] statements, (3) _____ apologizing and saying the article was "misleading". The documents, Facebook said, were "intended to help marketers understand how people express (4) _____ ."

According to *The Australian*, the data available to advertisers includes a young user's (5) _____ status, location, number of friends on the platform and how often they (6) _____ the site on mobile or desktop. The newspaper reported that Facebook also has information on users discussing "looking good and body confidence" and "(7) _____ out & losing weight". The report also claimed that Facebook knows how emotions are communicated at different points during a young person's week. "Monday to Thursday is about (8) _____ confidence; the weekend is for broadcasting achievements."

The story comes three years after the company (9) _____ significant criticism after it published the results of an experiment in which it manipulated information on 689,000 users' homepages and discovered it could change people's feelings. The company had (10) _____ conducted the research, which was criticised for purposefully exposing people to "negative emotional content". So when young people are using Facebook, they should (11) _____ take extreme care about what they post and how they respond to targeted advertising. It is important to consider talking directly to friends when feeling down to avoid exposing these emotions online. Being aware of the tactics used to target teenagers means less chance of falling victim to possible negative outside influences.

A	access	D	clearly	G	feelings	J	relationship	M	was
B	both	E	conduct	H	on	K	secretly	N	working
C	building	F	faced	I	people	L	themselves		

0	1	2	3	4	5	6	7	8	9	10	11
H											

b **Decide which of the four options best describes the article.**

The text is a …

1 summary of an article from another newspaper.
2 summary of a report the author has found.
3 report published by Facebook about its users.
4 report published in a psychology magazine.

---
[1] **contradictory:** widersprüchlich

SPEAKING **35** **Discuss the following questions with a partner:**

1 What products would be easier to sell to someone who feels:
   a nervous before a test?
   b insecure about their looks?
   c angry at their parents?
   d pleased about getting their first job?
2 How do you feel today? What could someone sell you more easily because of your feelings today?
3 Considering everything you've learned about online advertising, how are you going to change your behaviour online now?

36 **Work in pairs to interpret the cartoon below.**
Share your interpretations in class.

"One more time, Mr Claus – who sold you the data?"

> **S** **Strategies box**
>
> **Remember the four steps for interpreting a cartoon:**
>
> **Step 1:** Describe the people and events you can see in the cartoon.
>
> **Step 2:** Explain what the characters in the cartoon are saying.
>
> **Step 3:** Speculate what message the cartoonist is trying to convey. Why could it be funny?
>
> **Step 4:** Comment on the opinion expressed in the cartoon. Do you agree with it? Why?/Why not?

LANGUAGE **37** a Topic vocabulary: Media
Create a table of word families with these categories:

Noun (idea)	Noun (person)	Verb	Adjective
journal, journalism		—	

Now complete the table with the word families of the words below. Then note down more words from the unit and your own ideas.

a criticise
b investigative
c (mis)information
d monitoring
e (un)edited
f (un)verified (no noun/person)

b **Complete the word map about media issues on the next page with the expressions in the box, then add your own ideas.**

> bias ▪ democratic society ▪ exploits ▪ fake news ▪ journalists ▪
> minors ▪ online content ▪ provides ▪ uncover ▪ verify

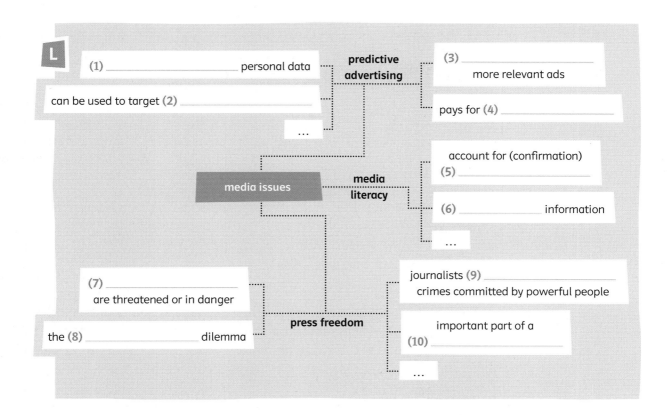

L

(1) _____ personal data

can be used to target (2) _____

...

predictive advertising

(3) _____
more relevant ads

pays for (4) _____

media issues

media literacy

account for (confirmation)
(5) _____

(6) _____ information

...

(7) _____
are threatened or in danger

the (8) _____ dilemma

press freedom

journalists (9) _____
crimes committed by powerful people

important part of a
(10) _____

...

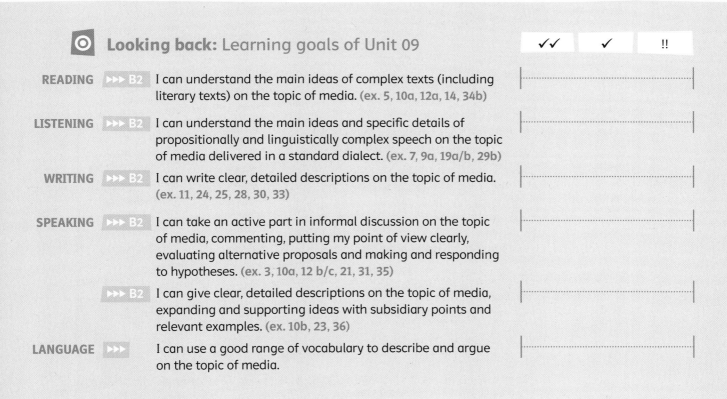

⊙ Looking back: Learning goals of Unit 09

| | ✓✓ | ✓ | !! |

READING ▶▶ B2 — I can understand the main ideas of complex texts (including literary texts) on the topic of media. (ex. 5, 10a, 12a, 14, 34b)

LISTENING ▶▶ B2 — I can understand the main ideas and specific details of propositionally and linguistically complex speech on the topic of media delivered in a standard dialect. (ex. 7, 9a, 19a/b, 29b)

WRITING ▶▶ B2 — I can write clear, detailed descriptions on the topic of media. (ex. 11, 24, 25, 28, 30, 33)

SPEAKING ▶▶ B2 — I can take an active part in informal discussion on the topic of media, commenting, putting my point of view clearly, evaluating alternative proposals and making and responding to hypotheses. (ex. 3, 10a, 12 b/c, 21, 31, 35)

▶▶ B2 — I can give clear, detailed descriptions on the topic of media, expanding and supporting ideas with subsidiary points and relevant examples. (ex. 10b, 23, 36)

LANGUAGE ▶▶ — I can use a good range of vocabulary to describe and argue on the topic of media.

Next time I read/watch the news, I will ...

What I find interesting about social media is ...

Unit 10
Iceberg and outback

 59x5ph

In this unit you will:
- expand your idea of culture
- look below the water line
- blog and talk about intercultural experiences
- appreciate indigenous achievements
- learn about Aboriginal Australians
- express negative emotions

READING + SPEAKING **1** How much do you know about cultures around the world? Take our quiz to find out! Circle your answers, then check with the key below. Compare your results with a partner.

1 *The 'culture' of a community can include*
A languages.
B food and drink.
C religion.
D all of the above.

2 *In which country are the most languages spoken?*
A Papua New Guinea
B India
C Indonesia
D China

3 *The first people to settle in Australia were*
A Spanish explorers around the year 1600.
B Maoris travelling from New Zealand.
C the British during the years of the Empire.
D Aboriginals around 50,000 years ago.

4 *Where are you least likely to greet your neighbour in the morning?*
A Hong Kong – it's not polite to look people in the eye.
B Namibia – by law houses must be built 1 km apart.
C Mongolia – there are only two people per square kilometre.
D Guyana – no one is allowed to speak before midday.

5 *Which of the following is not culturally acceptable in China?*
A Slurping your noodles loudly whilst eating.
B Boasting loudly about your achievements.
C Crossing the road whether the light's green or not.
D Taking a nap if you're tired – even at work.

6 *The Colombian culture of 'tranquilo' means*
A don't worry! Everything will work out.
B take it easy and have a sleep.
C be quiet! You're too noisy.
D you're being too quiet! Be louder!

7 *Toothpastes that whiten your teeth would never sell in some parts of Vietnam because*
A people think it's attractive to blacken their teeth with betel nuts.
B people never show their teeth when smiling.
C it's traditional to visit the dentist every month.
D no one cares what your teeth look like.

Answers: 1 D, **2** A (over 800 different languages are spoken here!), **3** D, **4** C, **5** B, **6** A, **7** A

WRITING **2** Do some research and make up a multiple-choice question yourself. Let your classmates guess the answer.

What is culture?

SPEAKING **3** **Discuss the following questions in small groups.**

1 What do you notice as being different when you meet young people from a different culture?
2 What do you understand by 'culture'? Make a list and compare it with members of other groups.

READING
SPEAKING **4** a **Read the quotations on culture below and match them with the summaries (1–4).**

1 You shouldn't look down on other cultures when protecting your own culture.
2 You can learn much about yourself by getting to know other cultures.
3 Though there are cultural differences, most human values are the same.
4 Learning about other people's lives helps you to understand each other.

> **A**
> "Culture makes people (1) *understand* each other better. And if they (2) *understand* each other better in their soul, it is easier to overcome the economic and political barriers. But first they have to (3) *understand* that their neighbour is, in the end, just like them, with the same problems, the same questions." (*Paulo Coelho*)

> **B**
> "Travel early and travel often. Live abroad, if you can. (4) *Understand* cultures other than your own. As your (5) *understanding* of other cultures increases, your (6) *understanding* of yourself and your own culture will increase." (*Tom Freston*)

> **C**
> "Preservation of one's own culture does not require contempt or disrespect for other cultures." (*César Chávez*)

> **D**
> "I'm not certain that I draw from any one culture more than others. Many myths and legends of many different cultures are really the same story when you get to the heart of it. They are often cultural cautionary tales[1] about how we should behave and how we should live." (*Robert Jordan*)

b **Which of the quotes above do you like best? Talk in pairs and give reasons for your choice.**

LANGUAGE **5** Avoiding repetition
Look at the words 'understand' and 'understanding' in quotes A and B and try to replace them with one of the expressions from the box below without changing the meaning too much. There might be more than one possible alternative.

p. 58

L	a appreciate	c be aware of	e know	g realise
	b appreciation	d get to know	f knowledge	h value

WRITING **6** a **Work in pairs. Person A writes down how Austrians see themselves, person B writes down how other cultures might see Austrians. Compare your ideas.**
Example: *A: Austrians are proud of their history, they are excellent skiers, traditions are important to most of them, …*
B: Austrians wear mainly Lederhosen and eat Wiener Schnitzel, …

b **Use some of the examples you have found to write an entertaining article of around 250 words on Austrian culture.**

---

[1]**cautionary tale:** warnende Geschichte (*wie Struwwelpeter*)

LANGUAGE **7** a Expand your vocabulary: Aspects of culture

p. 59

Look at the box below and discuss with a partner what these aspects of culture could mean. Illustrate your explanations with examples.

Example: *Art: could be a painting, a sculpture, a play.*
Attitude towards elders: The way you respect older people or take care of them.

a arts	**i** dress	**q** literature
b attitude towards animals	**j** education	**r** marriage rites
c attitude towards elders	**k** etiquette	**s** music
d celebrations & festivals	**l** food	**t** non-verbal communication
e class consciousness	**m** friendship	**u** rules
f competition vs. cooperation	**n** ideals of family life	**v** sports
g concept of beauty	**o** justice	**w** values
h display of emotions	**p** language	**x** methods of conflict resolution

b **Decide which of these aspects of culture are apparent (i.e. you can see, feel, hear, taste, smell or touch them), and which of them are not clearly recognisable at once.**

Example: *You can see art or watch celebrations, but it might take some time before you actually learn about the attitude towards elders in a family of a culture that is different to your own.*

SPEAKING **8** a **In his 'Iceberg Model of Culture', Edward T. Hall[2] suggests that just like an iceberg, culture is made of a visible and an invisible part. The visible or apparent aspects of culture are just the tip of the iceberg (10%). The aspects that actually constitute a culture, unseen, are beneath the surface (about 90%). Write some of the expressions from above into the picture below. Compare your ideas with a partner.**

celebrations

attitude towards elders

b **Together with a partner, think of more examples of aspects of culture that you could add to the lower part of the iceberg.**

[2] Edward T. Hall: *Beyond Culture*, 1976

SPEAKING **9** Discuss in small groups how the knowledge of these aspects of culture can improve mutual understanding and reduce potential conflicts.
Example: *Knowing that the meaning of body language such as hand gestures may have different meanings in other cultures.*

WRITING **10** Imagine you have hurt someone's feelings because you didn't understand his/her cultural background. (For instance, you have made a stupid remark about his/her literary tradition or concept of family life.) Write a note apologising.

LISTENING **11** ⊙ 27 a You are going to listen to a lecturer revising the Iceberg Model with his class. Write down three ideas that you think will be mentioned.

b Study the answers below. While listening, add suitable questions according to what you hear.

1 Q: _What did the group discuss in their last session?_

A: The Iceberg Model of Culture.

2 Q: _____

A: The aspects of culture you can't see.

3 Q: _____

A: Myths or thought patterns.

4 Q: _____

A: The cooking attempts to combine many flavours to achieve balance.

5 Q: _____

A: Attitudes towards hierarchies, older people or personal space.

6 Q: _____

A: Our own culture.

7 Q: _____

A: Cultural relativity.

8 Q: _____

A: Over time.

c How many of your ideas from 11a were mentioned in the lecture?

SPEAKING **12** a Together with a partner, discuss what you consider to be 'Austrian culture'. What values do most Austrians believe in?
Example: *Equality between men and women, no corporal punishment, same-sex marriage accepted, …*

b Talk to classmates with a different cultural background. What values do they believe in? Which values do you have in common and which of them are different?

LANGUAGE IN USE

pp. 58+60

13 a What tips would you give young people to learn and adapt to new cultures? Talk in groups.

b Read the text on learning about new cultures. Some words are missing. Change the word in brackets to form the missing word for each gap (1–10). Write your answers in the spaces provided. The first one (0) has been done for you.

How to learn and adapt to new cultures

by Sarah Johnson

There are (0) _____ (count) classes, books, articles and people that will claim they can teach you how to assimilate into a culture. In order to truly learn a culture, you have to shed any prior bias or judgements you might be bringing to the table. This can be one of the hardest things to do since often we are (1) _____ (aware) of our perceptions and tendencies. The best thing to do is not judge. Anytime you catch yourself thinking negatively about the way people act, when something they do seems (2) _____ (ridicule), just take a step back and consider how differently everyone sees the world. There is no right or wrong, just different ways of living life.

Learn the language. If you are (3) _____ (travel) anywhere, chances are that the native language where you're staying is not going to be English. Take the time to learn the language and show people you are interested in their culture. You might feel (4) _____ (anxiety) about speaking a foreign language, but even if you sound completely (5) _____ (fool), people will be happy that you tried. Plus, it can be pretty endearing – like when you're trying to roll your Rs while speaking Spanish to your new friends in Barcelona.

There are going to be things that you aren't used to, but instead of avoiding new experiences, you should embrace them. It's okay to be (6) _____ (comfort); in fact, it is one of the best things that you can ever do. Maybe the thought of eating a worm makes you feel (7) _____ (dread), but when you're in Namibia and they offer it to you as a gift because it's one of their country's dishes, you eat that worm with a smile. When you face (8) _____ (certain) head on, you learn how well you really can adapt to and learn a new culture.

You have to want to learn about another culture, or you never will. Watch people, marvel at the (9) _____ (exist) of anything that is new to you. Embrace new lifestyles and culture with wonder and (10) _____ (curious). You will find that you are learning things and shifting your perspective without even knowing it.

0	countless	6	
1		7	
2		8	
3		9	
4		10	
5			

SPEAKING **14** Prepare a short statement (about 90 seconds long): Do you agree with the advice given in the text? Why?/Why not? Share your statements in class.

WRITING **15** **a** On returning from a great journey abroad, you came across the quote on the right. It has inspired you to share your travel experiences in a blog post.

> "If you reject the food, ignore the customs, fear the religion and avoid the people, you might better stay home." (*James A. Michener*)

In your blog post you should:

- present a positive experience you had
- point out how it affected your journey
- encourage readers to visit the country you travelled to

Write around 250 words. Give your blog post a title.

b Write the same blog post in around 400 words adding details to the 250-word version. Or write the 400-word blog post first and then see how you can shorten it to a 250-word version. See *Writing coach*, pp. 182/183 on how this can be done.

S **Strategies box**

To encourage someone to do something means to **give them confidence** by **giving advice** or by letting them know that they are **doing the right thing**.

SPEAKING **16** *Individual long turn:* You have been asked to give a 5-minute talk on intercultural issues.

In your talk you should:

- compare the pictures
- recommend two ways of getting to know a different culture
- explain how young people might benefit from getting to know a different culture

17 *Paired activity:* Your English language assistant wants to know which aspects of culture you might find difficult to learn about when spending some time with a family with a different cultural background to your own. Discuss the aspects below and agree on two.

- attitude towards elders
- class consciousness
- etiquette
- ideals of family life
- attitude towards animals

Indigenous peoples

SPEAKING 18 Indigenous peoples, also known as first peoples, aboriginal peoples or native peoples, are ethnic groups who are the original inhabitants of a particular region, in contrast to groups that have settled, occupied or colonised the area more recently.

Look at the pictures below. They show indigenous people in different parts of the world. Discuss the following questions with a partner, then share your ideas in class.

> **!**
> *people*: men, women and children
> *a people*: a society, a culture, a nation

1 Which parts of the world do these people come from?
2 What do you think the people in the pictures have in common, how do they differ?
3 What do you know about these indigenous people's cultures, histories and societies?

A

B

C

READING 19 a **Read the information about indigenous peoples around the world. There are three pieces of false information in this text. Discuss what they could be with a partner.**

p. 62

Did you know …?

There are an estimated 370 million indigenous people in the world, living across 90 countries. Indigenous people make up more than 10 percent of the world's population. They speak over 40 percent of the estimated 6,700 languages used around the world. And most of them are in danger of disappearing as the younger generations often do not learn their traditional language anymore.

The sporting event 'World Indigenous Games' was held for the first two times in 2015 and 2017. Some of the disciplines include football, archery, canoeing, road bicycle racing, darts, spear throwing, log races and swimming. The competitors don't wear sports attire but compete barefoot and wearing body paint.

Indigenous communities thrive by living in harmony with the environment. Research shows that where indigenous groups have control of the land, forests and biodiversity grow and develop successfully. Their lifestyles in much of the world's tropical rainforests are more harmful and threatening to the environment than the lifestyles of industrialised countries.

b **Do some research to correct the false information in the text. Then check with your teacher.**

WRITING **20** Take a piece of paper and write down as much as you can about Australia, Australian people and Australian lifestyle and culture. Share your results in class.

SPEAKING **21** Indigenous people all over the world have created different kinds of art. On this page you can see examples of Aboriginal art as it can be found in parts of Australia. Get together in small groups and discuss the possible meaning(s) of the (cave) paintings. Consider the questions below.

1 Who might have created these images?
2 What could they have used to paint them?
3 Why did the Aborigines create these pictures?
4 What do you think the pictures show?

A

B

Remember how to speculate about the present and past:

This cave painting might show a scene from …
The Aborigines must have used paints made of …
This image could show an animal species that …

LANGUAGE **22** **a** Expand your vocabulary: Indigenous issues
Get together with a partner and come up with definitions of the five expressions below.

| a hunter-gatherer b European settlers c valuable resources d citizenship e remote territories |

b Summarise what you know about the problematic history of indigenous people in the USA/in Australia/New Zealand or African countries. Use the expressions. Then share your results in class.

LISTENING **23** **a** Listen to the sound parts of a BBC video about an Aboriginal community in Australia.
VIEWING Answer the questions below in note form.

BBC ⓞⅅ 09

1 What was found on the Aborigines' land?
2 What consequences did this find have for the people?
3 What aspects of 'typical' Australian culture do the two men list?
4 What does Pastor Geoffrey Stokes say about paying for the Australian lifestyle?

b Now watch the video. Then get together with a partner and describe what you could see about the life of Aborigines in this community. What problems do the Aborigines face in their daily lives?

READING 24 a **Read only the title and the first sentence of each paragraph of the article below. What is it about?**

p. 61

b **Read the article about the indigenous people of Australia. Some parts are missing. Choose the correct part (A–M) for each gap (1–10). There are two extra parts that you should not use. Write your answers in the boxes provided. The first one (0) has been done for you.**

Worlds apart

by Germaine Greer

Ever since white men set foot in Australia more than 200 years ago, they have persecuted, harassed, tormented and tyrannised the people they found there. The more cold-blooded (0) _____ of dealing with a galaxy of peoples who would never be able to adapt to the 'whitefella' regime was to eliminate them as quickly as possible, so they shot and poisoned them. Others believed that they owed it to their God to rescue the benighted savage, strip him of his pagan culture, clothe his nakedness, and teach him the value of work. Leaving the original inhabitants alone (1) _____; learning from them was beyond impossible. As far as the pink people were concerned, black Australians were primitive peoples, survivors from the Stone Age in a land that time forgot.

White settlers have never truly understood the Aborigines. By the time the newcomers registered the fact that the Aboriginal peoples belonged to something like 700 language groups, many of those groups consisted of only a handful of people. Officialdom has never (2) _____ with the multiplicity and complexity of Aboriginal culture. For groups who have jealously guarded their distinctness and carefully managed their intercommunal negotiations for 40,000 years, forcing them to live together in closed communities brings intense psychological stress. That includes the tragically high rates of suicide in Aboriginal communities. In 2015, suicide (3) _____, compared with 1.8% of other Australians.

For years, the extinction of the Australian Aborigine has been eagerly (4) _____ as about to happen soon. In fact, there are probably more Aboriginal people alive in Australia today than there were when Captain Cook planted the British flag at Botany Bay in 1770. But while their numbers are growing, so is their unending suffering. Aboriginal people are tough, and it is the fate of the toughest to suffer longest and hardest.

AUSTRALIAN ABORIGINES.

The Aboriginal peoples reacted to contact in different ways. Some were used to foreigners visiting their land. Most (5) _____ to their way of life and offered to help them find food and show them how to survive. Even when the Europeans brought diseases, there was no real attempt to drive the foreigners away. By the time the Aboriginal peoples (6) _____ to the whole country and everything in it, it was too late.

It did not occur to Aboriginal Australians that the newcomers (7) _____; they were outraged when they saw men whipped. In Aboriginal communities, a man who offended against tribal law was to be speared, but he was not to be beaten like a dog. The crushing blow that (8) _____ was the gradual realisation that the strangers they had accepted as human like themselves did not reciprocate their respect.

Because Aboriginal people had few visible possessions, their culture seemed simple. Hunter-gatherer morality does not permit the collection of possessions and even today does not recognise the value of money. Emily Kngwarreye, an indigenous Australian artist, once (9) _____ for a car for her nephew in payment for one of her paintings. The car was supplied, Kngwarreye gave it to her nephew, but a few weeks later the nephew had sold the new car for A$300. "Why did he sell the car, a new car, for just A$300?" her patron asked. "Because he only needed A$300," said Kngwarreye. Capitalism simply doesn't know how to deal with people like this.

Traditional Aboriginal people will take government money as part payment for what the whitefellas (10) _____, namely, everything, but they simply don't see that that gives the whitefellas the right to tell them what to do. This is not a sign of stupidity or wickedness but resistance – eternal, implacable, self-destructive resistance. When government officials take over the policing of the Aboriginal communities, they can expect more of the same. They will never defeat the Aboriginal peoples, but will surely increase the bitterness of their suffering.

A	did not consider them fully human	H	looked forward to and repeatedly described
B	assumed that the newcomers would adapt	I	was never an option
C	made any attempt to cope	J	feared and narrowly avoided
D	decided that the most humane way	K	destroyed Aboriginal self-esteem
E	sold them	L	took away from them
F	asked one of her patrons	M	realised that the newcomers had laid claim
G	accounted for 5.2% of Aboriginal deaths		

0	1	2	3	4	5	6	7	8	9	10
D										

25 **Which of the following statements best describes what the article is about? Discuss in class.**

a For centuries, the Aboriginal people have been abused by the white people, but the whites have finally gained the respect of the Aborigines.

b White people have oppressed the Aboriginal people for hundreds of years, and failed to understand them.

c Since the whites arrived in Australia, the number of Aboriginal people has dramatically decreased, with suicide being the number one cause of death.

d For thousands of years, the Aboriginal people have enjoyed living in tightly-knit social groups, collecting a range of personal possessions.

WRITING **26** **Although the Australians and Aborigines live in one country, their different ways of life can easily cause intercultural misunderstanding. Using the information from the last three pages, write three paragraphs: one describing 'Australian culture', one describing the Aboriginal way of life and one explaining how the two might be in conflict with each other. You can also do more research on these different lifestyles and include them in your paragraphs.**

LANGUAGE 27 a Expand your vocabulary: Adjectives, nouns and opposites
Write the nouns next to the adjectives on the left and the adjectives next to the nouns on the right.

b Match the words to their opposites.

1 primitive,
2 savage,
3 complex, *complexity*
4 tragic,
5 dead,
6 intelligent,

a survival,
b development,
c luck,
d stupidity,
e civilisation,
f simplicity, *simple*

c Check both the spelling and the meaning of the words with a dictionary.

LANGUAGE 28 a Expand your vocabulary: Negative emotions
There are a lot of ways to express negative emotions in English. Copy the nouns from the box to your notes and add a translation or explanation.

> **L**
> a anger
> b despair/desperation
> c disappointment
> d disgust
> e grief
> f jealousy
> g outrage
> h rage
> i resentment
> j shame
> k sorrow
> l suffering

b Add the adjectives to the nouns in your notes. Sometimes you can also add an opposite or a verb.

SPEAKING 29 a In pairs, find examples of situations in which someone might have the feelings above.

b Choose six of your examples to write conditional sentences with the feelings.
Example: *There would be less suffering among Aborigines if the Australians hadn't treated them so badly.*

WRITING 30 An international organisation is looking for young volunteers who are interested in an education project with Aborigines in Darwin, Australia. You are interested and have decided to write an email to Emma McFerguson, the organiser of the project.

In your email you should:

- explain why you are interested in the project
- specify your qualifications
- outline your idea for the project

Write around 250 words.

→ See *Writing coach, Formal email*, p. 178.

LANGUAGE 31 a Topic vocabulary: Culture/Indigenous people
Draw your own iceberg with the ten aspects of culture you want to remember most.

b Unscramble the letters of the mixed-up words in the word map on the next page. Then add more information about indigenous people from this unit (e.g. on indigenous art) and your own ideas.

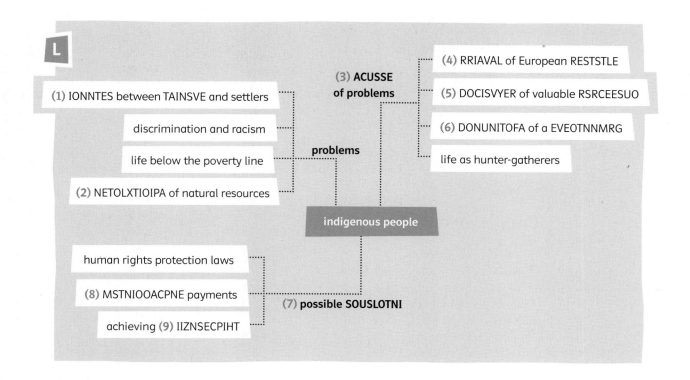

L

(1) IONNTES between TAINSVE and settlers

discrimination and racism

life below the poverty line

(2) NETOLXTIOIPA of natural resources

(3) **ACUSSE of problems**

problems

(4) RRIAVAL of European RESTSTLE

(5) DOCISVYER of valuable RSRCEESUO

(6) DONUNITOFA of a EVEOTNNNMRG

life as hunter-gatherers

indigenous people

human rights protection laws

(8) MSTNIOOACPNE payments

achieving (9) IIZNSECPIHT

(7) **possible SOUSLOTNI**

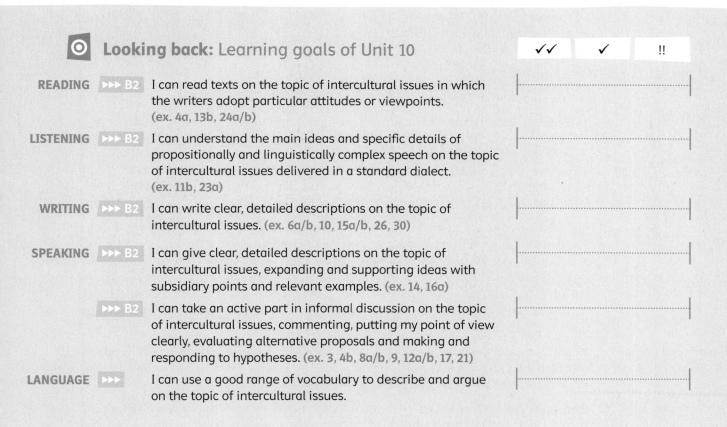

⊙ Looking back: Learning goals of Unit 10

	✓✓	✓	!!

READING ▶▶▶ B2 I can read texts on the topic of intercultural issues in which the writers adopt particular attitudes or viewpoints. (ex. 4a, 13b, 24a/b)

LISTENING ▶▶▶ B2 I can understand the main ideas and specific details of propositionally and linguistically complex speech on the topic of intercultural issues delivered in a standard dialect. (ex. 11b, 23a)

WRITING ▶▶▶ B2 I can write clear, detailed descriptions on the topic of intercultural issues. (ex. 6a/b, 10, 15a/b, 26, 30)

SPEAKING ▶▶▶ B2 I can give clear, detailed descriptions on the topic of intercultural issues, expanding and supporting ideas with subsidiary points and relevant examples. (ex. 14, 16a)

▶▶▶ B2 I can take an active part in informal discussion on the topic of intercultural issues, commenting, putting my point of view clearly, evaluating alternative proposals and making and responding to hypotheses. (ex. 3, 4b, 8a/b, 9, 12a/b, 17, 21)

LANGUAGE ▶▶▶ I can use a good range of vocabulary to describe and argue on the topic of intercultural issues.

The most surprising aspect of culture for me was . . .

Something I didn't know about Aboriginal Australians was . . .

Semester check 02

LESEN ▶▶▶ B2   Ich kann die Hauptaussagen von inhaltlich und sprachlich komplexen Texten, auch literarischen, zu konkreten und abstrakten Themen verstehen.

READING **1**   **Read the text about small parks on the side of streets. Complete the sentences (1–9) using a maximum of four words. Write your answers in the spaces provided. The first one (0) has been done for you.**

The power of parklets

The concept of the parklet – the conversion of a couple of curbside parking spots or other underused public spaces into a tiny park, complete with greenery and seating – got its start in San Francisco about 10 years ago. Since then, the idea has decidedly spread, in part through temporary 'Park(ing) Day' events, but also through more permanent efforts that have sprung up across the country, everywhere from Seattle to New York, Los Angeles to Minneapolis, even suburban New Jersey.

These urban innovations are not without their detractors or problems. One parklet, in San Francisco's Castro District, has proven to be a center of controversy thanks to nuisance activities (booze) and a small handful of unusual users (nudists). Another, in Boston, was eliminated because of a disagreement between two neighboring business owners: one liked the parklet, the other wanted the parking places given back to cars. But these are the outliers. In general, parklets have been well-received in communities all over the US.

But what exactly does a parklet achieve? For instance, how many people really use them? The folks at University City District, a non-profit neighborhood development organization in Philadelphia, wanted to find out. UCD worked with the city to install Philadelphia's first parklets in 2011, and currently operates several each season in partnership with local businesses. Now the group has released a report that analyzes detailed observations of six Philadelphia parklets during the 2013 season. UCD hopes to use the data to increase the positive impact such projects have on the community.

"We heard a lot of anecdotal reports about the parklets," says Seth Budick, policy and research manager at UCD. "One business owner said sales were up so much he had to hire new workers. What better economic development could you hope for than that?"

Anecdotes, however, weren't enough. Budick says the report aims to nail down a more sophisticated understanding of what works and what doesn't in the realm of parklets. And while studies in New York, Los Angeles and Chicago have looked at parklets in central business districts, this is one of the first serious efforts to examine them in a neighborhood setting.

What UCD found is that parklets located directly outside the right types of businesses can create a dynamic that brings a neighborhood together – picture families stopping for dinner or treats, lingering to socialize, and attracting passing acquaintances to stop and chat. The most successful parklet in the study, a 240-square-foot space located outside a taco shop and a popsicle store in a medium-density residential area, attracted as many as 150 individual users in a single day.

In particular, two parameters emerged as the strongest predictors of parklet success. The first was modest interior seating capacity within a main adjacent business, coupled with high turnover of that same interior seating. The second was large windows on the main adjacent business, which tend to increase the sense of connection between the business interior and the exterior parklet space.

The study also found that the parklets attracted a roughly even mix of men and women, a statistic that would indicate they are safe and welcoming spaces. And 20 to 30 percent of users were not customers of an adjacent business, answering concerns that the creation of a parklet removes street space from the public realm for the sole benefit of a private business.

For participating businesses, however, the benefits are clearly measurable. Owners reported a 20 percent increase in sales in the two weeks following a parklet installation, the report notes.

“Put all these things together and something new emerges,” says Budick. “All of a sudden everyone in the neighborhood is stopping there.”

0	To create a parklet, several parking spots are _____ .	*turned into a park*
1	The creation of parklets is becoming _____ .	
2	Parklets have been criticised because _____ . (Give <u>one</u> answer.)	
3	UCD works together with companies in the area to _____ .	
4	UCD has conducted a study to improve the _____ .	
5	After the installation of a parklet, a shopkeeper reported _____ . (Give <u>one</u> answer.)	
6	The UCD study in Philadelphia is focused on parklets in _____ .	
7	A parklet in a residential area can _____ .	
8	A parklet works especially well if the shop next to it _____ . (Give <u>one</u> answer.)	
9	About a quarter of parklet users _____ .	

✓✓   ✓   !!

HÖREN ▶▶▶ **B2**   Ich kann Hauptaussagen und spezifische Informationen von inhaltlich und sprachlich komplexen Redebeiträgen zu konkreten und abstrakten Themen verstehen, wenn Standardsprache gesprochen wird.

LISTENING **2**

radio **FM4**

⊙ 28

🌐

23u6mp

You are going to listen to an FM4 interview about a famous dog. First you will have 45 seconds to study the task below, then you will hear the recording twice. While listening, choose the correct answer (A, B, C or D) for each question (1–7). Put a cross (☒) in the correct box. The first one (0) has been done for you.

After the second listening, you will have 45 seconds to check your answers.

Prince Rupert's dog Boy

0 Some of the library's books

   A don't deal with dog-related topics. ☐
   B were written in the Middle Ages. ☒
   C tell you how to become a witch. ☐
   D are very badly damaged. ☐

1 The book about Boy is special because it

   A doesn't deal with dogs in general. ☐
   B was written before 1624. ☐
   C deals with the character of dogs. ☐
   D is the only known copy of the book. ☐

2 The word 'poodle'

   A was unknown in England then. ☐
   B is originally Czech. ☐
   C was created by Prince Rupert. ☐
   D is related to the work these dogs do. ☐

3 In the Civil War, Prince Rupert was

   A very frightened of witches. ☐
   B accused of being too religious. ☐
   C fighting in his uncle's army. ☐
   D famous for winning many battles. ☐

4 The book says Boy can

   A turn Prince Rupert invisible. ☐
   B talk to ghosts to learn secrets. ☐
   C find hidden items. ☐
   D only be killed by a special weapon. ☐

5 The librarian believes the book was

   A not meant to be taken seriously. ☐
   B written by Prince Rupert's enemies. ☐
   C making fun of Prince Rupert. ☐
   D a warning against witchcraft. ☐

6 The book shows that

   A people only cared about the dog. ☐
   B Prince Rupert was very unpopular. ☐
   C the author knew a lot about witches. ☐
   D Boy was extremely famous. ☐

7 At the battle of Marston Moor

   A Prince Rupert and Boy were killed. ☐
   B the King's army won. ☐
   C Prince Rupert was taken prisoner. ☐
   D Boy helped his master to survive. ☐

SPRECHEN ▶▶▶ **B2**   Ich kann zu einer großen Bandbreite von unterrichtsbezogenen Themen klare und detaillierte Beschreibungen
und Darstellungen geben, Ideen ausführen und durch
untergeordnete Punkte und relevante Beispiele abstützen.

▶▶▶ **B2**   Ich kann mich in vertrauten Situationen aktiv an informellen
Diskussionen beteiligen, indem ich Stellung nehme, einen
Standpunkt darlege, verschiedene Vorschläge beurteile,
Hypothesen aufstelle und auf Hypothesen reagiere.

SPEAKING **3** a **Individual long turn (5 minutes)**

Prepare for about 10 minutes, then give a 5-minute talk on art. Your partner will give you feedback with the checklist in the key.

In your talk you should:

- compare the pictures
- explain what you consider to be art
- suggest how to make art education attractive for students

b **Paired activity (8–10 minutes)**

Do the task below in a group of three. Two of you talk, the third person listens and gives you feedback with the checklist in the key.

You are taking part in an international discussion forum on challenges young people might have to face when they spend a gap year abroad. Discuss the aspects below with a partner and decide which of them could be the hardest to deal with. Agree on two or three.

- language
- food
- customs
- rules
- medical issues

✓✓ ✓ !!

▶▶▶ Ich kann auch komplexe grammatische, lexikalische und argumentative Strukturen erkennen und präzise anwenden.

LANGUAGE **4**
IN USE ■

Read the text about the Uluru/Ayers Rock. Some words are missing. Change the word in brackets to form the missing word for each gap (1–11). Write your answers in the spaces provided. The first one (0) has been done for you.

Uluru/Ayers Rock: Why names matter

Ask most Brits what the name of the **(0)** _____ **(credible)** giant rock formation that stands in the centre of the Australian outback is, and they will likely say Ayers Rock. However, you will often hear it called by a different name: Uluru. This is the name given to it by the Aboriginal people on whose **(1)** _____ **(extend)** land the rock stands. In 1873, Ayers Rock was named in honour of Sir Henry Ayers, the English-born premier of South Australia at the time. Then, in 1993, the Australian government changed the name to Ayers Rock/Uluru; in 2002 the titles were reversed and its current official name is Uluru/Ayers Rock. To some, these may seem like **(2)** _____ **(important)** name changes, but place names are a vital part of the **(3)** _____ **(culture)** fabric of a nation.

The name Uluru is of enormous significance to the local Aboriginal people. They are **(4)** _____ **(protect)** of it, being a key part of the Aboriginal story of creation – the Dreamtime. We rarely appreciate from our position of privilege just how important names are, but a little thought is all that is required to see how **(5)** _____ **(outrage)** and disempowering it is to be robbed of the power of naming the place you live. Even now the official name remains Uluru/Ayers Rock, an **(6)** _____ **(comfort)** reminder of the misappropriation of this landmark by European settlers. Many places in Australia still bear the names of the first **(7)** _____ **(Europe)** who stumbled across them, such as Botany Bay and Cooks River, rather than their ancient Aboriginal names.

Uluru is a hugely important site, and the indigenous people have a very strict set of customs regarding the climbing of this rock, which they don't climb for **(8)** _____ **(enjoy)**. At the bottom of the rock is a sign displaying a plea from local Aboriginal people not to climb Uluru. In fact, since 2019 there has been a total ban on tourists climbing Uluru, though prior to this only a minority of people did so after the indigenous people asked them not to. Obviously, the view from the top of the rock is **(9)** _____ **(beauty)** and would make a great Instagram photo.

But compare it to the emotional harm caused by (10) _____ (ignore) the spiritual customs which apply to this land and there's really no contest. It's just plain (11) _____ (responsible). It is vitally important that visitors to Australia are conscious of and respect the long and rich history of these people. Next time you wonder why the name of a place matters so much, bear this in mind.

0	incredible	6	
1		7	
2		8	
3		9	
4		10	
5		11	

SCHREIBEN ▶▶▶ B2
Ich kann unterschiedliche Texte schreiben, in denen Argumente für oder gegen einen bestimmten Standpunkt angegeben und die Vor- und Nachteile verschiedener Optionen erläutert werden.

WRITING 5 **Your English teacher wants to know whether he/she should organise a language trip to England for the whole class during the school year. He/She wants your opinion on this and has asked you to write an essay.**

In your essay you should:

- outline the advantages **or** disadvantages of going on a language trip to England
- discuss possible challenges of organising such a language trip for the whole class
- argue why this language trip should **or** shouldn't take place during the school year

Write around 400 words. Give your essay a title.

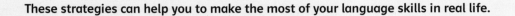

Reading and listening strategies

These strategies can help you to make the most of your language skills in real life.

Reading

Before you read

Determine the purpose of your reading. Are you looking for specific information, do you need to know the general meaning (gist) of the text, or are you simply reading for pleasure? The purpose of your reading will determine which technique works best for you.

Identify the type of writing. Is it a factual article or somebody's opinion? Is it a piece of fiction or a text relating real events? Why was it written? To inform? To entertain? To convince?

Think about what you already know about the topic of the text. This will help you relate the information to your present knowledge and make it easier for you to understand and remember what you read.

Make predictions about what the text will tell you. For this, you can use headlines or subheadings, pictures and the text below pictures if you read an article, or the title, cover and blurb[1] of a book. Your predictions will help you relate the information in the text to what you know already, and evaluate it more easily.

While you read

Depending on why you read the text, you will use different strategies.

Skimming (or reading for gist) means reading a text quickly to get **the main ideas**. You speed through the paragraphs to get an overall understanding of the text. Very often the main idea(s) can be found in the first and last paragraph of a text, or in the first sentences of each paragraph. Note, though, that some magazine or newspaper articles will start with an example, not the main idea(s).

Scanning means looking for **specific information** in a text. When you scan, you should think about what the information you want might look like. Are you looking for numbers or years, or names of people or places? This will help you to find the information quickly. Once you have found what you are looking for, you can stop reading.

Intensive reading (or reading for detail) means working with a text **in detail** to understand as much as possible. This means you will have to read the whole text, sometimes several times, from beginning to end and interact critically with the text by underlining keywords, writing notes or questions into the margin of the page or crossing out passages that are not important. This is easier if the text is on paper, but most e-readers also offer annotation and highlighting functions. Make yourself familiar with them.

Extensive reading (or reading for pleasure) is exactly that – reading for pleasure, so enjoy. It's a great way to consolidate your language skills and learn about the culture of a country. If you're not sure which book to read, start with one that you would read in German as well. If you're a fan of fantasy, don't go for hard core crime in the foreign language. Books that win prizes (the Man Booker Prize in the UK, for example, or the Pulitzer Prize in the US) are also almost always a good choice.

---

[1] **blurb:** Klappentext

Some general tips

Don't stop for every word you don't know but focus on the overall meaning of the passage. Very often words you don't know aren't essential for understanding the text. If you're interested, you can come back and look up these words after you've done everything else required.

Identify keywords – if you don't understand these, you have to look them up. Underline the keywords, and mark and interact with the text. For example, mark passages you aren't sure about with a question mark (?), passages you find interesting with an exclamation mark (!), and passages you want more information on with an arrow (→).

Learning from reading

Look for new grammar patterns – or grammar patterns you aren't sure about. Note how they are being used and write down examples.

Work with keywords – develop their word families and use a dictionary to look for synonyms and opposites.

Write a summary of the text using some of the keywords. Write a tweet about the content. Write a letter to the author/one of the characters/the next reader, etc.

Keep a reading journal and note down your responses to what you've read (this works best with fiction but can also be useful with factual texts).

Listening

Listening to announcements or recordings

When you listen to **loudspeaker announcements** or **films/videos**, communication is **one-sided** – you can't ask questions about anything you don't understand. Therefore, again, **think about what you're going to hear**. This will make understanding easier, especially in a noisy environment. At airports, train or bus stations, most announcements are supported by **visual information** (flight or train departures), which will help you follow them. In case of unexpected announcements (e.g. a change in platform or gate), **don't hesitate to ask other passengers** or the facility's staff.

With **films or video**, you can again rely on **visual clues** to help you understand the main points. If it's a recording, you can watch it multiple times. Most TV stations today also offer this possibility on their websites, as do most radio stations.

Listening to people

If you talk to a person, you can always **ask about the meaning of words** you didn't get. Don't hesitate to do so because misunderstandings just lead to complications.

Being a good listener also means **showing that you understand** through your **body language**, and through **keeping eye contact** and **being attentive** to your partner. Don't interrupt unless it is for clarifying meaning, but hear your partner out and ask questions to make sure you've understood correctly.

If you listen to a **lecture or a talk**, you can't ask for repetition, so it might be **useful to record it** if the details are important. If not, **focus on the main message**, and use the title to activate prior knowledge to make predictions about the content. **Taking notes** will also help.

Strategies for exam tasks

These strategies can help you to make the most of what you know in exams.

Reading

Always highlight the sentences in the text where you've found information on a question so you can check your answers quickly when you're done!

Reading – Multiple matching (sentence parts or paragraphs) (MM)

- Cross out options you've used. The task gets easier the more parts you've matched correctly.
- Only fill in answers you're sure of. Picking a wrong option could lead to another mistake elsewhere. If you're unsure, write down all possible options and decide at the end.

Reading – Multiple choice (MC)

- If you aren't sure about the answer to a question, eliminate the options you know are wrong and then take a guess. Always answer every question!

Reading – True/False/Justification (TFJ)

- The text will always give you information on each statement. A statement is considered 'false' if the text gives you different information on it.
- You must use the <u>first four words</u> of the sentence that gives you the information.
- A new sentence starts after a full stop. A word is everything between two spaces.
- Justify your answer for both true *and* false statements.

Reading – Four-word sentence completion/Four-word answers (4W)

- If the text gives you more than one possible answer, write in only one of them.
- Never write more than four words. No matter how good your answer is, it'd still be wrong.
- Don't worry too much about spelling or grammar, your answer only has to be clear.

Listening

- Before listening, read the task carefully and start thinking about what the recording will deal with. If you know what to expect, it will be much easier for you to understand the content.
- Read the items (options, questions, sentence parts, etc.) carefully. Brainstorm different ways of expressing the same ideas – the language used in the recording will be different from the language in the items.
- Highlight relevant keywords and phrases in the questions or options. This might help you.

Listening – Multiple matching (sentence parts or speakers) (MM)

- In tasks requiring you to match sentence parts, not all combinations make sense. You could try writing the letters of possible matches next to the first halves of the sentences before you listen.

Listening – Multiple choice (MC)

- You may hear expressions from all four options, but only one answer is correct.
- Try crossing out options that you've heard are wrong.

Listening – Four-word sentence completion/Four-word answers (4W)

- Think about possible answers when reading the task. Does the question ask for a name or a number? Does the sentence need an object, a person or an activity to complete it?

Language in use

Language in use – Banked gap fill (BGF)

- While reading, think of a word that could fit the gap, then check the words in the bank.
- Remember to check the sentence before and after the gap to make sure your word fits.

Language in use – Word formation (WF)

- First decide what kind of word (noun, verb, etc.) you need to complete the gap. Then change the given word to the correct form.
- Watch out in case a plural form, third person 's' or an opposite is required.
- Check your spelling!

Language in use – Multiple choice (MC)

- While reading, think of a word that could fit the gap, then check the four options.

Language in use – Editing (ED)

- Read the instructions carefully because the number of correct lines can vary.
- Look for short words like prepositions, modal verbs or adverbs.
- Reading a difficult line from right to left can help.
- The first and last word of a line are never wrong.
- A word that is in the line more than once is never wrong.

Language in use – Open gap fill (OGF)

- Every gap must be filled with exactly one word. Contractions such as *don't* or *I'm* are one word.
- If you can't think of a word right away, decide what kind of word (modal verb, linking word, article, etc.) you need to complete the gap. Then go through possible options in your head.
- Watch out in case a plural form or third person 's' is required.
- Check your spelling!

Grammar revisited

Talking about the future

There are several ways to talk about the future in English. Very often there is little difference in meaning.

Spontaneous decisions and predictions: *will* future

I, you, he/she/it we, they	+ will/won't + verb	I have no idea what this dish is, but I**'ll try** it anyway. We **won't need** a visa for this trip. You**'ll have** the time of your life in Costa Rica. **Will you be** OK travelling on your own?

Predictions based on evidence; Expressing intentions: *going to* future

I + am he/she/it + is you, we, they + are	+ going to + verb	Look at those dark clouds. It**'s going to rain**! Travelling by bus on these bumpy roads is awful. I think I**'m going to be** sick.

Timetables, programmes: Present simple

For planned, fixed events in the future (usually with a time expression).	The train **leaves** at 10.30. Does boarding **start** at 8 p.m.? The ferry **doesn't depart** until 11 p.m.

Arrangements: Present continuous

I + am he/she/it + is you, we, they + are	+ verb + -ing	Adam**'s going** back to the States next week. **Are you travelling** to Ireland this summer? I**'m not going** on another Interrail trip ever again.

Future events/actions in progress: Future continuous

I, you, he/she/it we, they	+ will/won't + be + verb + -ing	This time next year, I **will be backpacking** in Thailand. **Will he be waiting** for me when my plane lands? I **won't be living** here in 20 years.

Looking back on completed events from the future: Future perfect

I, you, he/she/it we, they	+ will/won't + have + past participle	By Easter, I **will have finished** my journey around the world. He still **won't have finished** organising the photos from his summer holidays by Christmas. **Will the rainforests have disappeared** by the time our children have grown up?

Useful phrases for talking about the future

There are a number of phrases that are useful for talking about the future. Some are followed by an infinitive, others by a gerund or noun.

Phrases that indicate that something is definitely going to happen

be bound to + infinitive *be due to* + infinitive *be sure to* + infinitive *be set to* + infinitive *be certain to* + infinitive	*Traditional family structures **are bound to change**.* *The new law **is due to come** into effect in September.* *Your sister **is sure to win** the game.* *The costs **are set to double** by the end of the year.* *They **are certain to get** married soon.*

Phrases that indicate that something will happen soon

be about to + infinitive *be on the brink of* + gerund/noun *be on the verge of* + gerund/noun *be on the point of* + gerund/noun	*We **were about to get** married when my fiancé changed his mind.* *The country **is on the brink of a civil war**.* *The economy **is on the verge of collapsing**.* *I **was on the point of giving up** when the letter arrived.*

Gerunds and infinitives

- You can use a gerund (verb + *-ing*) as the subject of a sentence or as an object, just like nouns.
  *Travelling is a lot of fun. – Tony enjoys **travelling**.*
- When you use two verbs together, the second verb is often a gerund.
  *Greg doesn't **like travelling** on rural roads./Tara **enjoys exploring** other cultures.*
- You always need a gerund when using a verb after a preposition (*by*, *from*, *without*, etc.).
  *I couldn't live **without travelling**./Why don't you give **up flying**?/I'll get used **to taking** the bus.*
- Whether you need to use an infinitive (*to invite*, *to take*) or a gerund often depends on the verb of the sentence.

Some **verbs** are **always** followed by a **gerund (with or without preposition):**	
▪ **likes and dislikes** ▪ **ideas and opinions** ▪ **starts and stops** ▪ **others**	*can't stand, dislike, enjoy, feel like, mind, prefer* *admit (to), consider, imagine, insist (on), recommend, suggest, understand* *delay, finish, give up, practise, put off, spend (time)* *avoid, can't help, deny, get used to, involve, mention, miss, risk*

Verb followed by a gerund without preposition:
*I **can't stand waiting** at airports for a long time.*
*When I travel, you wouldn't believe how much time I **spend writing** in my journal.*

Verb followed by a gerund with preposition:
*The tour guide **insisted on paying** for everyone's snacks.*
*The travel blogger **admitted to fabricating** all his stories.*

Some **verbs** are **always** followed by an **infinitive construction (infinitive with *to* or object + infinitive with *to*):**

▪ **mental activity**	*agree, choose, decide, encourage, forget, learn, teach, tell, want, warn, wish*
▪ **future arrangements**	*arrange, expect, hope, intend, manage, offer, plan, prepare, promise*
▪ **appearance**	*appear, pretend, seem, tend*
▪ **effort**	*afford, attempt, fail, hurry, manage, refuse*
▪ **interaction**	*ask, help, hesitate, invite, remind*

Verb followed by an infinitive with *to*:
*I **tend to fall** asleep on long train rides./I can't **afford to travel** to exotic destinations.*

Verb followed by an object and an infinitive with *to*:
*The famous traveller **encouraged** <u>young people</u> **to leave** their comfort zone.*
*He **taught** <u>me</u> **to be** open to new experiences.*

▪ **With some verbs, it makes no difference to the meaning whether a gerund or an infinitive follows.**
*begin, start; love, like, hate: She **started to laugh**. = She **started laughing**.*

▪ **With some verbs, it depends on the sentence structure whether a gerund or an infinitive follows.**
allow, permit, advise, forbid:
 – In general rules (when no object is specified), the verbs are followed by a gerund:
 *The airline **does not permit smoking** on planes./Doctors **advise exercising** regularly.*
 – When a specific person is addressed (when an object is specified), the verbs are followed by the object and an infinitive:
 *The flight attendant **didn't allow** <u>her</u> **to smoke**./Her GP **advised** <u>him</u> **to exercise** more.*

▪ **With some verbs, the meaning can change depending on whether a gerund or an infinitive follows.**

stop
+ gerund: *Mandy **stopped watching** the birds* = She's no longer watching the birds.
+ infinitive: *Mandy **stopped to watch** a little bird.* = She stopped walking so she could watch the bird.

remember
+ gerund: *Carrie still **remembers seeing** the pyramids in Egypt for the first time.* = Carrie remembers an experience she had in the past.
+ infinitive: *Next week, Carrie will **remember to show** her mum the picture she took of the pyramids.* = Carrie will do what she has promised to do and not forget it.

try
+ gerund: *I've lost my passport. I've **tried calling** the embassy, **emailing**, **sending** a letter – no reply.* = You have experimented with different methods of doing something.
+ infinitive: ***Try to stay** calm, it'll all work out.* = Make an effort to do something that is difficult for you.

go on
+ gerund: *After his first few trips abroad, Tony **went on travelling** for years.* = He continued doing the same thing.
+ infinitive: *After he finished his degree, Tony **went on to travel** around the world.* = He started to do something different.

regret
+ gerund: *I **regret booking** the cruise.* = I'm unhappy about something I did in the past.
+ infinitive: *I **regret to inform** you that the cruise is fully booked. We cannot accommodate you.* = I'm about to give you unpleasant news.

Modal verbs to express likelihood

You will remember that *can*, *could*, *may*, *might*, *must*, *will*, *would*, *shall*, *should* and *ought to* are all modal auxiliary verbs. You can use them to express ability, permission and obligation. (For a more detailed explanation of the use of modal verbs in different tenses, check your copy of *way2go!* 5.) You can also use modal verbs to express how sure you are that something (past or present) is true.

Present	
Assertion: You use these modal verbs to express that you're almost certain about something:	
When you are very sure that something is (not) true, you use: **must** or **can't** + **(continuous) infinitive**	*Tarik **must** still **be playing** football. Otherwise he would have come home already.* *There are no lights on. Sue **can't** be at home.*
Probable assumption: You use these modal verbs to indicate that you consider something likely:	
When you are fairly sure that something is probably (not) true, you use: **should/shouldn't/ought to** + **(continuous) infinitive**	*We **shouldn't have** trouble finding a taxi. There are enough around here.* *He left for university early, so he **should be sitting** in his economics lecture now.*
Possible or unlikely assumption: You use these modal verbs to say that something is possible, but you are not sure how likely it is:	
When you doubt that something is (not) true, or you believe that it's unlikely, you use: **could/may/might** + **(continuous) infinitive**	*Maggie hasn't arrived yet. She **could be having** trouble with her car.* *Paul **might come** to my birthday party, but I don't really think he'll show up.*
Past	
Assertion: You use these modal verbs to express that you're almost certain that something happened in the past:	
must or **can't** + **perfect infinitive**	*There are no lights on. Sue **must have left** already.* *Why are you handing in your test? You **can't have finished** yet.*
Probable assumption: You use these modal verbs to indicate that you consider it likely that something happened in the past:	
should/shouldn't/ought to + **perfect infinitive**	*Somebody **should have processed** your application by now. Why don't you call and find out?*
Possible or unlikely assumption: You use these modal verbs to say that it's possible that something happened in the past, but you are not sure how likely it is that it happened.	
could/may/might + **perfect infinitive**	*Sandra **might have missed** the train. Shall we call her and offer to get her?*

Mixed conditionals, wishes and regrets

You will remember the four most common types of conditionals ('*if*-sentences') and how they are used. (You can also check your copy of *way2go!* 5 for a more detailed description.)

Regular conditionals	
▪ If you talk about **cause and effect/things that are always true**, you use: **If/When + present simple → present simple**	*If you **drop** glass, it **breaks**.*
▪ If you talk about **real and possible situations in the future**, you use: **If + present simple → *will* future**	*If you **arrive** late at school, you'll **get** detention.*
▪ If you talk about **impossible things in the present** or **unlikely situations in the future**, you use: **If + past simple → *would/could/might* + infinitive**	*I'd **buy** a new car **if** I **won** the lottery.*
▪ If you talk about **things that didn't happen in the past** and their **imaginary consequences**, you use: **If + past perfect → *would/could/might* + *have* + past participle**	*I **wouldn't have called** if I **had known** you were working.*

In the four types of conditional sentences above, the *if*-clause (condition) and the main clause (consequence) refer to the same time. See also:

*If the college **had** a better reputation,*
past tense used to describe a present condition

*more students **would apply**.*
would + infinitive for a present consequence

*If he **had graduated** from a prestigious university,*
past perfect used to describe a past condition

*he **would have found** a good job immediately.*
would + *have* + past participle for a past consequence

This is not the case in so-called 'mixed conditionals':

Mixed conditionals	
An imaginary situation in the past has consequences for the present	
If you talk about an imaginary situation in the past that has consequences in the present, you use: **If/When + past perfect → *would/could/might* + infinitive**	*If Derek **had invested** money in the Google company, he **would be** rich today.* *We **would be** in Bali now **if** you **had won** the raffle last month.*
A present situation influences how you see an imaginary past situation	
If you talk about an imaginary past situation influenced by a present or ongoing state, you use: **If + past simple → *would/could/might* + *have* + past participle**	*If I **wasn't** worried about money, I **would have gone** to a college that charges higher fees.* *Dad **would have driven** you to the university for your exam **if** he **didn't have** so much work right now.*

An imaginary future situation has consequences for the present	
If you talk about an imaginary future situation that influences the present, you use: **If + past continuous → would/could/might + infinitive**	*If I **were taking** the exam tomorrow, I **would be** extremely nervous. I **could spend** all my money on fun stuff if I **wasn't buying** a new car next month.*

You use the same tenses as in the *if*-clauses above to express wishes about the present and regrets about the past with *I wish/If only*:

Wishes about the present: *I wish/If only* + past tense	
When something in the present is not the way you would like it to be, you use: **I wish/If only + past tense**	*I **wish** it **wasn't raining** today. (It's raining and you don't like this.) I **wish** I **knew** how to help you. (You don't know how to help and you are unhappy about that.)*
Regrets about the past: *I wish/If only* + past perfect tense	
When you say that you regret (not) doing something in the past, you use: **I wish/If only + past perfect tense**	*I **wish** I **hadn't picked** this college. (You picked a specific college and you regret that now.) **If only I'd studied** harder for the exam. Maybe I would've got a better mark. (You didn't study hard enough and you regret that.)*

Writing coach

Formal email

You write formal emails to give or ask for information, respond to a request, apologise, complain, make suggestions, state facts, or apply for a job. The recipient is usually someone that you don't know so well or don't know at all.

It is important that you are specific about the purpose of your email. It should be clear, polite and to the point. If necessary, let the recipient know what action you expect him/her to take before signing off.

These are the main points to remember when writing a **formal email**:
- Start with:
  From: your name and email address
  To: the person you are writing to
  Subject (*Re*): what the email is about
- Address the person you are writing to and sign off at the end in a formal way.
- Make your purpose for writing clear at the beginning of your email.
- Start a new paragraph for each content point (bullet point).[1]
- Highlight the personal significance of ideas/events at the beginning of each paragraph.

Sample task – formal email of enquiry

You and your classmates would like to do a music project together with a school in Ireland. Your music teacher has suggested that you contact Kenmore Traditional Music School, whose website you have spotted on the internet.

You have decided to write an email.
In your email you should:

- explain why you have chosen this particular school
- present your school's focus on music
- ask about a possible project you could do together

Write around 250 words.

Kenmore
Traditional Music School

Explore the possibilities!

Share music with friends from all over the world!

<office@kenmusic.ie>

---

[1] The content points are referred to as bullet points in the task.

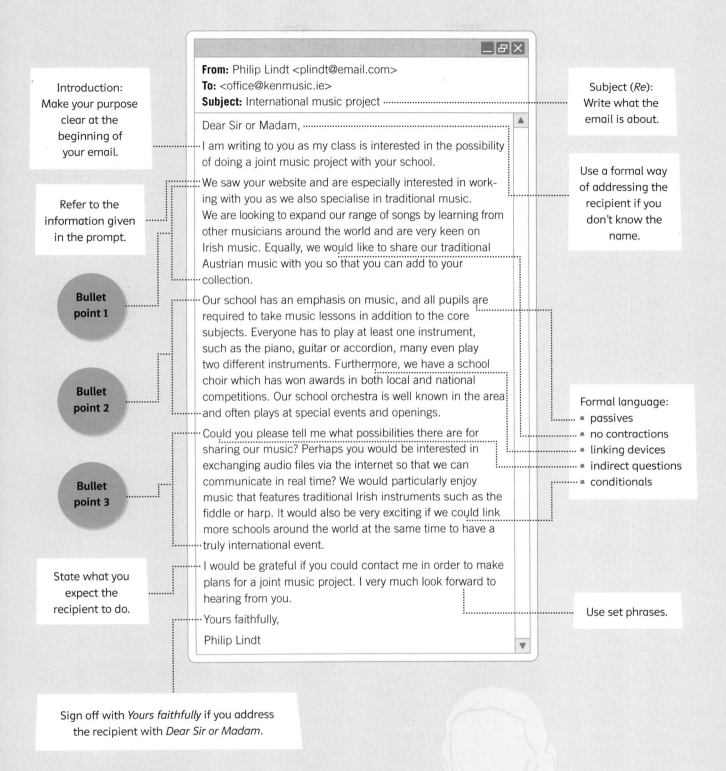

Introduction: Make your purpose clear at the beginning of your email.

Refer to the information given in the prompt.

Bullet point 1

Bullet point 2

Bullet point 3

State what you expect the recipient to do.

Sign off with *Yours faithfully* if you address the recipient with *Dear Sir or Madam*.

Subject (*Re*): Write what the email is about.

Use a formal way of addressing the recipient if you don't know the name.

Formal language:
- passives
- no contractions
- linking devices
- indirect questions
- conditionals

Use set phrases.

From: Philip Lindt <plindt@email.com>
To: <office@kenmusic.ie>
Subject: International music project

Dear Sir or Madam,

I am writing to you as my class is interested in the possibility of doing a joint music project with your school.

We saw your website and are especially interested in working with you as we also specialise in traditional music. We are looking to expand our range of songs by learning from other musicians around the world and are very keen on Irish music. Equally, we would like to share our traditional Austrian music with you so that you can add to your collection.

Our school has an emphasis on music, and all pupils are required to take music lessons in addition to the core subjects. Everyone has to play at least one instrument, such as the piano, guitar or accordion, many even play two different instruments. Furthermore, we have a school choir which has won awards in both local and national competitions. Our school orchestra is well known in the area and often plays at special events and openings.

Could you please tell me what possibilities there are for sharing our music? Perhaps you would be interested in exchanging audio files via the internet so that we can communicate in real time? We would particularly enjoy music that features traditional Irish instruments such as the fiddle or harp. It would also be very exciting if we could link more schools around the world at the same time to have a truly international event.

I would be grateful if you could contact me in order to make plans for a joint music project. I very much look forward to hearing from you.

Yours faithfully,

Philip Lindt

Blog

A blog is an interactive webpage for publishing writing online. Anybody who has access to the internet can write, read and comment on blogs. In a blog, you provide or respond to information, ask for or give advice and motivate readers to take action using formal or semi-formal language, depending on the topic and your readership. You may also address your readers directly and invite comments.

Blog post (blog entry)	Blog comment
You write a blog post to arouse interest, share experiences, express concern, persuade or convince readers, or offer your opinion on a particular topic. This could be of general interest, such as leisure, lifestyle and travelling, or more specific, such as technology or literature. You could give or ask for information or advice or other bloggers' opinions. In your conclusion, you might want to let the readers know what you would like them to do: comment on your blog post or take action, depending on your post.	You write a blog comment to react to a blog post or another blog comment. Make sure you have read it carefully and fully understand the writer's view before you comment on it. In your blog comment you start by referring to the blog post you have read. Then you may agree or disagree with the writer, criticise the writer's arguments, give or follow advice, make suggestions, or give your readers something to think about.

These are the main points to remember when writing a blog post:

Layout

- User name
- Title

Organisation

- Introduction
- Main body (address and expand the content points)
- Conclusion

These are the main points to remember when writing a blog comment:

Layout

- User name
- Email address

Organisation

- Introduction (refer to the blog post/comment)
- Main body (address and expand the content points)
- Conclusion

Blog post – sample task

More and more young people are deciding to spend some time studying or working abroad. You have just come home from a four-week stay in Australia and want to encourage other young people to go there by starting a blog.

In your blog post you should:

- point out why it is a great idea to spend some time abroad
- outline the advantages of staying with a host family
- convince your readers to choose Australia

Write around 400 words. Give your blog post a title.

Blog post – sample answer

User name ······· World_traveller

Title ······· **It's got to be Australia.**

Introduction: Let the reader know what you are going to write about.

'Down under' – it's the one place to go if you want to spend some time abroad. I just got back from the most amazing trip to Australia. Fabulous, I've got so much to tell you.

In a personal blog, you may use informal or neutral language and write in a chatty tone.

Bullet point 1

It's such a great idea to spend some time away from all your home comforts and spread your wings for a while. Why? Well, to start with, you'll learn some life skills and independence. For instance, having to get from A to B by yourself by using public transport can be a real challenge, but you'll be pretty pleased with yourself once you've done it. Plus, you'll make a ton of new friends as there's nothing like travelling to make people open up and start chatting. Also, you could be helping someone else while at the same time helping yourself. I volunteered at a koala sanctuary near Brisbane and had the time of my life helping out these cute little bears.

Bullet point 2

But what about accommodation? Well, take it from me, the best thing you can do is stay with an 'Ozzie' host family. I think they're just the most open and welcoming people on earth! You don't have to worry about looking for a bed and breakfast because this can be pretty expensive. My hosts made me feel like part of the family and introduced me to all their friends and relatives, which was really cool. They also took me sightseeing at the weekends, and we spent a lot of time on the beach. Having said that, they also gave me my space when I needed it. I had my own room, so I could stay there and read or take a nap whenever I felt like it. The best of both worlds, isn't it?

Address the reader.

So, listen up: Everyone should spend some time abroad to see things from a different point of view and get a taste of independence. Whether you're travelling for a month or a year, Australia is the perfect place to go. Fab weather, friendly people, endless beaches – it's got the lot. You can easily find a job volunteering with animal sanctuaries or some other organisation – the possibilities are endless. Then you'll get the chance to give something back while you're there. You can find more information online, or try asking around. Your friends are bound to know someone who's spent some time in Oz.

Bullet point 3

Conclusion: Move your audience to comment on your blog post or to take action.

Well, how about it? Why not start planning your Australian adventure today?

reply

<u>Blog comment – sample task</u>

Browsing blogs on leisure activities you have come across the blog post on the right.

You have decided to comment on this blog post. In your blog comment you should:

- discuss whether sports increase people's health
- examine the importance of sports for reducing stress
- point out the effect of sports on people's self-esteem

Write around 250/400 words.

Rashid_M

Sports? No, thanks!

… Doing sports – I've always hated it. There's always someone lecturing you how doing sports is healthy, how it reduces stress and boosts your self-esteem. Such nonsense! Well, running, cycling, swimming – it just isn't for me, and I'm perfectly healthy, thank you very much.

reply

<u>Blog comment – sample answer 250 words</u>

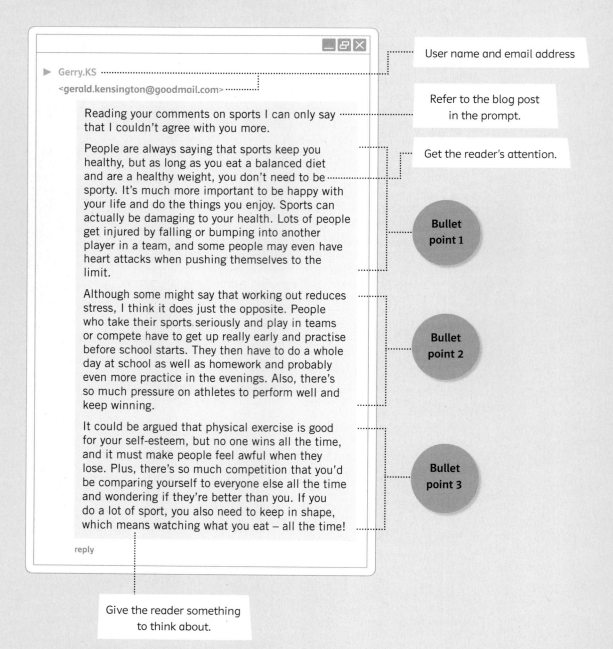

▶ Gerry.KS
<gerald.kensington@goodmail.com>

Reading your comments on sports I can only say that I couldn't agree with you more.

People are always saying that sports keep you healthy, but as long as you eat a balanced diet and are a healthy weight, you don't need to be sporty. It's much more important to be happy with your life and do the things you enjoy. Sports can actually be damaging to your health. Lots of people get injured by falling or bumping into another player in a team, and some people may even have heart attacks when pushing themselves to the limit.

Although some might say that working out reduces stress, I think it does just the opposite. People who take their sports seriously and play in teams or compete have to get up really early and practise before school starts. They then have to do a whole day at school as well as homework and probably even more practice in the evenings. Also, there's so much pressure on athletes to perform well and keep winning.

It could be argued that physical exercise is good for your self-esteem, but no one wins all the time, and it must make people feel awful when they lose. Plus, there's so much competition that you'd be comparing yourself to everyone else all the time and wondering if they're better than you. If you do a lot of sport, you also need to keep in shape, which means watching what you eat – all the time!

reply

User name and email address

Refer to the blog post in the prompt.

Get the reader's attention.

Bullet point 1

Bullet point 2

Bullet point 3

Give the reader something to think about.

Blog comment – sample answer 400 words

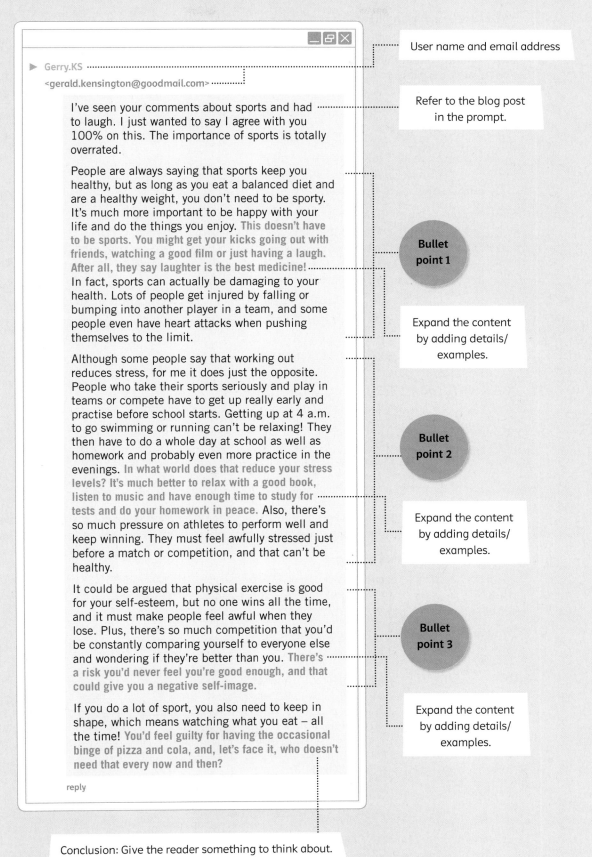

Gerry.KS
<gerald.kensington@goodmail.com>

User name and email address

I've seen your comments about sports and had to laugh. I just wanted to say I agree with you 100% on this. The importance of sports is totally overrated.

Refer to the blog post in the prompt.

People are always saying that sports keep you healthy, but as long as you eat a balanced diet and are a healthy weight, you don't need to be sporty. It's much more important to be happy with your life and do the things you enjoy. This doesn't have to be sports. You might get your kicks going out with friends, watching a good film or just having a laugh. After all, they say laughter is the best medicine! In fact, sports can actually be damaging to your health. Lots of people get injured by falling or bumping into another player in a team, and some people even have heart attacks when pushing themselves to the limit.

Bullet point 1

Expand the content by adding details/ examples.

Although some people say that working out reduces stress, for me it does just the opposite. People who take their sports seriously and play in teams or compete have to get up really early and practise before school starts. Getting up at 4 a.m. to go swimming or running can't be relaxing! They then have to do a whole day at school as well as homework and probably even more practice in the evenings. In what world does that reduce your stress levels? It's much better to relax with a good book, listen to music and have enough time to study for tests and do your homework in peace. Also, there's so much pressure on athletes to perform well and keep winning. They must feel awfully stressed just before a match or competition, and that can't be healthy.

Bullet point 2

Expand the content by adding details/ examples.

It could be argued that physical exercise is good for your self-esteem, but no one wins all the time, and it must make people feel awful when they lose. Plus, there's so much competition that you'd be constantly comparing yourself to everyone else and wondering if they're better than you. There's a risk you'd never feel you're good enough, and that could give you a negative self-image.

Bullet point 3

Expand the content by adding details/ examples.

If you do a lot of sport, you also need to keep in shape, which means watching what you eat – all the time! You'd feel guilty for having the occasional binge of pizza and cola, and, let's face it, who doesn't need that every now and then?

reply

Conclusion: Give the reader something to think about.

183

Essay

An essay is a factual piece of writing in which you discuss an issue or inform or convince the reader of your opinion. It is usually written as part of an exam or a competition and read by a teacher or a jury. The language is neutral or formal, and the reader is not addressed directly by (rhetorical) questions. There are no contractions, and personal pronouns (*I, you*) should be avoided. The title is supposed to be factual and state the topic.

An essay consists of three main elements:

1 Introduction: thesis statement

The first paragraph introduces the topic. It ends with the thesis statement that presents the arguments you intend to develop in the main body. The thesis statement makes clear what you think about the issue at hand.

2 Body: explaining and proving the thesis statement

The body consists of paragraphs (developing the content points) in which you discuss your ideas in detail. Each paragraph builds on one argument that reflects your opinion. You start a paragraph with a topic sentence and support it with relevant details (evidence, examples, reasons).

3 Conclusion: summary

The conclusion summarises (paraphrases) your opinion based on the arguments given in the main body. It does not introduce additional/new ideas.

Sample task

Your English class is discussing whether Austrians should be allowed to get their driving licence at 16. Your English teacher wants to know what you think about this and has asked you to write an essay.

In your essay you should discuss:
- whether getting their driving licence at 16 increases teenagers' mobility
- financial aspects of getting one's driving licence at 16
- if 16-year-olds are responsible enough to drive a car

Write around 400 words. Give your essay a title.

Factual title stating topic

No need for Austrians to get their driving licence at 16

Driving at 16 is allowed in some other countries, and many young Austrians wonder why this is not possible in Austria as well. However, as public transport in Austria is generally good, getting one's driving licence is costly and teenagers are probably not responsible enough drivers, it is not necessary for 16-year-olds to drive a car.

Thesis statement: It makes clear what you think about the issue at hand.

Bullet point 1

While being able to drive would give 16-year-olds their independence, it really is not necessary for them to have a driving licence. Young people that age should still be taking public transport as it is easy to use, and they can get a discounted student ticket. Especially in urban areas, going by tram, bus or underground is frequently faster than driving a car. If they are going out in the evening, it is surely more comfortable for them to be picked up by their parents, especially if they have had something to drink. Consequently, driving a car does not necessarily mean an increase in young people's mobility.

Topic sentence

Supporting detail 1

Supporting detail 2

Bullet point 2

Getting one's driving licence is comparatively inexpensive in other countries where driving lessons may be offered in school, but it is a financial burden for people in Austria. Driving lessons are costly, and parents might be reluctant to spend so much money as there are other expenses to be paid for 16-year-olds. Additionally, getting one's driving licence at 16 might create peer pressure between young people when one of them can afford to get it and perhaps also a car of their own. Others might feel compelled to do the same, and this might be a challenge for parents who may not have enough money to afford driving lessons, let alone a car.

Topic sentence

Supporting detail 1

Supporting detail 2

Bullet point 3

Although some may argue that 16-year-olds are old enough to control a vehicle, there is evidence that younger drivers are more likely to cause accidents. They are too young to recognise dangerous situations and cannot react quickly enough. They are more likely to be distracted by using their mobiles while driving and could pose a danger to others on the road. Other motorists would consider them inconsiderate and immature and would blame them for an increase in traffic accidents. More accidents could also result in higher insurance costs for everyone, which is totally unnecessary.

Topic sentence

Supporting detail 1

Supporting detail 2

In conclusion, it can be seen that there is no need for Austrians to get their licence at 16 as parents might want to use the money for more important things, teenagers have other methods of transport available to them and they can be a danger to themselves and others on the roads.

Conclusion: It summarises the arguments presented in the main body using a wording different from the thesis statement

Article (sample task + answer in the *Writing coach* of *way2go!* 6)

An article is an independent piece of writing usually published in an (online) magazine and read by a specific audience who is interested in the topic. It can be serious or amusing using lively and expressive language. Its purpose is to inform, entertain, convince, persuade or simply captivate the reader.

To attract the readers' attention, the article needs to have a catchy title which gives them an idea of what it is about. This can be a question or a surprising/provocative statement. The readership should be involved with direct or rhetorical questions, imperatives and exclamations. The article may include descriptions, anecdotes, examples and the writer's opinion if appropriate. The ending should give the readers the feeling that they have not wasted their time reading it. It could be a question, an answer to a question or a summary. It could also give them something to think about or encourage them to take action.

These are the main points to remember when writing an article:

- Give your article a catchy title.
- Write an introduction that pulls the reader right in.
- Involve your readership.
- Use lively and expressive language.
- Link the paragraphs: The reader should never lose interest in what you are writing.
- Finish your article by giving the reader something to think about.

Report (sample task + answer in the *Writing coach* of *way2go!* 6)

A report is a document that gives clear information on facts, projects, incidents or events and is based on evidence and research. It is written for an institution, an authority or a person in charge who has asked the writer to submit such a document. It is clearly structured, making use of sections and headings so that the information is easy to follow. A report uses formal and polite language.

In the introduction the *wh*-questions are addressed, such as what the report is about, why it is written and who it is for. The main body consists of paragraphs with a heading explaining what each paragraph is about. The conclusion may be a summary, a recommendation or a future outlook.

The ABC guideline for writing reports:

A – be **a**ccurate. The information has to be exact.
B – be **b**rief. Keep the report to the point.
C – be **c**lear. Make sure everybody understands it.

The (visual) layout:

From: Subject: Date:
Introduction
Heading Content point
Heading Content point
Heading Content point (Recommendation)
(Conclusion)

AE	American English	opp.	opposite	etw.	etwas
BE	British English	abbr.	abbreviation	jmdm.	jemandem
fml.	formal	sb.	somebody	jmdn.	jemanden
infml.	informal	sth.	something	jmds.	jemandes

Unit 01

	to manage sth.	etw. managen/verwalten
	overpaid	überbezahlt
	to become a pro at ...	ein Profi-... werden
	analysis [əˈnæləsɪs]	Analyse, Deutung
1	to be stressed out	gestresst sein
	peace and quiet	Ruhe und Frieden
	I need peace and quiet to prepare for the exam.	
	to appreciate [əˈpriːʃieɪt] sth.	etw. schätzen
	to have a go at sth.	etw. (einmal) ausprobieren
	to try your hand at sth.	sich an etw. versuchen
	to widen your horizons	seinen Horizont erweitern
2	satisfaction	Zufriedenheit
	appealing	ansprechend, reizvoll
	to let your imagination run free	seiner Fantasie freien Lauf lassen
	to take sth. up	etw. anfangen/beginnen
	My brother has recently taken up in-line skating.	
	outcome	Ergebnis
	college application	Bewerbung für die Universität
	to strike a balance	einen Mittelweg finden
	Try to strike a balance between working and socialising.	
	win-win (situation)	Win-win-Situation (*eine Situation mit beidseitigem Nutzen*)
	my way of doing sth.	meine Art, etw. zu tun
	Drinking a cup of tea in the afternoon is my way of relaxing.	
	to relieve stress	Stress abbauen
	to take advantage of sth.	etw. (aus)nutzen, von etw. Gebrauch machen
	They were offering free lunch, so I took advantage of it.	
	a paying job	ein bezahlter Job
3	to amuse [əˈmjuːz] sb.	jmdn. unterhalten
	equal [ˈiːkwəl]	gleich, gleichwertig
	original [əˈrɪdʒənəl]	originell, kreativ
	pastime [ˈpɑːstaɪm]	Zeitvertreib
	Football is Austria's national pastime.	
	to realise sth.	etw. erkennen/begreifen
6	to balance sth.	etw. in Einklang bringen/ im Gleichgewicht halten
	How do you balance work and family life?	
	consultant	Berater/in
	commitment	Verpflichtung

	pace [peɪs]	Tempo
	to focus on sth.	(sich) auf etw. konzentrieren
	demands	Anforderungen
7	breathing space	Atempause
	productivity	Produktivität
	me time	Zeit für mich
	to unwind [ʌnˈwaɪnd]	abschalten, sich entspannen
	to overtax yourself	sich zu viel zumuten
	to cut down on sth.	etw. reduzieren/ einschränken
	to schedule time for sth.	für etw. Zeit einplanen
	to set (clear) priorities	(klare) Prioritäten setzen
	rest	Ruhe, Erholung
	to procrastinate	Dinge aufschieben, etw. vor sich herschieben
9	wipe-off calendar	Kalender zum Abwischen
	to praise sb./sth.	jmdn./etw. loben
10	to put sth. off	etw. aufschieben
	overwhelmed [əʊvəˈwelmd]	überfordert, überwältigt
	I have so much work this week, I feel a little overwhelmed.	
	encouragement	Ermutigung, Anregung
	avoidance behaviour	Vermeidungsverhalten
	to short-circuit [ˌʃɔːtˈsɜːkɪt] sth.	etw. umgehen
	well-being	Wohlergehen
	to make up your mind to do sth.	einen Entschluss/Vorsatz fassen, etw. zu tun
	mindset	Einstellung, Mentalität
	frame of mind	Stimmung, Gemützustand
	resilient [rɪˈzɪliənt]	belastbar
	to be riled up	aufgebracht sein
	Avoid getting riled up when talking to your boss.	
	collaboration	Zusammenarbeit
	steady [ˈstedi]	ruhig, entschlossen
	tone of voice	Tonfall
	curiosity	Neugier
	to tap (into) sth.	sich etw. zunutze machen
	Rob is good at drawing; let's tap his talent for the poster.	
11	to be in a league of your own	eine Klasse für sich sein
	The whole group is very talented, but Lisa's in a league of her own.	
13	combat sport	Kampfsport
	to punch sb.	jmdn. mit der Faust schlagen
	self-defence	Selbstverteidigung
	to be accompanied by sth.	von etw. begleitet werden
	lightweight	leicht(gewichtig)

15	to **be supportive** (of sb./sth.) *Her trainer was very supportive.*	jmdn./etw. unterstützen
	hijab ['hɪdʒæb]	Hidschab
	the **Muslim community**	die muslimische Gemeinschaft
16	**controversial**	umstritten
18	**precious little**	herzlich wenig
	childcare	Kinderbetreuung
	toned	straff, durchtrainiert
	to **steer clear of sth.**	etw. aus dem Weg gehen
	illiterate [ɪ'lɪtərət]	analphabetisch; ungebildet
	menfolk (old-fashioned)	Mannsvolk
	to **straighten your back**	sich aufrichten/durchstrecken
	three-course meal	Drei-Gänge-Menü
	subsequently	anschließend
	occupied *I was so occupied with cleaning,* *I forgot to call you.*	beschäftigt
	kitbag	Sporttasche
	crossbow ['krɒsbəʊ]	Armbrust
	male/female territory	männliches/weibliches Territorium
	figure skater	Eiskunstläufer/in
	graceful	anmutig, graziös
	to **be pleasing to the eye**	schön anzusehen sein
	feminine ['femɪnɪn]	feminin, weiblich
	masculine ['mæskjəlɪn]	maskulin, männlich
	stamina ['stæmɪnə]	Ausdauer
	barrier ['bærɪə]	Barriere, Hindernis
	manufacturer	Hersteller/in
	financial backing	finanzielle/r Unterstützung/Rückhalt
	restriction	Einschränkung
	prestigious [pres'tɪdʒəs]	prestigeträchtig, angesehen
	status-conscious	standesbewusst
	admittedly	zugegebenermaßen
	garment	Kleidungsstück
	modesty	Anstand, Sittsamkeit
	to **suit sb.** *Green doesn't suit you, I think you* *should wear blue instead.*	jmdm. passen/stehen (Stil, Farbe)
	lap	Schoß
	to **broadcast sth.**	etw. übertragen (z.B. im Fernsehen)
	prejudice ['predʒədɪs]	Vorurteil
19	**force**	Zwang, Druck
21	**unsuitable**	ungeeignet
	westernised	verwestlicht, an die westliche Kultur angepasst
23	to **go for sth.**	auf etw. aus sein, es auf etw. abgesehen haben
24	**counterpart**	Pendant, Gegenstück
25	**insane** [ɪn'seɪn]	wahnsinnig, verrückt
	insanely priced	total/wahnsinnig überteuert
	long-standing	langjährig
	lucrative ['luːkrətɪv]	einträglich, lukrativ
	wear and tear [,weə ən 'teə]	Abnutzung, Verschleiß
	to **perfect** [pə'fekt] **sth.**	etw. perfektionieren
	to **fund sth.**	etw. finanzieren
	paycheck (AE), **pay cheque** (BE)	Gehaltsscheck

	salary	Gehalt
	at hand *You'll find everything you need* *close at hand.*	vorliegend, verfügbar
	to **come across as** ... *It's easy to come across as* *arrogant if you always talk about* *yourself.*	... rüberkommen, ... wirken
	the **issue at hand**	die Angelegenheit/Sache, um die es geht
	career span	Karrieredauer
	to **finance sth.** *You could take out a loan to* *finance the car.*	etw. finanzieren
	profitable ['prɒfɪtəbəl]	gewinnbringend, profitabel
26	**it comes as no surprise**	es ist nicht überraschend
	to **dream of sth.**	von etw. träumen, sich etw. erträumen
	deal	Vertrag, Abmachung
	to **purchase** ['pɜːtʃəs] **sth.** (fml.)	etw. erwerben/kaufen
	to **average around sth.** *The number of guests varies but* *averages around 50.*	durchschnittlich etw. betragen
	no regrets	ohne Bedauern
	gear [gɪə]	Ausrüstung
28	to **invest sth. in sth.**	etw. in etw. investieren
	contract ['kɒntrækt]	Vertrag
	to **confess sth.**	etw. gestehen
30	**exceptional**	außergewöhnlich; Ausnahme-...
	severe [sɪ'vɪə]	ernsthaft
	a great deal of ... *A typical chart includes a great* *deal of information.*	eine Menge ...
	a drop in ... *The company announced a drop* *in profits for the current year.*	ein Rückgang/Abfall von ...
	peak [piːk]	Höhepunkt
	effort	Anstrengung, Bemühung
	popularity	Beliebtheit
32	**bar chart**	Balkendiagramm
	pie chart	Tortendiagramm
	line graph	Liniendiagramm
	to **depict sth.**	etw. darstellen/zeigen
	to **illustrate sth.**	etw. veranschaulichen
	proportion	Anteil
	to **decline** *The number of accidents has* *declined in recent years.*	zurückgehen, (sich) verringern
	to **remain steady**	gleichbleibend sein
33	to **put considerable effort into sth.**	große/beträchtliche Anstrengungen in etw. stecken
	percentage [pə'sentɪdʒ]	Prozentsatz
	coverage *The project has had significant* *media coverage.*	Berichterstattung
	data	Daten
35	**appreciation**	Wertschätzung
	relieved *I'm so relieved you're back!*	erleichtert
	courage	Mut, Tapferkeit
36	to **reflect on sth.** *In these lessons, you learn to* *reflect on social issues.*	etw. reflektieren, über etw. nachdenken

Unit 02

	prediction	Vorhersage
	to get sth. across	etw. vermitteln/ rüberbringen
1	to have an argument	sich streiten, Streit haben
	to prevent sth.	etw. verhindern
	occasion [əˈkeɪʒən]	Gelegenheit
3	extended family	erweiterter Familienkreis
4	immediate family	engster Familienkreis, engste Angehörige, Kernfamilie
	to take after sb. *Jane's pretty tall already. She takes after her father.*	nach jmdm. kommen, jmdm. ähneln
	sibling	Geschwisterteil, Bruder oder Schwester
	relationship	Beziehung
	blended family	Patchworkfamilie
	great-aunt/-uncle	Großtante/-onkel
6	not necessarily *It's not necessarily true that you feel closer to your family than to your friends.*	nicht unbedingt
	blood relative	Blutsverwandte/r
	household	Haushalt
	a close bond *I've got a close bond with my grandfather.*	eine enge Bindung
	inseparable [ɪnˈsepərəbəl] *Joe and his dog are inseparable.*	unzertrennlich
	separation	Trennung
	nuclear family	Kernfamilie
	dysfunctional family	zerrüttete Familie, Problemfamilie
	related	verwandt
	pigsty [ˈpɪgstaɪ]	Saustall
	to depend on sb. *I can always depend on my grandma for good advice.*	sich auf jmdn. verlassen
	to crack jokes	Witze reißen
	to stick together *We can get over this problem if we stick together.*	zusammenhalten
	when push comes to shove	wenn es hart auf hart kommt
	madness	Wahnsinn
	to be attached to sb. *He's really attached to his uncle, but they don't see each other very often.*	an jmdm. hängen
	strong ties	starke Verbindung
	upbringing	Erziehung
	confidant/e [ˈkɒnfɪdænt] *I can tell Marie all my secrets; she's my confidante.*	Vertrauter/Vertraute
	crucial [ˈkruːʃəl] *A child's early years are crucial to their development.*	entscheidend, essenziell
7	adolescence [ædəˈlesəns]	Jugend, Pubertät
10	to do well	ein gutes Leben führen, sich gut machen
	biologically related	biologisch verwandt

	variant [ˈveəriənt] *There are several spelling variants of the name 'Isabel'.*	Variante, Abwandlung
	at best *The service at the restaurant was satisfactory at best.*	bestenfalls
	same-sex parents	gleichgeschlechtliche Eltern
	reproductive technology	Fortpflanzungstechnologie
	stigmatised	stigmatisiert, gebrandmarkt
	to raise a child	ein Kind großziehen
	dedicated	engagiert, hingebungsvoll
	casually *Our meeting wasn't planned – we met quite casually.*	zufällig, beiläufig
	parenting	(Kinder-)Erziehung
	characteristics	Eigenschaften
	to harm sb./sth.	jmdm./etw. schaden
	to put sb. at risk	jmdn. in Gefahr bringen
	to contradict sb./sth. *Don't contradict me! I'm telling you, he's a thief!*	jmdm./etw. widersprechen
	wisdom [ˈwɪzdəm]	Weisheit
	to confirm sth. *Studies confirm that good parenting is hard work.*	etw. bestätigen
12	backbone (of society)	Stütze (der Gesellschaft)
	professional	Fachkraft (*Berufstätige/r mit qualifizierter Ausbildung*)
	breadwinner	Geldverdiener/in
	living space	Lebensraum, Wohnraum
	living costs	Lebenshaltungskosten
	urban [ˈɜːbən]	urban, städtisch
15	to speculate (about sth.)	Vermutungen (über etw.) anstellen
16	father-in-law	Schwiegervater
	spouse [spaʊs]	Ehegatte/Ehegattin
	ancestor [ˈænsestə]	Vorfahre/Vorfahrin
	to stand by sb./sth. *I stand by my decision, even if you disagree.*	zu jmdm./etw. stehen
	to keep sb. company	jmdm. Gesellschaft leisten
	hospitable [hɒsˈpɪtəbəl]	gastfreundlich
18	to be on the brink/verge/point of sth. *She's on the verge of breaking the record.*	kurz vor etw. stehen
	single (person) household	Einpersonen-/Single-Haushalt
19	divorce rate	Scheidungsrate
22	How does that register?	Wie kommt das (bei jmdm.) an?
24	to make money	Geld verdienen
	to enquire about sth. *I would like to enquire about the price of concert tickets.*	sich nach etw. erkundigen
	to be crap (*infml.*)	Mist/schlecht sein
25	tedious [ˈtiːdiəs]	langatmig, mühsam
	to be a real drag (*infml.*)	echt stinklangweilig sein
	sth. sucks (*infml.*)	etw. ist beschissen
	rubbish (*infml.*)	Blödsinn, Mist
27	formality	Förmlichkeit
	slip-up	Ausrutscher, Fehler

	to **laugh** sth. **off** *He made fun of me, but I just laughed it off.*	etw. mit einem Lachen abtun, über einen Fehler lachen
	to **overlook** sth.	über etw. hinwegsehen
	tricky	knifflig, heikel
	to **take on** sth. *I'd like to take on more responsibility at work.*	etw. annehmen/übernehmen
	to **demonstrate** sth. *Let me demonstrate how this new mobile phone works.*	etw. aufzeigen/beweisen
	experienced	erfahren, sachkundig
	interpreter [ɪn'tɜːprətə]	Dolmetscher/in
	to **master** sth.	etw. meistern/beherrschen
	to **rely** [rɪ'laɪ] **on** sb./sth. *My grandpa relies on me to bring his shopping each week.*	auf jmdn./etw. bauen, von jmdm./etw. abhängig sein
	to **progress** [prə'gres] *You'll never progress if you don't practise.*	Fortschritte machen, voranschreiten
	to **evolve** [ɪ'vɒlv] *These days, technology is evolving really quickly.*	sich weiterentwickeln
	linguist	Sprachwissenschaftler/in
29	to **misjudge** [ˌmɪs'dʒʌdʒ] sb./sth. *I misjudged the situation;* *I shouldn't have yelled at him.*	jmdn./etw. falsch einschätzen
31	to **reveal** sth.	etw. offenbaren/preisgeben
	appeal [ə'piːl]	Appell, Aufforderung, Bitte
32	**doubtless** ['daʊtləs]	zweifellos
	to **transmit** sth. *Water transmits sound faster than air.*	etw. übertragen/übermitteln
	to **anticipate** sth. *We didn't anticipate such a big crowd at the event.*	etw. erwarten/vorhersehen
	misinterpretation	Fehldeutung, Missverständnis
	explicit [ɪk'splɪsɪt] *He was explicit in his instructions.*	explizit, deutlich
	defensive	abwehrend, verteidigend
	matter-of-fact *He spoke in a matter-of-fact way about their divorce.*	sachlich, nüchtern
	to **swing back and forth**	hin- und herpendeln
	to **emphasise** sth.	etw. betonen
	mismatching	nicht zusammenpassend
	implicit [ɪm'plɪsɪt]	implizit, unausgesprochen
	whereas [weər'æz] *She enjoys meeting people, whereas he prefers a quiet life.*	während, hingegen
	junction ['dʒʌŋkʃən]	(Straßen-)Kreuzung
	to **get going** *I enjoy jogging once I get going.*	losstarten, in Gang kommen
	square	Viereck, Quadrat
	to **confuse** sb.	jmdn. verwirren
	to **clarify** sth. *Please clarify what you're proposing. I don't understand.*	etw. klarstellen
	standpoint	Standpunkt
	annoyance *She completely ignored me, much to my annoyance.*	Ärgernis
	attentive	aufmerksam
	to **move on to** sth. **else**	zu etw. anderem übergehen

	neither ['naɪðə] *Neither parent speaks English.*	kein/e; keiner/keine/keines der beiden …
	to **arise** (fml.) *Problems arise if you don't pay your share of the rent.*	sich ergeben, entstehen, aufkommen
36	to **know the medium**	das (Kommunikations-)-Mittel kennen

Unit 03

	to **move out**	ausziehen
1	**flatmate** (BE), **roommate** (AE)	Mitbewohner/in
	to **rent** sth. **out**	etw. vermieten
	to **be OK with** sth.	mit etw. einverstanden sein
	fellow … *The girl got on well with her fellow students.*	Mit-…; gleichgesinnte/r/s …
	kitchen cabinet	Küchenkasten
	to **brew** [bruː] **beer**	Bier brauen
	to **seize** [siːz] **a chance**	eine Chance ergreifen
	to **whistle** ['wɪsəl]	pfeifen
	well-behaved	gut erzogen
	vacuum cleaner	Staubsauger
	semi-weekly	zweimal wöchentlich
	food dispenser	Futterautomat
4	**living arrangement**	Wohnsituation
	accommodation	Unterkunft, Quartier
	campus	Campus, Hochschulgelände
	common room	Gemeinschaftsraum
	to **commute** [kə'mjuːt]	pendeln
	costly	teuer
	dorm (AE)	Studentenwohnheim
	to **move** *I want to move to the USA after I've finished school.*	umziehen, ziehen nach …
	to **move in with** sb.	bei jmdm. einziehen, mit jmdm. zusammenziehen
	on your own *I really don't mind going to the theatre on my own.*	alleine
	rent	Miete
	studio flat	Garçonnière, Einzimmerwohnung
6	**suitable** *Sports cars are hardly suitable for families with children.*	geeignet, passend
	upside/downside	Vorteil/Nachteil
8	**privacy** ['prɪvəsi]	Privatsphäre
	luxury ['lʌkʃəri]	Luxus
	tenant ['tenənt]	Mieter/in
	resident *The residents in my building are really nice.*	Bewohner/in
	facilities *Luckily my new place has basic cooking facilities.*	Einrichtung, Geräte
	to **be well off** *I wish my family was well off.*	wohlhabend sein
	on the top floor	im obersten Stock
	as far as I'm concerned, …	was mich betrifft, …
	to **have a roof over your head**	ein Dach über dem Kopf haben

to store sth.	etw. lagern	
commute	Pendelzeit, Arbeitsweg	
I have a 45-minute commute to the place where I work.		
environmentally friendly	umweltfreundlich	
bookshelf	Bücherregal	
en-suite bathroom [ˌɒnˈswiːt ˈbaːθruːm]	eigenes/separates Badezimmer	
Our guest room has an en-suite bathroom.		
necessity [nəˈsesəti]	Notwendigkeit, Muss	
communal kitchen	Gemeinschaftsküche	
allowance	finanzielle Unterstützung, Zuschuss, Taschengeld	
ready-made	fertig, vorgefertigt	
tidy/untidy	ordentlich/unordentlich	
to vacuum [ˈvækjuːm]	(Staub) saugen	
Please vacuum the carpet.		
to do the laundry	Wäsche waschen	
to do your share	seinen Beitrag leisten	
Flatsharing means everyone does their share of cleaning.		
electrician [ˌɪlekˈtrɪʃən]	Elektriker/in	
to install sth.	etw. installieren	
socket	Steckdose	
to plug sth. in	etw. (an den Strom) anstecken	
I need to plug in my mobile.		
low-cost	kostengünstig; Billig-...	
Low-cost airlines are a major cause of climate change.		
fully furnished	vollständig möbliert	
junk	Krempel, Müll	
independence	Unabhängigkeit	
to make ends meet	über die Runden kommen	
They were a poor family struggling to make ends meet.		
utility bill	Strom-/Wasser-/Gasrechnung	
home insurance [ɪnˈʃʊərəns]	Haushaltsversicherung	
messy	unordentlich, schlampig	
household chore [ˌhaʊshəʊld ˈtʃɔː]	Hausarbeit	
to do the dishes	das Geschirr abwaschen	
central heating	Zentralheizung	
landlord/landlady	Vermieter/in	
plumber [ˈplʌmə]	Installateur/in	
loft (apartment)	Dachgeschoßwohnung	
part-time job	Teilzeitjob	
stylish	stilvoll, modisch	
amenities [əˈmiːnətiz]	Annehmlichkeiten; Ausstattung	
The flat has all the necessary amenities.		
dryer	Trockner	
air conditioning	Klimaanlage	
spacious [ˈspeɪʃəs]	geräumig	
residential area	Wohngegend	
housekeeper	Haushälter/in, Reinigungskraft	
(real) estate agent	Immobilienmakler/in	
construction site	Baustelle	
on-campus	auf dem Universitätsgelände	
On-campus cafeterias are cheaper than fancy restaurants off campus.		

	hall of residence (BE)	Studentenwohnheim
	cockroach	Kakerlake
14	to split sth.	(sich) etw. teilen
	When we go for coffee, we always split the bill.	
	to come by	vorbeikommen, jmdn. besuchen
	Why don't you come by later?	
	to drop off sth.	etw. vorbeibringen/abgeben
	Could you drop off this sweater at Jenny's house on your way home?	
	to sleep in	ausschlafen
	housekeeping	Reinigung, Reinigungsfirma
	to clear sth. out.	etw. ausräumen
	to show off (sth.)	(mit etw.) angeben
17	city-dweller	Stadtmensch
	dweller	Bewohner/in
18	the case for ...	Argumente für ...
	Let's hear the case for owning pets.	
	glamour	Zauber, Glanz
	balderdash (old-fashioned)	Blödsinn, Quatsch
	single digits [ˌsɪŋgəl ˈdɪdʒɪts]	einstelliger Betrag
	The price of movie tickets used to be in single digits, now they're over 15 pounds.	
	to (not) have a clue	(k)eine Ahnung haben
	to be this year's season	derzeit in Mode sein
	thimble [ˈθɪmbəl]	Fingerhut
	yard (AE)	Garten (AE)
	yard (BE)	(betonierter) Hof (BE)
	firefly	Glühwürmchen
	to go sledding	Rodeln gehen
	trodden (tread – trod – trodden)	zertrampelt, ausgetreten
	(star) constellation	Sternenkonstellation
	poop (infml.)	Kacke
	frankly	offen gesagt
	Quite frankly, I don't think you're making sense.	
	to put it another way, ...	um es anders auszudrücken, ...
	income inequality	Einkommensungleichheit
	to get by	gerade so durchkommen
	Sometimes it's hard to get by on a student budget.	
	to be aware of sth. (opp. unaware)	sich etw. bewusst sein
	to be reliant [rɪˈlaɪənt] on sth.	auf etw. angewiesen sein
	I can walk to work, I'm not reliant on public transport.	
	squashed	eingequetscht
	suspicious [səˈspɪʃəs]	misstrauisch
	grocery store (AE)	Lebensmittelgeschäft
	concern	Sorge, Bedenken
	Your mum's concern is that you don't sleep enough.	
	to size sb. up	jmdn. einschätzen/mustern
	The boys sized each other up, trying to decide who would win a fight.	
	résumé [ˈrezjuːmeɪ]	Lebenslauf
	genuine [ˈdʒenjuɪn]	echt, wahrhaftig
	retired	pensioniert

	a semblance of	so etwas wie …, ein Anschein von …
	I've just managed to restore a semblance of order to my flat after last night's party.	
	on a weekly basis	wöchentlich
	to be stuck in traffic	im Verkehr feststecken
	underdog	Außenseiter/in, Verlierer/in
	bigotry ['bɪgətri]	Engstirnigkeit
	dating prospects	Aussichten, eine/n Partner/in zu finden
	In rural areas, mobile apps can improve your dating prospects.	
	it would be a shame …	es wäre (doch) schade/ eine Schande …
	dismal ['dɪzməl]	erbärmlich
	to be thick-skinned	eine dicke Haut haben, nicht empfindlich sein
	to faze sb.	jmdn. belästigen/stören
	Traffic noise doesn't faze me.	
	to get even with sb.	es jmdm. heimzahlen
	empathy ['empəθi]	Empathie, Mitgefühl
	fragile ['frædʒaɪl]	zerbrechlich
	drawback	Nachteil
	idyllic [ɪ'dɪlɪk]	idyllisch
	You're mistaken.	Du täuschst dich.
	back-breaking work	Knochenarbeit
	thankless	undankbar
	dawn [dɔːn]	Morgendämmerung
	in the middle of nowhere	irgendwo im Nirgendwo, am Ende der Welt
	to scrutinise sb./sth.	jmdn./etw. sehr genau beobachten/unter die Lupe nehmen
	hermit ['hɜːmɪt]	Eremit/in, Einsiedler/in
25	safety	Sicherheit
	crime	Verbrechen
	recreational facilities	Freizeiteinrichtungen
	busy nightlife	lebendiges Nachtleben
	availability	Verfügbarkeit
	university graduate ['grædʒuət]	Universitätsabgänger/in
27	peaceful	friedlich
	lawn [lɔːn]	Rasen
	misty	dunstig, nebelig
	welcoming	einladend
	urban	urban, städtisch
	prohibitively expensive	unverschämt teuer
	Going out in this country is prohibitively expensive.	
	rational	rational, vernünftig
	rural ['rʊərəl]	ländlich
	thrilled	begeistert
	mansion ['mænʃən]	Villa
	priceless	unbezahlbar, unvergleichlich
28	to attract sb./sth.	jmdn./etw. anziehen/ anlocken
	The beautiful views in this area attract a lot of visitors.	
	to extend sth.	etw. ausbauen/ausdehnen
	They are extending the train station, so all trains are late.	
	extension	Ausbau, Verlängerung
	to impress sb.	jmdn. beeindrucken
	to negate sth.	etw. zunichtemachen/ aufheben; etw. verneinen
	Drinking alcohol can negate the effects of some medicines.	

29	standard of living	Lebensstandard
	housing	Behausung, Unterbringung
	human right	Menschenrecht
	slum	Armenviertel
	abandoned	leer stehend, verlassen
	to squat	ein Haus (illegal) besetzen
	to sleep rough (BE)	auf der Straße schlafen
30	inadequate [ɪ'nædɪkwət]	mangelhaft, unzureichend
	sanitation	sanitäre Einrichtungen; Hygiene
	poverty	Armut
	spreading of diseases	Verbreitung von Krankheiten
	crime rate	Verbrechensrate
	vulnerability	Verwundbarkeit, Anfälligkeit, Schutzlosigkeit
	child mortality	Kindersterblichkeit
	vulnerable	verletzlich, anfällig, schutzlos
31	Arab ['ærəb]	arabisch; Araber/in
	trading post	Handelsposten
	to establish sth.	etw. gründen/errichten
	The trading company was established in 1883.	
	to deal in sth.	mit etw. handeln
	Traders in the 19th century dealt in ivory and slaves.	
	slave	Sklave/Sklavin
	to descend into war	im Krieg versinken
	civil war	Bürgerkrieg
	widespread	weitverbreitet, großflächig
	devastation	Verwüstung, Zerstörung
32	occupant ['ɒkjəpənt]	Besetzer/in; Bewohner/in
33	to cope (with sth.)	(mit etw.) zurechtkommen
	It's been two months since he lost his job – how's he coping?	
36	think-tank	Thinktank, Denkfabrik
	pond	Teich
37	anonymity [ænɒn'ɪməti]	Anonymität

Unit 04

	on the move	in Bewegung
	pooch [puːtʃ]	Köter, Hündchen
	valid ['vælɪd]	gültig
	My passport is valid for another year.	
1	conductor	Schaffner/in
	to be left-/right-handed	Links-/Rechtshänder/in sein
	to dodge the fare	schwarzfahren
	to swallow sth.	etw. (ver)schlucken
	identification card (ID)	Ausweis
	to work undercover	verdeckt ermitteln
3	unlimited	unbegrenzt
4	embassy	Botschaft
	currency ['kʌrənsi]	Währung
	to hitchhike	autostoppen
	to ensure [ɪn'ʃɔː] sth.	etw. sicherstellen, sichergehen
	Passengers must ensure that they have a valid ticket.	
	for safety reasons	aus Sicherheitsgründen

	to encounter sb./sth. *If travellers stick to the rules, they shouldn't encounter any problems.*	auf jmdn./etw. stoßen, jmdm./etw. begegnen
5	street pedlar *(BE)*, street peddler *(AE)*	Straßenverkäufer/in
6	cane	(Blinden-)Stock
8	amusing	amüsant, lustig
9	to accompany sb. *Let me accompany you to the bus stop.*	jmdn. begleiten
10	to get in *What time did Lisa get in yesterday morning?*	ankommen, hineinkommen
	to get around	herumkommen
	to be off *Your train leaves in half an hour, you should be off now.*	weg sein, weggehen
	to run into sb.	jmdm. über den Weg laufen
	to catch up (with sb.)	Versäumtes nachholen, auf den neuesten Stand kommen
	to turn back	umdrehen, zurückgehen
	to stop over (somewhere) *We're stopping over in Rome to see a former colleague.*	(irgendwo) einen Zwischenstopp einlegen
	to walk off (with sth.)	(mit etw.) abhauen
	to make sth. up	etw. erfinden
	to run out of sth. *I've run out of ideas.*	etw. nicht mehr haben, (etw. „geht aus")
	to run for sth. *Is she running for mayor this year?*	für etw. kandidieren
	to run on sth. *Electric cars run on electricity.*	von etw. angetrieben werden
	to run on	weitergehen, sich hinziehen
	to run sth. by sb. *I'd like to run this idea by my boss first.*	etw. mit jmdm. abklären, etw. mit jmdm. kurz besprechen
	to run over sb./sth.	jmdn./etw. überfahren
11	to head out	aufbrechen, sich auf den Weg machen
	shopping spree	Einkaufstour
	to lift sb.'s mood	jmds. Stimmung heben
	to be on the road	unterwegs sein
	to take a surprise turn	eine überraschende Wendung nehmen
	to be a boost to sb./sth.	jmdm./etw. Auftrieb geben
	Absence makes the heart grow fonder.	Die Liebe wächst mit der Entfernung.
	inclined *Now I know the facts, I am inclined to agree with you.*	geneigt, bereit
	to strike up a conversation	ein Gespräch beginnen
	boundary	Grenze
	to have a break from sth.	eine Pause von etw. machen
	prevalent ['prevələnt] *Wi-Fi is becoming increasingly prevalent on transport systems.*	weitverbreitet, vorherrschend
	phone reception	Handyempfang
	liberating	befreiend
	day-to-day *Doing sports helps you to cope with your day-to-day problems.*	(all)täglich; Tages-…
	tension ['tenʃən]	Anspannung

	to value ['vælju:] sth. *You can find happiness if you value the little things in life.*	etw. (wert)schätzen
	awe [ɔː]	Ehrfurcht
	to recall sth. *People love recalling all the happy events of childhood.*	sich an etw. erinnern
	to sustain sth. *Living abroad makes it hard to sustain contact with family.*	etw. aufrechterhalten
	contentment	Zufriedenheit
	content(ed)	zufrieden
	in the long run	auf lange Zeit gesehen
	to jet off *Let's jet off to Dublin for an exciting weekend trip.*	wegfliegen
	broad-mindedness	Aufgeschlossenheit, Toleranz
	reflective *Hearing the bad news put me in a reflective mood.*	nachdenklich, besinnlich
	to wear off *Jet lag symptoms start to wear off as the body adapts to the new time zone.*	abklingen, nachlassen
18	carbon footprint	CO_2-Fußabdruck
	convenient [kən'viːniənt]	praktisch, bequem
	delay	Verspätung
	parking space	Parkplatz
	petrol *(BE)*, gasoline/gas *(AE)*	Benzin
	sustainable	nachhaltig
19	to do your bit	seinen Beitrag leisten, seine Pflicht tun
	straightforward *Stop being difficult! Just give me a straightforward answer.*	einfach, naheliegend
	to contribute sth. *Tim didn't contribute to the project, so he won't get an A.*	etw. beitragen
	one-way system	Einbahnsystem
	to sit back *Why don't you just sit back and relax?*	sich zurücklehnen
	tendency	Tendenz
	contrary to popular belief *Contrary to popular belief, public transport is faster than driving in rush hours.*	entgegen der allgemeinen Auffassung
	tax costs	Steuerausgaben
	expense(s)	Ausgaben, Unkosten
	scarce [skeəs] *Fresh water was scarce in the hurricane area.*	rar
	to hop out	raushüpfen
	all things considered, … *All things considered, I think we made the right choice.*	alles in Allem, …, unterm Strich …
23	trial [traɪəl] *Getting anywhere during rush hour can be a trial.*	Belastung, Herausforderung
	population density	Bevölkerungsdichte
24	affordable	leistbar
	mobile-friendly	handyfreundlich
26	reasonable travel time	zumutbare Reisedauer

	to **take a step towards** …	einen Schritt in Richtung … machen
	transport link	Verkehrsverbindung
	apprenticeship [ə'prentɪʃɪp]	Lehre, Ausbildungsstelle
	to **overcome an obstacle** ['ɒbstəkəl]	ein Hindernis überwinden
	crucial ['kruːʃəl]	ausschlaggebend
	policymaker	politische/r Entscheidungs-träger/in
27	**time-consuming**	zeitaufwendig
28	**punctuality** [ˌpʌnktʃu'æləti]	Pünktlichkeit
	comfort ['kʌmfət] *Travelling by train offers more comfort than travelling by bus.*	Komfort, Bequemlichkeit
29	**goods**	Waren, Güter
	llama	Lama
	rhinoceros [raɪ'nɒsərəs]/**rhino**	Nashorn
	bike courier ['baɪk ˌkʊriə]	Fahrradkurier/in
	delivery	Zustellung, Lieferung
	drone	Drohne
	freight train ['freɪt ˌtreɪn]	Frachtzug
	long-haul … *Have you ever been on a long-haul flight?*	Langstrecken-…
	lorry *(BE)*, **truck** *(AE)*	Lastwagen
30	**mode of transport(ation)**	Transportmittel
31	**rail network**	Eisenbahnnetz
32	to **fail to do sth.** *I failed to show up in time due to heavy traffic.*	etw. nicht tun (können), an etw. scheitern
	to **pretend to do sth.**	vorgeben, etw. zu tun
	surroundings	Umgebung
	to **take some time off** *I've been working too hard. I need to take some time off.*	sich freinehmen
	spontaneous [spɒn'teɪniəs] *My friends came by the apartment spontaneously.*	spontan
	local *When I'm on holiday, I always try to meet the locals.*	Einheimische/r
33	**scuba diving** ['skuːbə ˌdaɪvɪŋ]	Sporttauchen, Gerätetauchen
	tempting	verlockend
	to **manage to do sth.** *I won't manage to get all my chores done today.*	etw. schaffen/vollbringen
	train ride	Zugfahrt
	to **attempt sth.**	etw. versuchen
34	to **broaden your mind**	seinen Horizont erweitern
37	**hassle** ['hæsəl] *(infml.)* *Getting tickets online saves a lot of time and hassle.*	Schererei, Theater
	to **cough** [kɒf] **sth. up** *What? You've swallowed the candy? Cough it up at once!*	etw. (aus)husten
	to **take to the skies**	sich in die Lüfte schwingen
	carry-on baggage	Handgepäck
	cargo ['kɑːgəʊ]	Fracht
	undertaking	Vorhaben, Unternehmung
	furry ['fɜːri]	pelzig
	carrier box	Transportbox
	to **bark**	bellen
	to **meow** *(AE)*/**miaow** *(BE)* [mi'aʊ]	miauen

	spoiled	verwöhnt
	estimated *Brazil is home to an estimated 200,000 street children.*	geschätzt
	hateful	hasserfüllt, gehässig

Unit 05

	to **have a say (in sth.)**	(bei etw.) ein Mitspracherecht haben
1	**foundation**	Fundament, Basis
	philosopher [fɪ'lɒsəfə]	Philosoph/in
	growth	Wachstum
	to **cease** [siːs] *(fml.)* *When the fighting ceased, there was silence.*	enden, aufhören
	physicist ['fɪzɪsɪst]	Physiker/in
	values	Werte, Moral
	community	Gemeinschaft, Gesellschaft
	psychologist [saɪ'kɒlədʒɪst]	Psychologe/Psychologin
4	to **foster sth.** *The teacher hoped to foster interest in his pupils.*	etw. fördern/hegen
7	**critical thinking**	· kritisches Denken
	distracted	abgelenkt
	to **investigate sth.**	etw. untersuchen
	implication *The implications of global warming are extremely disturbing.*	Auswirkung, Tragweite
	to **make an informed decision** *I need all the facts before I can make an informed decision.*	eine wohlüberlegte/fundierte Entscheidung treffen
	fixed belief(s)	feste Überzeugung(en)
	to **weaken** ['wiːkən] **sth.**	etw. schwächen
	parental [pə'rentəl]	Eltern-…; elterlich
	to **undermine sb.'s authority** *If you disagree with me in front of everyone, you undermine my authority.*	jmds. Autorität untergraben
	sex education	Sexualkunde, Aufklärungs-unterricht
	to **oppose sth.** *Standardised tests were opposed by many teachers.*	etw. ablehnen
	disguised [dɪs'gaɪzd]	getarnt, verkleidet
	inconsistency	Widersprüchlichkeit
	reasoning ['riːzənɪŋ] *I understand your reasoning, but I still don't want to do it.*	Argumentation, Gedankengang
	consistent	stimmig, konsequent
	to **adapt sth.**	etw. anpassen
	justification	Rechtfertigung
	recipient [rɪ'sɪpiənt]	Empfänger/in
	rigorous ['rɪgərəs] *Organic food products are rigorously controlled.*	rigoros, gründlich, streng
	to **question sth.**	etw. hinterfragen
	finding	Erkenntnis, Resultat
	workplace	Arbeitsplatz, Arbeitsstätte
15	to **reward sth.** *His kindness was rewarded with a dinner invitation.*	etw. belohnen
16	**disrespectful**	respektlos

to **set work** *The teacher set work for the following week.*	Arbeitsaufträge verteilen
to **sit an exam** *(BE)*	eine Prüfung ablegen
degree	akademischer Titel/ Abschluss
to **nag sb. (to do sth.)**	jmdm. auf die Nerven gehen (bis er/sie etw. tut); an jmdm. herumnörgeln
scholarship [ˈskɒləʃɪp]	Stipendium
fee	Gebühr
desperate [ˈdespərət]	verzweifelt
to **struggle with sth.**	mit etw. kämpfen, sich mit etw. abmühen
progress [ˈprəʊgres]	Fortschritt(e)
tutor	(Nachhilfe-)Lehrer/in
18 **tough love** [ˌtʌf ˈlʌv]	„liebevolle Strenge"
cruelty [ˈkruːəlti]	Grausamkeit
excellence *He has won awards for excellence in research.*	Spitzenleistung, hervorragende Qualität
to **reject sth.** *The company rejected his application for a job.*	etw. zurückweisen/ ablehnen
account *I was asked to give an account of the night's events.*	Schilderung, Bericht
disbelieving	ungläubig, zweifelnd
buzz [bʌz] *The band created a buzz by giving away their new album for free.*	Aufregung
outrageous [ˌaʊtˈreɪdʒəs] *It's outrageous of you to accuse me of stealing!*	empörend, schockierend
defiance [dɪˈfaɪəns] *She returned late in defiance of her strict parents.*	Trotz
authoritarian parenthood	autoritärer Erziehungsstil
to **hit a sore spot**	einen wunden Punkt treffen
to **lose ground to sb.**	jmdm. gegenüber an Boden/Einfluss verlieren
rising power	aufsteigende Macht
play date	Verabredung zum Spielen (*für Kinder*)
sleepover	Übernachtung, Pyjamaparty
outraged	empört
cub [kʌb]	Welpe, Junges, (Tier-)Baby
to **rule the world**	die Welt beherrschen
offspring *Kate's brother came over on Sunday with all his offspring.*	Nachkomme/Nachkommin/ Nachkommenschaft
weak-willed *I'd love to go jogging every day, but I'm too weak-willed.*	willensschwach
indulgent [ɪnˈdʌldʒənt] *My indulgent grandma let me do anything I wanted.*	nachgiebig, milde
ill-equipped *The tourists were ill-equipped for hiking and got lost.*	schlecht vorbereitet/ gerüstet
tender-hearted	sanftmütig
merciless	gnadenlos
harshness [ˈhɑːʃnəs]	Härte, Strenge
mocking *He imitated the man's speech in a mocking way.*	spöttisch

to **confess sth.** *I have to confess, I've never really liked her.*	etw. gestehen/beichten
bad-tempered	schlecht gelaunt, launisch
disadvantaged	benachteiligt
harsh [hɑːʃ]	hart, streng
19 to **excel** [ɪkˈsel] **(in sth.)** *Laura excels in sports.*	hervorragend (in etw.) sein, sich bei etw. hervortun
to **defy** [dɪˈfaɪ] **(sb./sth.)** *He defied his parents by not going to school.*	sich jmdm./etw. widersetzen
defiant [dɪˈfaɪənt]	trotzig, aufmüpfig
apparent *Her nervousness was apparent to everyone.*	offensichtlich, sichtbar
20 **absent** [ˈæbsənt]	abwesend
to **underestimate sb./sth.**	jmdn./etw. unterschätzen
bullying	Mobbing
to **look back fondly at sth.**	sich gerne an etw. erinnern
23 **tertiary** [ˈtɜːʃəri] **education**	tertiäre Bildung, Hochschulausbildung
24 **federal** *Federal laws apply to all people in the USA.*	Bundes-…; bundesstaatlich
federally-funded	staatlich gefördert
economics [ˌiːkəˈnɒmɪks]	Wirtschaftswissenschaften
to **deepen your understanding of sth.**	sein Verständnis von etw. vertiefen
(academic) field	(wissenschaftliches) Gebiet, Fachgebiet
thesis [ˈθiːsɪs] *What's your Master's thesis about?*	Abschlussarbeit
graduate	Absolvent/in, Akademiker/in
to **hold a degree**	einen akademischen Titel tragen
University of Applied Sciences	Fachhochschule
applied computer science	angewandte Informatik
engineering [ˌendʒɪˈnɪərɪŋ]	Maschinenbau, Bautechnik, Ingenieurwesen
to **gain admission** *You have to do an interview to gain admission to some universities.*	aufgenommen werden
instruction	Schulung, Unterweisung
Bachelor's/Master's degree	Bachelor-/Mastertitel
business studies	Betriebswirtschaftslehre
tuition [tʃuːˈɪʃən] **fees**	Studiengebühren
in exchange (for) *The farmer gave free food in exchange for working in the fields.*	als Entschädigung (für), im Tausch (für)
26 **study** *Anthropology is the study of human behaviour.*	das Lernen, das Studieren
27 **graduation** [ˌgrædʒuˈeɪʃən]	Studien-/Ausbildungsabschluss
world leader	internationale/r Politiker/in, führende/r Regierungschef/in
32 to **acquire** [əˈkwaɪə] **sth.**	sich etw. aneignen
to **justify sth.** *Politicians need to justify their decisions to the public.*	etw. rechtfertigen/belegen
to **tackle sth.** *Let's tackle Unit 6 next week.*	etw. in Angriff nehmen/ angehen
ethics [ˈeθɪks]	Ethik, Moral, Sittenlehre
tricky	knifflig, schwierig

Unit 06

4	editorial meeting	Redaktionssitzung
5	glamorous	glamourös, glanzvoll
	mainstream	Mainstream-…, Durchschnitts-…
	affluent ['æfluənt] *Only rich families can afford to live in this affluent area.*	wohlhabend, vermögend
	fast-paced	hektisch, schnelllebig
	lavish ['lævɪʃ] *He enjoys throwing lavish parties.*	verschwenderisch, aufwendig
	mindful	bewusst, achtsam
	nomadic [nəʊˈmædɪk]	nomadisch, nicht sesshaft
	sedentary ['sedəntəri] *A sedentary lifestyle contributes to many health problems.*	sitzend
	spiritual	spirituell, geistig
	toxic	giftig
6	to advocate sth. *Many YouTubers advocate unlimited use of the internet.*	etw. verfechten, für etw. eintreten
8	to survey sth.	etw. erheben/erfassen
	age-old *Countless students have been struggling with this age-old problem.*	uralt
	spending	Ausgaben
	to work in finance	im Finanzsektor arbeiten
	conversely	umgekehrt
10	idiom	Redewendung
	goose (*pl.* geese)	Gans
	chase	(Verfolgungs-)Jagd
	share	Anteil
	guinea pig	Meerschweinchen
11	kennel	Hundezwinger
	librarian	Bibliothekar/in
	breed	Rasse, Sorte
	sheep dog	Hütehund
13	command	Kommando, Befehl
15	responsibility *Kate takes her responsibilities as a doctor very seriously.*	Pflicht, Aufgabe, Verantwortung
	to disrupt sth.	etw. stören
	to tax sb./sth. *All you have to do is iron a few shirts – that shouldn't tax you too much.*	jmdn./etw. strapazieren/belasten
	(sense of) responsibility *Taking care of a pet can help children to develop a sense of responsibility.*	Verantwortungsbewusstsein
	Whose turn is it?	Wer ist an der Reihe? Wer ist dran?
	to clean sth. out	etw. ausräumen/reinigen
	cage	Käfig
	to do your part	seinen Beitrag leisten
	to be reluctant to do sth.	etw. nur widerwillig tun
	disagreement	Meinungsverschiedenheit
	to exceed sth. *Eating out three times a week will exceed your budget.*	etw. überschreiten
	pricey	kostspielig, teuer

	(fish) tank	Aquarium
	lead [liːd]	Leine
	collar	Halsband
	veterinary bills	Tierarztrechnungen
	check-up	ärztliche Kontrolluntersuchung
	to lack sth. *The problem is that he lacks experience with horses.*	etw. vermissen lassen, etw. nicht haben
	maturity	Reife
	living being	Lebewesen
	needs	Bedürfnisse
	to socialise with friends	Freundschaften pflegen
	to meet sb.'s needs	jmds. Bedürfnisse befriedigen
	to be suited for/to sth.	für etw. geeignet sein
16	factual	sachlich
	thesis statement	Kernaussage, These
	to arouse interest	Interesse wecken
	to paraphrase sth.	etw. mit anderen Worten ausdrücken
	in the margin	am Rand
18	Calm down.	Beruhige dich.
19	approval/disapproval	Zustimmung/Ablehnung
	to be willing/unwilling to do sth.	gewillt/nicht gewillt sein, etw. zu tun
	to deny sth. to sb.	jmdm. etw. verweigern
	to disapprove of sth. (*opp.* to approve of sth.)	etw. ablehnen/missbilligen
	to judge ['dʒʌdʒ] sb.	jmdn. beurteilen, über jmdn. urteilen
	to speak your mind	offen seine Meinung sagen
	likewise *I'm trying to keep the flat tidy, and I'd ask you to do likewise.*	ebenso, gleichermaßen
	viewpoint	Sichtweise, Standpunkt
	to take sth. seriously	etw. ernst nehmen
	hesitant ['hezɪtənt]	zögerlich
	resistance	Widerstand
21	ever-present	allgegenwärtig
	to feud [fjuːd] (with) sb.	mit jmdm. in Fehde liegen
	to get out of hand	außer Kontrolle geraten
	to misbehave	sich schlecht benehmen, ungezogen sein
	nobleman/noblewoman	Adelige/r
	born out of wedlock	unehelich (geboren sein)
	troubled	problembeladen
	military	Militärs-…; militärisch
	new-found *University students often struggle with their new-found freedom.*	neu (gefunden)
22	wealthy	wohlhabend
	to gatecrash a party	uneingeladen zu einer Feier auftauchen
	love at first sight	Liebe auf den ersten Blick
	opposing	gegnerisch
	daring	waghalsig
	friar [fraɪə]	Mönch, Ordensbruder
	fuss [fʌs]	Wirbel, Theater
	disgraceful	schändlich, skandalös
	to bury ['beri] sb.	jmdn. begraben

	dagger	Dolch
	tomb [tu:m]	Grab
	heartbroken	untröstlich, todunglücklich
24	adventurous	abenteuerlich
	cautious ['kɔːʃəs]	vorsichtig
	conscious	bewusst
	courageous [kəˈreɪdʒəs]	couragiert, mutig
	disastrous	katastrophal
	furious ['fjʊəriəs]	wutentbrannt
	obvious	offensichtlich
	poisonous	giftig
	prosperous	wohlhabend; erfolgreich
	The town became prosperous through tourism and trade.	
	rebellious	rebellisch
28	to matter	von Bedeutung sein
	Education matters if you want to get a well-paid job.	
	shareholder	Miteigentümer/in, Aktienbesitzer/in
	playwright	Dramatiker/in, Bühnenautor/in
	Shakespeare is the most important English playwright.	
	legacy ['legəsi]	Erbe, Vermächtnis
	Tom found it hard to live up to his father's legacy.	
	royalties ['rɔɪəltiz]	Autorenhonorar, Tantiemen
	to be embedded in sth.	in etw. eingebettet/ eingebaut sein
	There are many rocks embedded in the soft ground of the valley.	
	relatable	nachempfindbar, nachvollziehbar
	This tale of growing-up is relatable for all teenagers.	
	ruthlessness	Rücksichtslosigkeit
	confusion	Verwechslung, Verwirrung
	set of twins	Zwillingspaar
	arguably	wohl
	Technology is arguably more important than ever.	
	enduring [ɪnˈdʒʊərɪŋ]	beständig, dauerhaft
	The song is an enduring fan favourite that has been popular for decades.	
	investigation	Untersuchung, Nachforschungen
	pragmatic	pragmatisch, praxisorientiert
	to act decisively	entschlossen handeln
	to delay sth.	etw. verzögern/aufschieben
	to have proof of sth.	einen Beweis für etw. haben
	to prompt sb. to do sth.	jmdn. veranlassen, etw. zu tun
	We don't know what prompted him to say that.	
	to reside in sth. *(fml.)*	in etw. liegen, etw. innewohnen
	bard [bɑːd]	Barde, Dichter
	humanity	Menschheit
	subtlety ['sʌtəlti]	Feinsinn, Raffinesse
	Their jokes lacked subtlety and were embarrassing.	
	assumption	Annahme; Weltanschauung
32	senseless	sinnlos
	arranged marriage	arrangierte Ehe

	first-hand	aus erster Hand
	The book is a first-hand account of the author's experiences in Africa.	
	devastated	am Boden zerstört
35	ownership	Besitz, Eigentum
	breeder	Züchter/in
	champion dog	preisgekrönter Zuchthund
	dog from rescue ['reskjuː]	„geretteter Hund", Hund aus einem Tierheim
	master	„Herrchen"/„Frauchen", Hundebesitzer/in
	service dog	Assistenzhund
	to make demands on sb.'s time	jmds. Zeit stark beanspruchen

Unit 07

1	robbery	Raub(überfall)
	civilian [sɪˈvɪljən]	Zivilist/in
	murder	Mord
	murderer	Mörder/in
	theft	Diebstahl
	poaching	Wilderei
	unlicensed protesting	Protestieren ohne Genehmigung
	to protest (against sth.)	(gegen etw.) protestieren
	to disobey sb./sth.	jmdm./etw. nicht gehorchen
	Don't disobey the law or you'll have to go to prison.	
	police order	polizeiliche Anordnung
	to riot ['raɪət]	Unruhe stiften, randalieren
	torture ['tɔːtʃə]	Folter
	genocide ['dʒenəsaɪd]	Genozid, Völkermord
3	pavement	Gehsteig
4	local council	Gemeinderat
5	offence	Straftat, Regelverstoß
	Minor offences are often punished with a fine.	
	unwelcome sight	unwillkommener Anblick
	To many people in cities, graffiti is an unwelcome sight.	
	to cause trouble	Unruhe stiften
	to be outlawed	gesetzlich verboten sein
	nuisance ['njuːsəns]	Störung, Ärgernis
	loitering	unerlaubtes Herumlungern
	to issue a fine	eine Geldstrafe verhängen
	justified measure	gerechtfertigte Maßnahme
	troubling	besorgniserregend
	The increasing number of homeless people is a troubling development.	
	violence	Gewalt
7	mayor	Bürgermeister/in
8	arson ['ɑːsən]	Brandstiftung
	drug trafficking	Drogenhandel
	fraud [frɔːd]	Betrug
	hacking	(Computer-)Hacken
	plagiarism ['pleɪdʒərɪzəm]	Plagiat, geistiger Diebstahl
	vandalism	Vandalismus, vorsätzliche Sachbeschädigung
	to break into sth.	in etw. einbrechen

	to **deceive** [dɪˈsiːv] **sb.** *He was deceived by an email to send his personal data.*	jmdn. täuschen	
	to **frighten sb.**	jmdm. Angst einjagen	
	to **set sth. on fire**	etw. in Brand setzen	
	to **shoplift** *Judy was arrested for shoplifting a bag last week.*	Ladendiebstahl begehen	
	to **trade in sth.** *Samuel got rich trading in bitcoins.*	mit etw. handeln	
9	**petty offence**	Bagatelldelikt, kleines Vergehen	
	prison sentence	Gefängnisstrafe	
11	to **get caught**	erwischt werden	
12	**security**	Sicherheit, Schutz	
	to **approach sth.** *I want to approach this school year differently than the last.*	an etw. herangehen	
	offender *He is a first-time offender, so he'll get a light sentence.*	Täter/in	
	to **prioritise sth.**	etw. den Vorrang geben	
	property	Besitz	
	to **commit a crime**	ein Verbrechen begehen	
	surveillance [səˈveɪləns]	Überwachung	
	valuables [ˈvæljəbəlz]	Wertsachen	
	visible *(opp. invisible)*	sichtbar	
	domestic waste	Haushaltsabfälle	
	commercial [kəˈmɜːʃəl]	gewerblich	
	to **mark sth.**	etw. markieren/beschriften	
	to **upgrade sth.**	etw. aufwerten/verbessern	
	fence	Zaun	
	to **remain unseen**	ungesehen bleiben	
	watchful	wachsam	
	ladder	Leiter	
	wheelie bin *(BE)*	Mülltonne	
	to **be out of reach** *Chemicals should be kept out of reach from children.*	außer Reichweite sein	
15	**legend** [ˈledʒənt]	Legende	
	non-violent resistance	gewaltloser Widerstand	
	oppressed	unterdrückt	
	folk tale [ˈfəʊk ˌteɪl]	Volkssage	
16	**regret**	Bedauern	
17	**crime scene**	Tatort	
	intruder [ɪnˈtruːdə] *Fences and alarm systems can keep out intruders.*	Eindringling, Einbrecher/in	
19	**gun law**	Waffengesetz	
	constitution	Verfassung	
	mass shooting	Massenschießerei	
	amendment	Zusatz, Nachtrag	
	gun control (law)	Reglementierung von Waffenbesitz	
20	to **bear** [beə] **arms**	Waffen bei sich tragen	
21	**gun ownership**	Waffenbesitz	
	to **keep sb. from harm**	jmdn. vor Gefahr schützen	
	to **record** [rɪˈkɔːd] **sth.** *The police have to record every emergency phone call they receive.*	etw. aufzeichnen/erfassen	
	to **violate the law**	gegen das Gesetz verstoßen	
23	**perpetrator**	Straftäter/in	

	in the first place *Cliff-jumping was dangerous, and we shouldn't have done it in the first place.*	von vornherein	
	ID badge	Ausweis *(zum Anstecken)*	
	functioning *We need a functioning security system to keep the house safe.*	funktionsfähig, funktionierend	
	bullet-resistant	durchschusshemmend	
	panel [ˈpænəl]	Platte, Vertäfelung	
	to **mount sth.** *Cameras are mounted above each entrance.*	etw. befestigen/anbringen	
	to **vacate** [vəˈkeɪt] **sth.** *(fml.)* *In case of a fire, vacate the building quickly.*	etw. räumen/verlassen	
	armed	bewaffnet	
	deterrent [dɪˈterənt]	Abschreckung	
	shooter	Schütze/Schützin	
	in the event of … *In the event of an accident, an airbag can save lives.*	im Falle von …	
	educator	Erzieher/in, Pädagoge/ Pädagogin	
	to **negotiate** *We'll have to negotiate until we come to an agreement.*	verhandeln	
	harassment [ˈhærəsmənt]	Belästigung, Schikane	
	hostile [ˈhɒstaɪl] *Sam's quite hostile towards his parents, although they mean well.*	feindselig	
	law enforcement officer	Gesetzeshüter/in	
	bulletproof	kugelsicher	
	peace of mind	Seelenfriede, innere Ruhe	
	falsely *Robert falsely accused Ms Morrison of unfair treatment.*	fälschlicherweise	
	assault rifle [əˈsɒlt ˌraɪfəl]	Sturmgewehr	
	to **dare (to do) sth.** *Nobody dared to say a word.*	etw. wagen	
26	**civil disobedience**	ziviler Ungehorsam	
27	**equality**	Gleichheit	
	injustice	Unrecht, Ungerechtigkeit	
	non-violence	Gewaltfreiheit	
	sit-in	Sitzstreik, Besetzung	
	to **witness sth.**	etw. bezeugen/miterleben	
	throughout history	quer durch die Geschichte	
	deliberately *You deliberately gave me the wrong address so I would be late! That's so mean!*	absichtlich, ganz bewusst	
	unjust/just	ungerecht/gerecht	
	to **initiate** [ɪˈnɪʃieɪt] **sth.** *Public protests are often initiated by young people.*	etw. initiieren, etw. anstoßen/auslösen	
	clash	Zusammenprall	
	camp-in	Besetzung	
	march [mɑːtʃ]	Marsch, Demonstration	
	hunger strike	Hungerstreik	
	threat [θret]	Bedrohung	
	public safety	öffentliche Sicherheit	
	protester	Protestierende/r	
	to **resist sth.** *The protesters didn't resist being carried off the road.*	sich etw. widersetzen, etw. Widerstand leisten	

mace [meɪs]	Tränengas, Pfefferspray	
club	Knüppel	
arrest [əˈrest]	Festnahme	
to beat sb.	jmdn. schlagen	
to go unnoticed	unbemerkt bleiben	
to be at your disposal	zur Verfügung stehen	
The car will be at your disposal for the next eight hours.		
mankind	Menschheit	
mighty	mächtig	
ingenuity [ˌɪndʒəˈnjuːəti]	Einfallsreichtum	
man	der Mensch, die Menschheit	
Man wasn't made to live alone.		
30 antonym [ˈæntənɪm]	Gegenteil, Gegenwort	
to unlock sth.	etw. entriegeln/aufsperren	
After he had unlocked the door, we could finally see what was behind it.		
31 credible (*opp.* incredible)	glaubhaft	
literate (*opp.* illiterate)	lese- und schreibkundig	
33 construction	Bau, Errichtung	
oil pipeline	Ölpipeline, Ölleitung	
34 to launch [lɔːntʃ] sth.	etw. starten/in Gang setzen	
movement	Bewegung (*Gruppe von Menschen, die sich für etw. einsetzen*)	
elders	Ältere, die Ältesten	
tribal council	Stammesrat	
tepee	Tipi (*traditionelles Zelt amerikanischer Ureinwohner*)	
prayer	Gebet	
sacred [ˈseɪkrɪd]	heilig	
purity [ˈpjʊərəti]	Reinheit	
The purity of gold is measured in karats.		
spirit	Geist	
recognition	Anerkennung	
relay run [ˈriːleɪ ˌrʌn]	Staffellauf	
scattered	verstreut	
My family is scattered all over Europe.		
reservation	Reservat	
to revive sth.	etw. wieder aufleben lassen	
blizzard [ˈblɪzəd]	Schneesturm	
to hold a ceremony	eine Zeremonie abhalten	
spokesman/spokeswoman	Sprecher/in	
to line up for sth.	sich für etw. anstellen	
to reunite [ˌriːjuːˈnaɪt]	sich wiedervereinigen	
failure [ˈfeɪljə]	Scheitern, Versagen	
suicide [ˈsuːɪsaɪd]	Suizid, Selbstmord	
to pray	beten	
drug abuse	Drogenmissbrauch	
struggle	Kampf	
The struggle against racism isn't over yet.		
prophecy [ˈprɒfəsi]	Prophezeiung	
to symbolise sth.	etw. symbolisieren	
alcoholism [ˈælkəhɒlɪzəm]	Alkoholismus	
barrel	Fass	
beneath [bɪˈniːθ]	unter(halb)	
I love the beach and feeling the sand beneath my toes.		

source	Quelle	
drinking water	Trinkwasser	
downstream	flussabwärts	
Any pollution will affect all other villages downstream.		
crisis (*pl.* crises)	Krise	
to inherit sth.	etw. erben	
Our kids should inherit a world that is not polluted.		
to unite sb.	jmdn. (*eine Gruppe von Menschen*) vereinigen/ zusammenführen	
chief [tʃiːf]	Häuptling	
unlikely	unwahrscheinlich	
tight-knit	eng verbunden, verschworen	
In small villages, you often find a very tight-knit community.		
nationwide	landesweit	
growing	wachsend	
to underlie sth.	etw. zugrunde liegen	
Mental problems very often underlie illnesses.		
to resort to violence	auf Gewalt zurückgreifen	
to be wiped out	ausgelöscht werden	
to race	rasen, um die Wette fahren	
to throw yourself at sb./sth.	sich auf jmdn./etw. stürzen	
tear gas [ˈteə ˌgæs]	Tränengas	
36 admiration	Bewunderung	
37 to reconstruct sth.	etw. rekonstruieren/ wiedergeben	
to clash	zusammenprallen	
The government and the opposition clashed over.cuts in education.		
38 to stress sth.	etw. betonen	
40 to burgle sth.	in etw. einbrechen	
legalisation	Legalisierung	
to offend	eine Straftat begehen	
This project helps young people who have offended.		
to criminalise sth.	etw. zur Straftat erklären	
Some US states have criminalised protesting against infrastructure projects.		

Unit 08

culture vulture (*infml.*)	Kulturfreak	
loo	Klo, Toilette	
1 remarkable	bemerkenswert	
simplicity	Einfachheit	
to refill sth.	etw. wieder auffüllen	
2 to receive rave reviews	von der Kritik hoch gelobt werden	
division (between)	Kluft, Spaltung (zwischen)	
3 profession	Beruf	
4 artistic endeavour [ɑːˈtɪsɪk enˈdevə]	künstlerische Bestrebung	
commercial	kommerziell, wirtschaftlich	
crossover	Crossover (*Vermischung von unterschiedlichen Musikstilen*)	
Her band plays a crossover between indie and jazz.		
electronic amplification	elektronische Verstärkung	
entertainer	Unterhalter/in	

	an expression of …	ein Ausdruck von …
	iconic [aɪˈkɒnɪk] *The Statue of Liberty is an iconic picture of New York.*	ikonisch, kultig
	to interpret sth.	etw. interpretieren/deuten
	inner self	inneres Ich
	joint experience	gemeinsames Erlebnis
	perception *The film could change the perception of hip-hop.*	Wahrnehmung, Auffassung
	rehearsal [rəˈhɜːsəl]	Probe
7	contemporary *Christopher Marlowe was a contemporary of Shakespeare.*	Zeitgenosse/Zeitgenossin
	reputation	Ruf
	the authorities	die Obrigkeit, die Behörden
	breeding ground *Dirty bathrooms are a breeding ground for infections.*	Brutstätte, Nährboden
	the plague [pleɪg]	die Pest
	indecent [ɪnˈdiːsənt] behaviour	unsittliches Verhalten
	prostitute	Prostituierte/r
	courtyard	Innenhof
	inn	Gasthaus
	disloyal	illoyal, untreu
	imprisonment	Inhaftierung
	execution	Exekution, Hinrichtung
	cannon	Kanone
	to rediscover sth.	etw. wiederentdecken
	reconstruction	Wiederaufbau
	to hold sth. *Modern football stadiums can hold up to 100,000 people.*	etw. fassen/beinhalten
	pit	*hier:* Stehplatzbereich
	artificial lighting	künstliche Beleuchtung
	to relieve yourself	sich erleichtern *(die Toilette benutzen)*
	sewage [ˈsuːɪdʒ]	Abwasser, Schmutzwasser
	pit	Grube
	to dispose of sth. *You should recycle plastics and not dispose of them in your household rubbish.*	etw. entsorgen
	improper sanitation	unzureichende sanitäre Einrichtungen
	outbreak *During the Renaissance, Europe suffered from several outbreaks of the plague.*	Ausbruch, Beginn
	burial [ˈberiəl]	Beerdigung
	to cater to sb. *This restaurant caters to both vegetarians and vegans.*	auf jmdn. ausgerichtet sein, auf jmdn. abzielen
	to endure [ɪnˈdjʊə]	andauern, Bestand haben
	age	Zeitalter, Epoche
	health risk	Gesundheitsrisiko
	to give religious rites	religiöse Zeremonien durchführen
10	odds *What are the odds she'll win?*	Wahrscheinlichkeit(en), Chancen
	to tremble [trembəl]	(er)zittern
11	in spite of *In spite of nationwide protest, the president allowed the oil pipeline to be built.*	trotz

	replacement	Ersatz
	to call sth. off *The meeting has been called off.*	etw. absagen
	to tolerate sth.	etw. tolerieren/dulden
	to postpone [pəʊstˈpəʊn] sth. *Let's postpone our walk until tomorrow.*	etw. verschieben
	to request sth. *May I request another meeting?*	um etw. bitten, etw. verlangen
	to obtain sth. *(fml.)* *You need to obtain special permission to park here.*	etw. erhalten
14	superstition	Aberglaube
	bad luck	Pech
15	a superstitious bunch	ein abergläubiger Haufen (Menschen)
	to bear [beə] sth. in mind *Please bear in mind that the shops are closed on Sundays.*	etw. bedenken/ berücksichtigen
	peacock [ˈpiːkɒk]	Pfau
	exception	Ausnahme
	unsuspecting *It's fairly easy to surprise an unsuspecting person.*	ahnungslos, nichts ahnend
	scenery [ˈsiːnəri]	*hier:* Bühnenbild
	by accident	aus Versehen, unabsichtlich
	Take care!	*hier:* Pass auf!; Mach's gut!
18	humorous	humorvoll, komisch
19	groundbreaking *Many groundbreaking discoveries were made in the 19th century.*	bahnbrechend
	to cross genres [ˈʒɑːrez]	Genregrenzen überschreiten
	prolific *With her 40 books, she's a really prolific author.*	produktiv
	prose [prəʊz]	Prosa
	established *He's an established writer.*	etabliert, bekannt
	highest honour	höchste Auszeichnung/Ehre
	quirk [kwɜːk]	Eigenheit, Macke
21	to nod (your head)	nicken
	supernatural being	übernatürliches Wesen
	plot	Handlung
22	miracle [ˈmɪrəkəl]	Wunder
23	charity event	Wohltätigkeits- veranstaltung
25	educational value	pädagogischer Wert, Lernwert
26	to be common knowledge	allgemein bekannt sein
	damp	feucht
	marsh	Sumpf, Moor
	to catch your death	sich den Tod holen *(krank werden)*
	evasive [ɪˈveɪsɪv]	ausweichend
	imaginative [ɪˈmædʒɪnətɪv]	einfallsreich
	wasteland	Ödland, Brachland
	obedient [əˈbiːdiənt]	folgsam
	to irritate sb. *Do ticking clocks irritate you?*	jmdn. stören/irritieren
	chapel [ˈtʃæpəl]	Kapelle
	spire [spaɪə]	Kirchturm, Spitzturm
	fallen leaf	zu Boden gefallenes Blatt
	holy [ˈhəʊli]	heilig

faith [feɪθ] *People who weren't of Christian faith were buried outside Christian graveyards.*	(religiöser) Glaube
inquisitive [ɪnˈkwɪzətɪv]	wissbegierig, neugierig
indeed *He is very rich indeed.*	in der Tat
to be in a good/bad mood	gute/schlechte Laune haben
to dislike sth.	etw. ablehnen/nicht mögen
27 decay [dɪˈkeɪ]	Verfall
morality	Moral, Sittlichkeit
29 to be highly regarded *His books are highly regarded by critics and the public.*	hoch angesehen sein
entertaining	unterhaltsam

Unit 09

bias [ˈbaɪəs]	Voreingenommenheit, Vorurteil(e)
fake news	Fake News *(falsche oder irreführende Nachrichten)*
to share sth.	etw. (mit)teilen
1 to unveil [ʌnˈveɪl] sth. *The artist unveiled her latest masterpiece.*	etw. enthüllen, etw. bekanntmachen
floating	schwebend, schwimmend
unwittingly *He's often unwittingly funny because of his accent.*	unwissend
search party *The search party found the missing five-year-old in time.*	Suchtrupp
highway *(AE)*	Autobahn
to be starving	am Verhungern sein
bald head	Glatze
to leap [liːp]	springen
to knock sb. unconscious	jmdn. bewusstlos schlagen
investigator	Ermittler/in
to trace sth. (back) to sth. *Many fears can be traced to bad childhood experiences.*	etw. auf etw. zurückführen, etw. von etw. herleiten
outdated	veraltet, überholt
5 media literacy [ˈmiːdiə ˌlɪtərəsi]	Medienkompetenz *(die Fähigkeit, kritisch mit Medien umzugehen)*
limitless	unbegrenzt
undistorted *Do we have a true, undistorted picture of reality?*	unverzerrt, unverfälscht
to spot sth. *Fake news is sometimes difficult to spot.*	etw. erkennen/ausmachen
misleading [ˌmɪsˈliːdɪŋ]	irreführend
sensationalist	sensationslüstern
judgement	Urteilsvermögen
knowingly	wissend
biased [ˈbaɪəst]	voreingenommen
confirmation bias	Bestätigungsfehler
to verify sth. *You can verify news easily by looking at several sources.*	etw. verifizieren, etw. (auf Richtigkeit) überprüfen
truthfulness	Wahrheit, Wahrhaftigkeit

to take sth. into account	etw. berücksichtigen
7 objective	objektiv, vorurteilsfrei
9 Middle Eastern	nahöstlich
the Middle East	der Nahe Osten
duty [ˈdʒuːti]	Verpflichtung
to doubt [daʊt] sth. *Never doubt your abilities.*	etw. anzweifeln
to communicate sth. *It's important to communicate your message clearly.*	etw. vermitteln
10 understanding	Verständnis
crappy *(infml.)*	beschissen
transcript	Abschrift, Niederschrift
angle [ˈæŋgəl]	Blickwinkel, Standpunkt
self-involved	egozentrisch, ichbezogen
12 freedom of the press	Pressefreiheit
to hold sb. to account *The opposition should hold the government to account.*	jmdn. zur Verantwortung ziehen
public affairs	öffentliche Angelegenheiten
advocate [ˈædvəkət]	Befürworter/in
14 Reporters Without Borders	Reporter ohne Grenzen
to face sth.	mit etw. konfrontiert sein
hostility [hɒsˈtɪləti]	Feindseligkeit
dictatorship	Diktatur
hatred [ˈheɪtrɪd]	Hass
prominent *She's a really prominent blogger on politics.*	prominent, herausragend
to assassinate sb.	jmdn. ermorden
investigative reporter	Enthüllungsjournalist/in
fiancé/e [fiˈɒnseɪ]	Verlobter/Verlobte
to shoot sb. to death	jmdn. erschießen
shake-up	Weckruf, Aufrüttelung
to expose sth. *The journalist exposed the government's role in illegal activities.*	etw. aufdecken/entlarven
to collaborate	zusammenarbeiten
to harass [ˈhærəs] sb.	jmdn. belästigen/ schikanieren
chilling	abschreckend
to intimidate sb. *The new teacher is quite strict, but don't let her intimidate you.*	jmdn. einschüchtern/ bedrohen
to denounce sth. *The president must publicly denounce the use of violence.*	etw. anprangern
unfavourable coverage	unvorteilhafte Bericht-erstattung
to adopt sth. *The newspaper has adopted a rather left-wing approach.*	etw. annehmen/ übernehmen
leader	Herrscher/in
correlation *There's a direct correlation between smoking and cancer.*	Zusammenhang, Wechselbeziehung
stable democracy	stabile Demokratie
corruption	Korruption
substantial decline	erheblicher Rückgang
censorship	Zensur
to take sth. to new heights	etw. auf die Spitze treiben

to **rank**		einen Platz/Rang erreichen, sich einreihen
Austria ranks in the top 20 countries for press freedom.		
dissent [dɪ'sent]		Dissens, abweichende Meinung
Totalitarian regimes do not tolerate dissent.		
to **be based on sth.**		auf etw. basieren
Her article was based on interviews with eye-witnesses.		
pluralism ['plʊərəlɪzəm]		Pluralismaus, gesellschaftliche Vielfalt
to **monitor sth.**		etw. überwachen/beobachten
A few NGOs monitor human rights worldwide.		
to **be champion of sth.**		Meister/in in etw. sein
Norway is a champion of press freedom worldwide.		
22	**jail**	Gefängnis
	raid [reɪd]	Razzia, Durchsuchungsaktion
	to **report on sth.**	von etw. Bericht erstatten
	catastrophic	katastrophal
	catastrophe [kə'tæstrəfi]	Katastrophe
	to **suspend a sentence**	eine Strafe aussetzen/aufheben
	distinguished	bemerkenswert, ausgezeichnet
	to **confiscate** ['kɒnfɪskeɪt] **sth.**	etw. konfiszieren/beschlagnahmen
	The police have confiscated fifteen pounds of cocaine.	
25	**foreign correspondent**	Auslandsberichterstatter/in
26	**big business**	lukratives Geschäft
	a big business	ein Großunternehmen
27	**commercial**	Werbespot
	continuing popularity	anhaltende Beliebtheit
	to **reach a wide audience**	ein großes Publikum erreichen
	to **track sth.**	etw. nachverfolgen/nachvollziehen
	to **personalise sth.**	etw. personalisieren/individuell anpassen
	target audience	Zielpublikum, Zielgruppe
	search engine ['sɜːtʃ ˌendʒɪn]	Suchmaschine
	classified ad	Kleinanzeige
	state-of-the-art	hochmodern, auf dem neuesten Stand (der Technik)
	I have a state-of-the-art computer at the office.	
	advertorial	Advertorial (*Werbeanzeige, die aussieht wie ein Zeitungsartikel*)
	influencer marketing	Marketing durch Influencer/-innen („Beeinflusser/innen")
	to **create a demand for sth.**	für etw. Nachfrage erzeugen
	appalling [ə'pɔːlɪŋ]	entsetzlich
	viral ['vaɪərəl]	viral, sich schnell verbreitend
	The latest Beyoncé video went viral within minutes.	
29	**predictive**	vorhersagend; Prognose-…
	data hunter	Datenjäger/in
	to **prove to be sth.**	sich als etw. erweisen
	None of the news stories proved to be true.	

to **relate to sb.**		zu jmdm. einen Zugang finden, eine Beziehung zu jmdm. herstellen
repeatedly		immer wieder, wiederholt
32	to **leak** [liːk] **sth.**	etw. unerlaubt veröffentlichen/durchsickern lassen
	He leaked the news of his girlfriend's pregnancy before she wanted it known.	
	to **conduct sth.**	etw. durchführen
	We need to conduct a survey before we create a new product.	
	to **gather sth.**	etw. sammeln
	They'll have to gather more data before they can reach a decision.	
	to **release** [rɪ'liːs] **sth.**	etw. herausgeben/veröffentlichen
	Her new book will be released in August.	
	criticism ['krɪtɪsɪzəm]	Kritik
	oversight	(Flüchtigkeits-)Fehler, Versehen
	government official	Regierungsbeamte/r
34	**worthless**	wertlos
	internal	(firmen)intern
	to **make sth. public**	etw. öffentlich machen
	in real time	in Echtzeit
	defeated [dɪ'fiːtɪd]	geschlagen
	insight	Einblick, Erkenntnis
	in response to sth.	als Antwort auf etw.
	In response to your question, I won't run for president.	
	contradictory statement	widersprüchliche Aussage
	to **broadcast sth.**	etw. hinausposaunen/an die große Glocke hängen
	I don't want this broadcast to the whole family.	
	purposeful	absichtlich, vorsätzlich
	to **expose sb. to sth.**	jmdn. etw. aussetzen
	Make sure the baby isn't exposed to the sun too much.	
	to **fall victim to sth.**	etw. zum Opfer fallen
37	**verified**	bestätigt
	to **exploit sth.**	sich etw. zunutze machen
	minor ['maɪnə]	Minderjährige/r
	to **uncover sth.**	etw. aufdecken/enthüllen
	The police uncovered a series of crimes.	

Unit 10

the outback		australisches Hinterland
indigenous [ɪn'dɪdʒɪnəs]		indigen; … der Ureinwohner/innen
Aboriginal Australians		Ureinwohner/innen Australiens
1	to **settle somewhere**	sich irgendwo niederlassen
	explorer	Entdecker/in, Forschungsreisende/r
	to **slurp** [slɜːp]	schlürfen
	whilst [waɪlst] (*fml.*)	während
	I fell asleep whilst waiting.	
	to **boast** [bəʊst] **about sth.**	mit etw. angeben
	to **take a nap**	ein Nickerchen machen
	to **take it easy**	es ruhig angehen
	to **whiten sth.**	etw. weiß machen/bleichen
	to **blacken sth.**	etw. schwärzen
4	**soul**	Seele, Innerstes

	to overcome barriers	Hindernisse überwinden
	preservation	Erhaltung, Pflege
	contempt [kən'tempt]	Geringschätzung, Verachtung
	disrespect	Respektlosigkeit
7	class consciousness	Klassenbewusstsein
	concept of beauty	Verständnis von Schönheit
	display of emotions	Zeigen von Gefühlen
	etiquette ['etɪket]	Etikette, Benimmregeln
	justice ['dʒʌstɪs]	Gerechtigkeit
	marriage rites	Hochzeitsrituale
	conflict resolution	Konfliktlösung
8	the tip of the iceberg	die Spitze des Eisbergs
11	thought pattern(s)	Gedankenmuster
	hierarchy ['haɪərɑːki]	Hierarchie, Rangordnung
	personal space	Diskretionsabstand, persönliche Distanzzone
	over time	mit der Zeit
12	corporal punishment	körperliche Züchtigung, Prügelstrafe
13	to assimilate into sth.	sich in etw. einfügen, sich an etw. anpassen
	to shed sth. *Trees usually shed their leaves in November.*	etw. ablegen
	prior ['praɪə] *I had no prior knowledge of Finish when I moved there.*	vorhergehend; Vor-…
	to bring sth. to the table	etw. mitbringen
	ridiculous	lächerlich
	foolish	närrisch, albern
	endearing [ɪn'dɪərɪŋ] *He has an endearing smile.*	liebenswert, einnehmend
	dreadful ['dredfəl]	fürchterlich, schrecklich
	uncertainty	Unsicherheit
	to face sth. head on	sich etw. stellen, etw. direkt angehen
	to marvel at sth. *I marvel at the way he makes time for all his hobbies.*	über etw. staunen
	wonder	Staunen, Verwunderung
	countless	zahllos
18	indigenous peoples	indigene Völker, Ureinwohner/innen
19	discipline ['dɪsəplɪn]	(sportliche) Disziplin, Sportart
	spear throw ['spɪə ˌθrəʊ]	Speerwurf
	log race	Baumstammrennen
	barefoot *I love walking barefoot on the grass.*	barfuß
	to thrive [θraɪv] *In order to thrive, plants need sunlight.*	gedeihen, aufleben
21	cave painting	Höhlenmalerei
22	hunter-gatherer	Jäger und Sammler
	settler	Siedler/in
	citizenship	Staatsbürgerschaft
	remote territory	abgelegenes Territorium
24	to set foot in sth.	etw. betreten
	to persecute ['pɜːsɪkjuːt] sb.	jmdn. verfolgen (aus politischen/religiösen Gründen)
	to torment [tɔː'ment] sb.	jmdn. quälen

	to tyrannise ['tɪrənaɪz] sb.	jmdn. tyrannisieren
	cold-blooded	kaltblütig
	humane [hjuː'meɪn]	menschlich
	to poison sb.	jmdn. vergiften
	savage ['sævɪdʒ]	Wilde/r
	newcomer	Neuankömmling, Fremde/r
	to guard sth.	etw. hüten/beschützen
	distinctness	Einzigartigkeit
	negotiation	Verhandlung
	extinction	Auslöschung, Aussterben
	suffering	Leiden
	foreigner	Fremde/r, Ausländer/in
	to drive sb. away	jmdn. vertreiben
	to whip [wɪp] sb.	jmdn. auspeitschen
	possession	Besitz, Eigentum
	patron ['peɪtrən]	Kunde/Kundin; Mäzen/in
	eternal [ɪ'tɜːnəl]	ewig
	self-destructive	selbstzerstörerisch
	to assume sth. *We can't assume that what they say is the truth.*	etw. annehmen, von etw. ausgehen
	to cope with sth.	mit etw. umgehen
	self-esteem	Selbstwertgefühl
	to lay claim to sth./to claim sth.	auf etw. Anspruch erheben
25	to abuse sb.	jmdn. missbrauchen
	to oppress sb.	jmdn. unterdrücken
27	survival [sə'vaɪvəl]	Überleben
	stupidity	Dummheit
28	despair/desperation	Verzweiflung
	disgust [dɪs'gʌst]	Ekel
	grief [griːf]	Trauer
	resentment	Verbitterung, Groll
	jealousy ['dʒeləsi]	Eifersucht, Neid
	shame	Scham, Schande
	sorrow ['sɒrəʊ]	Kummer, Leid
31	below the poverty line	unter der Armutsgrenze
	exploitation	Ausbeutung
	compensation payment	Entschädigungszahlung

Writing coach

	personal significance	persönliche Bedeutung
	to have an emphasis on sth.	einen Schwerpunkt auf etw. haben
	koala sanctuary ['sæŋktʃʊəri]	Koalareservat
	to bump into sb.	mit jmdm. zusammen-stoßen
	mobility	Mobilität, Bewegungsfreiheit
	financial burden	finanzielle Last
	to feel compelled to do sth.	sich gezwungen sehen, etw. zu tun
	motorist ['məʊtərɪst]	Fahrer/in

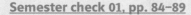

Semester checks – answer key

Semester check 01, pp. 84–89

READING 1 **How a Mumbai slum became a riot of colour (T/F/J)**

Key: 1 T, The odd pot plant; 2 T, Having persuaded Snowcem Paints; 3 F, No one had ever/ Others wondered if coloured/Some neighbours refused at; 4 F, In December 2017, over; 5 T, One shows a group; 6 T, Tours of Asalpha will/Local women will earn; 7 F, People have got carried/The comparison is far-fetched

LESEN ▶▶ B2 Ich kann längere Texte, auch Berichte und Artikel, zu aktuellen Fragen sowie literarische Texte selbstständig lesen und verstehen.

7–6: ✓✓   5–4: ✓   3–0: !!

What next? Now that you know the correct answers and where they are in the text, compare the expressions used in the text with those in the task. Are there any synonyms you didn't know that prevented you from getting the answer correct? For example, in item 1 it says "The majority of Mumbai's inhabitants" – how does the text express the same idea?

LISTENING 2 **Birdwatching (4W)**

Key:
1 a crow's nest/a crow
2 drum(ming) on metal/use metal not wood
3 their back stories/what they've seen/their experiences
4 grew up in London/raised in inner city/learned about birds himself
5 a book on birds
6 widening the diversity/reaching a wider audience
7 that there is beauty/beauty is close by

HÖREN ▶▶ B2 Ich kann längeren Redebeiträgen und komplexer Argumentation folgen, sofern die Thematik einigermaßen vertraut und der Rede- oder Gesprächsverlauf durch explizite Signale gekennzeichnet ist.

7–6: ✓✓   5–4: ✓   3–0: !!

What next? Listen to the recording again and stop after every question. Write down the language the speakers use to communicate the idea of the questions. For example, item 2 asks how woodpeckers have changed their behaviour while Lindo says, "Some woodpeckers have learned to drum on metal."

SPEAKING 3 a **Individual long turn**

SPRECHEN ▶▶ B1+ Ich kann eine Argumentation, auch in Form einer Präsentation, gut genug ausführen, um die meiste Zeit ohne Schwierigkeiten verstanden zu werden.

Study the list on the next page before your partner starts with his/her long turn. Tick the questions while your partner is speaking. Give honest feedback by telling your partner what went really well and what needs improving.

Did your partner . . .	Yes	No
1 describe the **nature of the chart** including all information (e.g. title) given?		
2 use **quantifiers** (*a large proportion, …*) describing the survey?		
3 focus on the **essential information** discussing the chart?		
4 give two or three **good reasons with supporting details** when talking about bullet point 2?		
5 make two or three **useful suggestions with supporting details** when talking about bullet point 3?		
6 use **modal verbs/conditionals** when talking about bullet points 2 and 3?		
7 speak **fluently without** reading from **notes** he/she has made?		
8 speak for about **4 minutes** (a bit more than 1 minute for each bullet point)?		

b Paired activity

SPRECHEN ▶▶▶ B1+ Ich kann ein Gespräch oder eine Diskussion aufrechterhalten und dabei kurz zu den Standpunkten anderer Stellung nehmen, Vergleiche anstellen und verschiedene Möglichkeiten angeben.

Ask a friend to give you and your partner honest feedback based on the tables below.

Student A . . .	Yes	No
considers the **situational context**.		
listens to what B says.		
invites B to give his/her **opinion**.		
reacts to B's arguments **politely** and competently.		
gives **good reasons** and **supporting details** for all content points.		
speaks **fluently**.		
doesn't dominate the discussion.		

Student B . . .	Yes	No
considers the **situational context**.		
listens to what A says.		
invites A to give his/her **opinion**.		
reacts to A's arguments **politely** and competently.		
gives **good reasons** and **supporting details** for all content points.		
speaks **fluently**.		
doesn't dominate the discussion.		

LANGUAGE **4** **Do you have a growth mindset? (MC)**
IN USE

Key: **1** C, **2** D, **3** D, **4** B, **5** A, **6** B, **7** C, **8** B, **9** D, **10** C

SPRACH- ▶▶▶ Ich kann ein hinreichend breites Spektrum an sprachlichen Mitteln korrekt erkennen und
VERWENDUNG anwenden.
IM KONTEXT

10–9: ✓✓   **8–7:** ✓   **6–0:** ‼

What next? Find reasons why only the correct answer to each item fits the text. Especially for the answers you got wrong, find out what grammatical structure or expression you didn't know. Here are some examples:

- Item 1 needs to complete a conditional clause about an imaginary situation in the past. You can see this because the main clause uses the verb form *would have passed*, so the conditional clause can only be in the past perfect (*had* + past participle of the verb).
- On the other hand, item 4 needs to complete a fixed phrase with the correct preposition. If you discover you don't know a phrase like that, immediately record it in your notes for revision.

WRITING 5   **Blog post**

SCHREIBEN   ▶▶▶ B1+   Ich kann mit einer gewissen Sicherheit größere Mengen von Sachinformationen über vertraute Routineangelegenheiten und über weniger routinemäßige Dinge zusammenfassen, darüber berichten und dazu Stellung nehmen.

Look at the blog post you have written and tick the questions.

Did you ...	Yes	No
1 state your **user name** and give the blog post a catchy **title**?		
2 get the **reader's attention** in your **introduction**?		
3 write **three paragraphs** (one for each bullet point) of about equal length?		
4 add **relevant supporting details**?		
5 use **semi-formal** or **neutral language**?		
6 use a variety of **linking devices**?		
7 engage the reader with (rhetorical) **questions** and **imperatives**?		
8 observe the **function words**?		
9 "**invite" the reader to comment** on your blog post or **take action** in your **conclusion**?		
10 **proofread** your blog post for common mistakes you might have made?		

<u>Semester check 02, pp. 162–167</u>

READING 1   **The power of parklets (4W)**

Key:
1 more popular/more widely accepted/more common
2 people drank alcohol there/it blocked parking/nudists spent time there
3 operate parklets/manage parklets (NOT: build parklets)
4 positive impact of parklets
5 increased sales/demand for more workers
6 neighbo(u)rhood settings (NOT: central business districts)
7 bring a neighbo(u)rhood together
8 has lots of customers/has large shop windows/has few seats indoors
9 aren't customers/don't shop there

LESEN   ▶▶▶ B2   Ich kann die Hauptaussagen von inhaltlich und sprachlich komplexen Texten, auch literarischen zu konkreten und abstrakten Themen verstehen.

9–8: ✓✓   7–5: ✓   4–0: !!

What next? Items 3 and 6 of this task are most difficult to get right because they ask about very specific information. In item 3, the question is what UCD does for businesses, not the local council. They installed parklets for the city in the past but currently only manage them together with local businesses. Item 6 asks about the topic of the current UCD study, not past ones by other organisations. Only the past studies were about parklets in business districts.

LISTENING 2   **Prince Rupert's dog Boy (MC)**

Key: 1 A, 2 D, 3 C, 4 C, 5 A, 6 D, 7 C

HÖREN ▶▶▶ B2   Ich kann Hauptaussagen und spezifische Informationen von inhaltlich und sprachlich komplexen Redebeiträgen zu konkreten und abstrakten Themen verstehen, wenn Standardsprache gesprochen wird.

7–6: ✓✓   5–4: ✓   3–0:   !!

What next? Some of the information given in the recording is quite complex and specific. For the items you got wrong, listen to the parts where they are discussed multiple times. You might even want to copy down parts of the text in writing for practice.

SPEAKING **3** **a** Individual long turn

SPRECHEN ▶▶▶ B2   Ich kann zu einer großen Bandbreite von unterrichtsbezogenen Themen klare und detaillierte Beschreibungen und Darstellungen geben, Ideen ausführen und durch untergeordnete Punkte und relevante Beispiele abstützen.

Study the list below before your partner starts with his/her long turn. Tick the questions while your partner is speaking. Give honest feedback by telling your partner what went really well and what needs improving.

Did your partner ...	Yes	No
1 say what the pictures have in **common** and what is **different** about them? (bp1)		
2 use the **present continuous** when describing what the people are doing? (bp1)		
3 **speculate** how the people **might feel** about the paintings? (bp1)		
4 **support** his/her opinion with **examples (evidence) and reason**? (bp2)		
5 use a **variety** of **sentence starters** avoiding the overuse of *I think* ...? (bp2)		
6 make **one or two good suggestions supporting them with relevant details** instead of offering a variety of suggestions without any details? (bp3)		
7 speak **fluently without** reading from **notes** he/she has made?		
8 speak for about **5 minutes** (a bit less than 2 minutes for each bullet point)?		

b **Paired activity**

SPRECHEN ▶▶▶ B2   Ich kann mich in vertrauten Situationen aktiv an informellen Diskussionen beteiligen, indem ich Stellung nehme, einen Standpunkt darlege, verschiedene Vorschläge beurteile, Hypothesen aufstelle und auf Hypothesen reagiere.

Ask a friend to give you and your partner honest feedback based on the tables below.

Student A ...	Yes	No
considers the **situational context**.		
listens to what B says.		
invites B to give his/her **opinion**.		
reacts to B's arguments **politely** and competently.		
gives **relevant supporting details** (examples, evidence, reason) **for each content point**.		
speaks **fluently**.		
doesn't dominate the discussion.		

Student B ...	Yes	No
considers the **situational context**.		
listens to what A says.		
invites A to give his/her **opinion**.		
reacts to A's arguments **politely** and competently.		
gives **relevant supporting details** (examples, evidence, reason) **for each content point**.		
speaks **fluently**.		
doesn't dominate the discussion.		

LANGUAGE IN USE **4**

Uluru/Ayers Rock: Why names matter (WF)

Key: 1 extensive, 2 unimportant, 3 cultural, 4 protective, 5 outrageous, 6 uncomfortable, 7 Europeans, 8 enjoyment, 9 beautiful, 10 ignoring, 11 irresponsible

SPRACH-VERWENDUNG IM KONTEXT

Ich kann auch komplexe grammatische, lexikalische und argumentative Strukturen erkennen und präzise anwenden.

11–10: ✓✓   **9–6:** ✓   **5–0:** ‼

What next? Look up and study the complete word family (nouns, verbs, adjectives with their opposites, etc.) of all items in the task. Then look at the sentence around the gaps again and write down the kind of word that needs to go there. Does the sentence still need a verb, a noun, an adverb? Find out if your mistakes come from not knowing the right forms or from not understanding the sentence structure, then continue studying from there.

WRITING **5**

Essay

SCHREIBEN **B2**

Ich kann unterschiedliche Texte schreiben, in denen Argumente für oder gegen einen bestimmten Standpunkt angegeben und die Vor- und Nachteile verschiedener Optionen erläutert werden.

Look at the essay you have written and tick the questions.

Did you . . .	Yes	No
1 write **five paragraphs**?		
2 write around **400 words**?		
3 give your essay a **factual** (not catchy, not sensational) **title**?		
4 conclude your **introduction** with a **thesis statement**?		
5 state your **opinion** in the **thesis statement**?		
6 start **each paragraph** with a **topic sentence**?		
7 support each of the **topic sentences** with **relevant details** (evidence/examples and reasons)?		
8 **summarise** your arguments in the **conclusion**?		
9 use a variety of **linking devices**?		
10 use **neutral** or **formal language** without contractions?		
11 **avoid personal pronouns** (I, you)?		
12 **proofread** your essay for common mistakes you might have made?		